$15⁰⁄₆

CHRISTIE'S

Review of the Season 1985

A group of fine French furniture and English pictures on view at Christie's King Street saleroom in London, summer 1985

CHRISTIE'S

Review of the Season 1985

Edited by Mark Wrey

PHAIDON · CHRISTIE'S

OXFORD

Copyright © Christie, Manson & Woods Ltd., 1985

Distribution through Phaidon · Christie's Ltd.,
Littlegate House, St. Ebbe's Street, Oxford OX1 1SQ

British Library Cataloguing in Publication Data
Christie's review of the season.—1985
    1. Art – —Periodicals
    I. Wrey, Mark
    705   N1
ISBN 0-7148-8024-8

Distribution in USA and dependencies by Salem House,
99 Main Street, Salem, NH 03079

Design and layout by Norman Ball,
Logos Design, Datchet, Berkshire

Phototypeset in Compugraphic Baskerville by
J&K Hybert, Maidenhead, Berkshire

Printed and bound in The Netherlands by
Drukkerij Onkenhout b.v., Hilversum

Endpapers:
JOHANN HEINRICH RAMBERG
German 1763–1840
The Royal Family at the Academy
Signed and dated 1787
Pencil, pen and grey ink and watercolour, on two
adjoining sheets, laid down on a contemporary mount
$4^{3}/_{4} \times 19^{1}/_{2}$ in. (12 × 49.5 cm.) overall
Sold 9.7.85 in London for £23,760 ($32,788)
By order of the Trustees of the Harewood Charitable
Trust

**All prices include the buyer's premium where
applicable. The currency equivalents given throughout
the book are based on the rate of exchange ruling at
the time of the sale.**

Contents

Foreword

PAUL WHITFIELD

Christie's new saleroom in
Park Avenue, New York,
opened May 1985

The season under review has been one in which attention has been focused by vendors, buyers, the press and the public on the effects of the strength of the US dollar. Certainly, there is no denying that demand for works of art at sales in London and Europe has been extraordinarily strong and that much of the strength of that demand has stemmed from the United States, or perhaps more accurately from those denominating their spending in dollars. But it would be wrong to attribute too much to this factor; it has been particularly noticeable that in London there has been a growing number of private buyers in many fields, and it is gratifying that this should be so, for we are paying great attention to encouraging this trend.

An important event in our history came in May when the newly extended salerooms in New York were inaugurated, virtually doubling our available space and giving us undoubtedly the finest centrally located premises in New York. The outstanding moment of the season, which we shall long remember, was the sale of Andrea Mantegna's *The Adoration of the Magi* in April for £8.1 million ($10.4 million), the highest price paid for any painting. The fragile, haunting beauty of the 480-year-old picture captured us all. Other significant achievements for Old Masters

The Hon. Patrick Lindsay holding a press conference after the sale of Andrea Mantegna's *The Adoration of the Magi*, which had just been auctioned for a record price for any picture

have been £486,000 ($626,940) for the extraordinarily detailed and fresh village market scene by Jan Brueghel the Elder and no fewer than three Canalettos, which totalled over a million pounds between them. Dutch painters (and sales) have been prominent, with a small interior by Nicolaes Maes at £410,400 ($529,416), a Salomon van Ruysdael river landscape at $418,000 (£366,666) in New York and another in Amsterdam at D.fl.1,083,000 (£246,136), a record sum for a picture sold in the Netherlands.

The demand for fine furniture continues, and Christie's reputation for important sales in this area with it. $220,000 (£177,419) was paid in New York for an extremely fine English satin-wood library bookcase of *c.*1775, and £388,880 ($505,440) for a sombre and magnificent Louis XVI bureau plat by Joseph Baumhauer from the collection of Edmond de Rothschild. High prices for Boulle furniture have again been seen. American furniture can be amongst the most expensive and the $363,000 (£283,590) paid for the Hollingsworth family walnut high chest of *c.*1779, by the great Thomas Affleck of Philadelphia, attests to this.

British Pictures appeal very strongly on both sides of the Atlantic and we have been fortunate to handle some masterpieces this season: no less than three by Joseph Wright of Derby, including his lovely portrait Mr and Mrs Coltman which fetched £1,404,000 ($1,740,960); and splendid works by Van Dyck, Zoffany, Gainsborough, and Turner. The Modern British School has also come to prominence recently, with sales regularly exceeding £1 million in total.

Jewellery of all kinds has been hotly competed for in all our salerooms. Although the vast majority of items fetch no more than the price of a small car, the Sw.fr.11 million (£3,548,387) paid by a jeweller of Jeddah will remain beyond most people's ambitions. It was the highest price at auction for a single stone. Jewellery of the Renaissance period was represented in Geneva by a Parisian jewelled and enamelled pendant of *c.*1540 at Sw.fr.1,320,000 (£425,806), also

Two connoisseurs taking a
close look at the Mantegna

Photo: Ken Towner (The Standard)

a record price. Other precious items to hit the headlines were the Paul Storr gold christening font known as the Portland Font, sold in London for £950,400 ($1,311,552), a silver Papal presentation dish of 1670, sold in Geneva for Sw.fr.1,100,000 (£354,840), and a Parisian gold and enamel box of 1747–8, sold for Sw.fr.297,000 (£95,806).

Works of art produced in this century become more and more important to collectors. Picasso's *Femme assise au chapeau*, sold in New York (although consigned from London) for $4,290,000 (£3,351,562), was the most prominent, but sales of Contemporary Painting have been very successful both in New York and London, as have sales of Modern Decorative Arts, Contemporary Ceramics and Photographs. But how does one categorize the Walt Disney celluloid of 1938, *Brave Little Tailor*, which fetched $20,900 (£17,131)?

Individual collections almost always bring higher than average prices. The season has included such diverse and remarkable groupings as: The Piccus Collection of Annamese Ceramics; The John Basmajian Collection of Walt Disney Animation Art; The Norweb Collection of Coins; the extraordinary Calvin Bullock Collection of Napoleonic and Nelson material, which totalled £1,781,811 ($2,191,627); The Rouët Cellar of Fine Wines; The F.J. Sandbergen Collection of Modern Pictures in Amsterdam; and Ancient Glass formerly in the Kofler-Truniger Collection, which included the minute cameo flask of 25 BC – AD 25 which fetched the far from small £324,000 ($356,400). Another distinguished glass collection was that formed by the Earl of Bradford, sold in London for £198,666 ($256,280).

These of course represent only the tip of the iceberg. It is the sheer breadth of what we offer in a season, rather than the prices, which makes the auctioneer reel in recollection. Lots passed under the hammer during the season covering every aspect of collecting and interest. To sell a lovely yellow Tiger Moth biplane one day, a distinguished collection of Old Master prints another, and all the time a continuous stream of furniture, pictures, silver, porcelain and much else, is a complex, demanding and responsible business. But all of us at Christie's love what we are doing, and we hope that this Review will serve as a reminder of another full and successful season, our 219th, and to encourage both buyers and sellers in the future.

I.O. Chance

I.O. Chance (1910–85)

RICHARD KINGZETT

Marshal Lyautey is said to have demanded of his officers that they possessed the quality of *panache*. If this is true, Peter Chance would have been a welcome member of the Marshal's staff, and it was a quality which served him well when he became chairman of Christie's in 1958. Internal complications, the new building risen like a phoenix from the flames, hampering currency restrictions and the emergence of Sotheby's as a major threat to his firm's 200 year virtual monopoly as auctioneers of pictures – these were the challenges he faced. When he retired 16 years later, Christie's has assumed their present active roles in New York and Geneva, had established offices (with varying degrees of success) in every corner of the world, had vastly increased their London premises, personnel and turnover, and had gone public.

It would however be wrong to remember him only at Christie's. Wartime service in the Coldstream Guards involved him in the glorious charge across Europe by the Guards Armoured Division which culminated in the liberation of Brussels. There he was photographed astride a tank like Brigadier Gérard waving a bottle of champagne to the cheering populace. Shortly afterwards he was wounded by a sniper's bullet, when fortunately, in his own words, 'the swine couldn't even shoot straight'.

'Swine' was a favourite epithet, and one that he used with relish to describe those of whom he disapproved. In public he liked to assume the persona of an elderly club-man who thought that the world had gone irrevocably to the dogs, but in fact he was someone who fought hard and in a very practical way for the things in which he believed. These included the National Trust, whom he served wholeheartedly as Chairman of the Properties Committee. In that role no journey was too arduous nor enquiry too trifling, but probably the cause closest to his heart was the Georgian Group of which he had been a founder member and eventually also became Chairman.

He had acquired great knowledge of 18th-century art in all its aspects and it was a period in which he felt instinctively at home. Alone in his generation he put together a beautiful group of those English mezzotints so admired by Pierpont Morgan and so neglected today. Seeing the enchanting rococo objects which adorned every corner of his London flat visitors may have felt that these represented the real focus of Peter's taste, but when shown the magnificent Hondecoeter in his country home, they came to realise its wider horizons.

He was a lively and generous host, who loved to entertain and he even continued to do so during the last year of his life, much of which was spent in great pain in hospital. There from his bed he welcomed visitors with all his old *élan* and listened eagerly to news of the saleroom and the art world. Some people had criticized his unabashed hedonism and had found affected the consciously stylish way in which he dressed and chose food and wine. Perhaps they were right, but there was style too in the way in which in retirement he bought a grand but crumbling Georgian house with a decaying garden, restored both to their original splendour with the passionate energy of a Wittlesbach, and bequeathed the result to the National Trust. It was his final splendid gesture of gratitude to the particular aspect of English life from which he had derived such very special pleasure.

Reprinted by kind permission of 'Apollo' magazine

A Quarter Century of Reviews

JOHN HERBERT

'It is hoped that in a time of acute financial depression the publication of Christie's *Annual Review* from November 1930 to the end of July 1931 will prove a much needed tonic.' Thus wrote one of the partners in 1931.

To settle the tremors of the abandonment of the Gold Standard and the fall of the Macdonald Government seems today to be asking too much of any book, but the confidence of Christie's partners was well founded. The 1931 Review, like those of 1928, 1929 and 1930, was a sumptuous volume of some 350 pages; no colour illustrations of course in those days, but high quality photogravure and very well printed. These Reviews were written on Christie's behalf by one A.C.R. Carter, who first started writing about art sales – believe it or not – in 1888, and yet was still on *The Daily Telegraph* when I became their most junior reporter in 1951. He was a larger-than-life figure in his Edwardian suit, wing collar and stock, and enormous moustaches. I well remember him because he would burst into the News Room shouting at anyone who got in his way 'dastardly poltroon'. When at Christie's, he stationed himself in front of the rostrum as if he might himself be put up for sale.

Thus, when in 1959 at the end of my first year the late Peter Chance, then chairman, said, 'John, I think we better have a Review on the year's best sales – have a look at A.C.R. Carter's,' I had a terrible feeling of inadequacy. A complete new boy to the art market I suggested that someone more experienced would do it better. To no avail: 'Nonsense, just the job for the Press Office [everything always seemed to be just the job for the Press Office, which consisted of me and one secretary]. You were even on the same paper as Carter.'

There had been no Reviews after 1931 because of what now are called euphemistically 'difficult trading conditions', but which really meant that the firm came close to the worst. Arthur Grimwade, father confessor and friend to so many raw recruits apart from myself, tells me that in 1932 there was a 10 per cent cut in salaries, which in his case would have meant that he got 18 shillings a week. Happily, generous counsels prevailed as he had joined so recently on agreed terms of £1 a week, and these were honoured. Then followed the war, when apart from the Red Cross sales little business was done and there was certainly no money for a Review.

Thus the 1959 Review, slim as it was compared with Carter's splendidly written hardbacked volumes, was not only a challenge for me but a significant policy move. Peter Chance was determined in the face of strong competition to reassure old clients and persuade new ones that Christie's was the best place to sell their works of art when the time came.

Being thrown in at the deep end is quite a salutary experience even for a swimmer. In the case of the Review it meant not only becoming closely involved with works of art, but also learning about printing, correcting proofs, and the time (then) taken for colour blocks to be made. The final product in 1959 certainly caused moments of anxiety and nervous exhaustion. It consisted of 6,000 words – not much for a professional journalist provided he knows his subject – but I didn't; the editorial was divided into sections on every department, which meant not only

John Herbert with *Portrait of the Artist's Son Titus* by Rembrandt, at the time of its sale on 15 March 1965 when it fetched 760,000 gns. ($2,234,400), then a record auction price for a picture

Copyright: BBC Hulton Picture Library

studying every catalogue but talking to the respective expert in order to make sure that I had not missed some vital sale. Thus began the close relationship with my colleagues which is such an essential element in the day-to-day work of the Press Office, let alone the Review. In this respect it often seemed that I had embarked upon an Open University course in an Alice in Wonderland atmosphere.

Looking at the 1959 Review today – fortunately hardly anyone has one save me – makes embarrassing reading, notwithstanding the colour reproduction of Turner's beautiful watercolour of the Lake of Lucerne, which we had sold for the world-record price of 11,000 gns., but which today would obviously fetch considerably more. I say embarrassing reading because prices by themselves can gradually cause the eyes to become glazed with boredom. However, I did not have any of Carter's knowledge of the art market or the vendors or of the history of the works of art with which to interlard the prices and thus make them more digestible. The perfect example of what I would have liked to produce is what that doyen of saleroom writers, Frank Davis, in spite of being over 90 years of age, still provides for the readers of *Country Life* each week – a beautifully rounded article.

However, in spite of its simple format the 1959 Review appeared to satisfy the Chairman and even my colleagues, who regarded me with deep suspicion, as I had suggested among other things that selling in guineas in such an international market was old fashioned and bad for our image. The amazing thing about the first Review was that it ever came out at all. What Peter Chance had not told me was that because the auction season runs from October to the end of July, leaving August and September for holidays, the refurbishment of the buildings and even some business-getting for the autumn, the editing, checking of proofs, and the production of a dummy with illustrations would have to be done on my holidays.

Having managed to deliver my 6,000 words to the printer within a week of the season ending, I and my family set off for Cornwall, leaving my gallant secretary to check the captions of the photographs and send them with 'galleys' of the editorial to our hotel on the Helford River, which in spite of its Victorian plumbing and furnishings had a very good menu: crêpe Suzettes filled with Cornish cream and liberally soaked in Grand Marnier. Having received the huge package from London and much to the amazement of the proprietrix and other guests, I started on my dummy. It was a real scissors-and-paste job, and by the end of each morning the lounge was littered with scraps of paper and smelt of paste. It was then sent by express post to the printer, who had a page proof ready by the time our holiday was over. That's how it was done for seven years; always a holiday task, a fact which was either not recognized or taken for granted. Over this time gradual improvements were made: hard covers, endpapers, and at long last proper articles by our technical staff. However, the 'labour ward' was still the hotel on the Helford River, so that regular guests became quite interested in it.

It was not until 1967/8 that we took the momentous decision to seek the help of a professional publisher. The Review had grown to just over 300 pages with quite a lot of colour illustrations. At long last a professional programme was introduced and a designer engaged, all of which was a considerable help. For the last few years the book has been 504 pages with the majority of illustrations in colour, which has meant even more careful planning. No publisher would normally undertake to produce such a book in three months; six would be nearer the mark. A schedule for the next book is drawn up immediately after the last one has been printed and from then on the precision of a military operation, now capably handled by Mark Wrey and a computer, is necessary. This is an opportunity for me to thank all the co-editors and their assistants at the various publishers we have used before our association with Phaidon Press (to whom thanks as well), and in particular Norman Ball, our designer for many years.

From the start – even from the 1959 season – there have been certain unforgettable works of art: the Burghley Net, which appealed for its nautical details as well; a dreamlike Boudin; drawings from the collection of the Marquess of Northampton, including a Giovanni Bellini – then a name unknown to me! But over the years the kaleidoscope of works of art has taught me to recognize many styles and techniques: Paul Storr and Paul De Lamerie; the great French *ébénistes* such as Oeben, Riesener and Carlin; even the subtle differences between minimalist and conceptual art.

Until 1967/8 the Reviews were given away to anyone who subscribed in the smallest way to our catalogues, which explained the sudden rush of Arms and Armour subscribers – it was the cheapest category – during the summer! Now the huge cost of production makes this impossible, and instead the books sell all over the world and are also distributed free to favoured clients. The attractions of the Review are, firstly that for the art historian or serious collector they build up into a useful reference series showing market trends. Secondly, the mere size of the book today compared with that of the sixties demonstrates the tremendous increase in the interest in collecting, and with it the explosion of prices. Thirdly, the Reviews show the many swings of fashion over the years; for instance, the renewed interest some years ago in Pre-Raphaelite pictures; the more recent boom in the Orientalist School and in Scandinavian pictures; and even more amazing the interest in 20th-century decorative art, and all the new collecting fields which Christie's South Kensington and Christie's East in New York have developed so successfully.

In conclusion, I admit I am pleased to have been thrown in at the deep end by Peter Chance and am proud to have been given the responsibility of editing the Reviews for so long, although my dear mother, 94 last September, still finds it somewhat surprising remembering my reports from school.

I am sure you will enjoy the 1985 Review. It is a very different matter from 1959 and the lounge of the Helford River hotel. Time in fact for me to bow out.

Negotiated Sales

CHRISTOPHER R. PONTER, LL.B

The financial climate over the past year or two has not been very encouraging for those owners anxious to explore private treaty sales or acceptances in lieu of tax. The Minister for the Arts in July 1985 announced that the earlier constraint on new offers is to be lifted, in that there should be recourse to the public expenditure Reserve where the heritage items on offer are of national importance and such a call on the Reserve is justified on merit. We await with some interest to see how this new criterion will be applied.

However, a number of important private treaty transactions were completed during 1984–5, and two of the works involved are illustrated. The exquisite painting of a young woman, *La Pensée*, by Renoir was accepted in lieu of a gross value in the region of £2 million ($2.8 million) and has been allocated to the Barber Institute, Birmingham. Also, the magnificent tulipwood bonheur-du-jour by Martin Carlin, *c.* 1770, was accepted from Lady Anne Cavendish Bentinck in part payment of the tax levied on the estates of her parents, the late Duke and Duchess of Portland, and this has been allocated to Bowes Museum at Barnard Castle, Durham.

The late Sir Geoffrey Keynes was renowned for his lifelong interest in the work of William Blake, and we were pleased to negotiate the transfer of his important collection of paintings, drawings and prints by William Blake in lieu of tax, and this collection has now been transferred to the Fitzwilliam Museum, Cambridge, in accordance with Sir Geoffrey's wishes. Among the more important private treaty sales negotiated during the year, there was the sale to the National Gallery of a rare religious painting of *Charity* by Anthony van Dyck, painted in 1627 following his return to Antwerp. Acquired by Sir James Lowther in 1763, it was last shown in public in 1823 and was sold by the Lonsdale Estate Trustees.

Following their acquisition of Belton House, near Grantham, and many of its contents, the National Trust acquired by private treaty an important group of paintings by Melchior D. Hondecoeter, a Reynolds portrait of Sir John Cust, and various tapestries to complete the essential furnishings of the house. Other private sales included an important pair of portraits of a gentleman and his wife by Marten van Heemskerk to the National Museum of Wales, Cardiff; an interesting group of 11 drawings of his children and others by Ford Madox Brown, together with his Accounts Book, to Walker Art Gallery, Liverpool; a group of five paintings by John Constable (including a self-portrait) direct from the Constable family to the Tate Gallery, London; and a portrait of the Emperor Franz Joseph to the Government to be retained in the British Embassy in Vienna.

PIERRE AUGUSTE RENOIR
French 1841–1919
La Pensée
c. 1877
Oil on canvas
$25\frac{1}{2} \times 21\frac{1}{4}$ in. (64.8 × 54 cm.)

Tulipwood bonheur-du-jour
By Martin Carlin
*c.*1770
Inset with 17 Sèvres porcelain plaques
25½ in. (64.8 cm.) wide
Probably bought by the 3rd Duke of Portland in the 1780s, it is hoped that this particular table
may prove to be the one formerly belonging to Mme du Barry, the mistress of Louis XV. If so,
the allocation to Bowes Museum will be very apt for it was the Château du Barry at Louveciennes
that John Bowes gave to his wife Josephine on their marriage in 1852, and the table may rejoin
the remaining contents then in the Château in 1770.

Treasure Houses of Britain: the Washington Exhibition and the Role of the Auctioneer in the Evolution of Taste

FRANCIS RUSSELL

The great exhibition of treasures from British houses that is being held in Washington this winter offers a unique opportunity for the American public to survey the history of patronage and collecting in this country. It illustrates many facets of taste, familiar and unfamiliar, and the reader of the catalogue will soon observe how central the role of Christie's has been in the development of these since James Christie set up in business in 1766.

The earliest purchase from Christie's in the exhibition is Guercino's celebrated *Erminia finding the wounded Tancred,* sent from Paris for sale by Comte de Lauraguais in 1772: this was bought for the 5th Earl of Carlisle, whose purchases in the saleroom quickly outshone his grand tour acquisitions, and happily remains at Castle Howard (see fig. 1). Other collectors were more interested in the northern schools. Sir John Griffin Griffin spent 20 gns. on van Goyen's *Coast at Egmond aan Zee* (Audley End) in 1773, while a year later Horace Walpole was astounded when Cuyp's great *View of Nijmegen* (Woburn Abbey) fetched the unprecedented price of 290 gns. at the sale of a bankrupt financier, Sir George Colebrooke. Subsequently acquired by the politician Richard Rigby, the latter picture returned to Christie's after his death in 1788 and was bought for 250 gns. by the 5th Duke of Bedford. The saleroom not only reflected changing patterns of taste, it also could influence those of patronage. Thus the 2nd Viscount Palmerston's purchase in 1771 at Christie's of a work by Joseph Wright of Derby was followed a year later by his decision to purchase an oustanding work from the artist, *The Iron Forge,* which is still at Broadlands.

In the 18th century, when capital taxes did not exist, a frequent reason for the sale of collections was the lack of a direct male heir. This was the case with Rigby and also with the banker William Fauquier, who died in 1788. Much of his collection was offered for sale a year later, when Chardin's remarkable *Le Faiseur du Châteaux de Cartes* of 1735 (Stanton Harcourt) was bought in at £5.15s. It was subsequently given to a family friend, the 2nd Earl Harcourt. Similarly, after the death without issue of Welbore Ellis Agar in 1805, his remarkable collection was sent to Christie's. Such was the excitement caused by the impending auction that Robert, 2nd Earl Grosvenor, later 1st Marquess of Westminster, determined to buy the collection *en bloc* for his gallery at Grosvenor House, thus acquiring a celebrated series of Claudes, represented in the exhibition by *Morning* and *Evening,* and Velázquez's *Don Balthasar Carlos in the Riding School,* which has also been lent by the Duke of Westminster.

From the late 18th century many pictures were commissioned by publishers who intended to profit from the sale of engravings made after them. The retirement of such a publisher led to the sale of Wheatley's poignant tableau, *John Howard Visiting and Relieving the Miseries of a Prison,* at Christie's in 1809. The sale casts an interesting light on the political complexion of the times, for the purchaser was the Pittite Lord Harrowby, who was an early convert to the movement against slavery and, as leader of the 'waverers', was in 1832 to facilitate the passage of the Reform Bill.

There were many reasons for sales in the early 19th century, but financial imprudence was evidently among the more compelling. Thus much of the pioneering collection of works of the English school formed by Lord Leicester de Tabley was auctioned in 1827; John Martin's *Destruction of Pompeii and Herculaneum* (Tabley House) was one of the few important pictures to be retained. Two years later the 6th Duke of Bedford, another generous patron of artists of the day, found it expedient to prune the collection he had inherited. Fortunately for his descendants, Poussin's noble *Moses trampling on Pharoah's Crown* failed to reach its reserve of 400 gns. and is still at Woburn.

Because they are on panel and should not be moved unnecessarily, Italian primitives, of which there were such spectacular auctions at Christie's in the mid and later 19th century, are not represented in the exhibition. But other facets of the taste of Victorian collectors can be vividly experienced. Dutch pictures, which had been consistently fashionable for over a century, continued to be popular with the owners of great houses. Thus the Duke of Cleveland, who 'restored' Raby Castle so energetically, spent 440 gns. in 1860 on Teniers' *Artist Painting in a Gallery* (Raby Castle), which had been acquired in the mid-18th century by Sampson Gideon, the first of the long sequence of Jewish connoisseurs who have so enriched the history of collecting in Britain. Tin mines were responsible for the wealth of Charles Pascoe Grenfell of Taplow Court who secured Philips de Koninck's *Panoramic Landscape* (Firle) in 1859; this cost 380 gns. and was bought to serve as pendant to a similar landscape Grenfell had acquired a few years earlier. The 3rd Marquess of Bute, the builder of Cardiff Castle and so many other architectural extravaganzas, had inherited the pioneering collection of Dutch pictures of his ancestor the 3rd Earl. He rarely bought pictures and apparently only acquired Hobbema's unique *Winter Scene*, which was sent for sale in 1895 and cost 1,450 gns., because it had previously been in the collection.

Seventeenth-century Dutch landscapes continued to be admired and so, albeit on less extravagant terms than previously, was Claude. The Altieri Claudes, the celebrated pendants of which the later in date, *Landscape with the Arrival of Aeneas at Pallenteum* of 1675 (Anglesey Abbey), is included in the exhibition (see fig. 2), were sold in 1884 with the collection formed earlier in the century by P.J. Miles for Leigh Court. They then fetched 3,800 gns. The market for Italian pictures of the *seicento* was more capricious as the fate in the same auction of Domenichino's great *Saint John the Evangelist* (Glyndbourne) indicated: so admired when first imported earlier in the century, this was bought in for 700 gns. and finally sold for only 70 gns. in 1899. By contrast, when the great collection at Blenheim was so tragically dispersed in 1886 two favourite works by Carlo Dolci were bought in at exceptional prices; of these the vibrant *Adoration of the Magi* (950 gns.) has remained at Blenheim, previously overlooked by scholars.

A spirited collector of the Edwardian period who sought to replace the gallery his ancestor had sold at Christie's in 1827 was the 5th Earl of Carysfort. The visitor to Washington can see two of his purchases at King Street, O'Neil's *Eastward Ho*, 1857 (Elton Hall), which cost 200 gns. in the Leatham sale of 1901, and Alma-Tadema's concentrated masterpiece *A Dedication to Bacchus* (Elton Hall), which at 5,600 gns. was the star of the posthumous sale of the influential dealer Ernest Gambert in 1903.

Changing economic forces and subsequently the incidence of taxation has weakened the tradition of connoisseurship and patronage in this country and many old collections have been lost, never to be replaced. Occasionally a masterpiece was saved by default, as when Romney's neo-classical masterpiece *Sir Christopher and Lady Sykes* (Sledmere) failed to reach expectations aroused by the sale of his *The Misses Beckford* for 52,000 gns. a few months earlier and was bought in for 27,000 gns. in 1920. Other pictures were rescued in the saleroom by public institutions, Zoffany's *Charles Towneley in his Gallery at Park Street* (Towneley Hall) for 1,250 gns. in 1939 and Scott's *Building of Westminster Bridge* and *Old London Bridge* (Bank of England) for 3,800 gns. in 1944.

A major development of the post-war years has been the role of the National Trust as conserver of great houses and their collections. Often the sale of contents has been negotiated privately with the Trust or the Treasury through Christie's. Thus it was at Hardwick (1959), with the celebrated silver furniture at Knole (1966), and at Uppark (1965 and later), represented in the exhibition by one of the exceptional set of Vernets. A recent sale of the kind was that of Belton (1984), which included Mercier's enchanting Tyrconnel group of *c.*1726, in the background of which the house itself appears (see fig. 3).

In recent years a number of great houses have been vested in private charitable trusts and Christie's contributed to the negotiations which in 1980 established the precedent that pictures could be accepted in lieu of tax and remain in houses held by such trusts. Of the five works thus saved for Arundel Castle, Mytens' great portraits of the Earl and Countess of Arundel dominate the Long Gallery in the exhibition.

It is equally reassuring that notable pictures have continued to be acquired for country house collections in the post-war years. The Altieri Claudes, which the Duke of Kent had acquired at King Street for 700 gns. in 1940, were purchased at the Duchess's sale in 1947 for 2,100 gns. by Lord Fairhaven, who formed a wide-ranging collection for Anglesey Abbey which he bequeathed to the National Trust. Others have had the determination to build on ancestral collections:

1. Giovanni Francesco Barbieri, il Guercino: *Erminia finding the wounded Tancred.* Castle Howard Collection

2. Claude Lorraine: *Landscape with the Arrival of Aeneas at Pallenteum.* The National Trust, Anglesey Abbey

3. Philip Mercier: *Viscount Tyconnel with his Family.* The National Trust, Belton House

Lord Hopetoun secured Dance's conversation piece of *Charles Lord Hope, the Hon. James Hope and their Tutor William Rovett* (Hopetoun House), when this was sold by the latter's heir for 10,000 gns. in 1970. It is perhaps fitting that this survey should end with Edward Lear's *Forest of Bavella, Corsica* (Beaufront Castle), sold for 7,500 gns. in 1973, just over 200 years after the sale of the Castle Howard Guercino and the birth in Corsica of Bonaparte, whose triumphant European rampages so ironically enriched British collections.

   The history of taste is of extraordinary complexity: some great collectors adhered to the fashions of their times while others, whether from whim or vision, have sought to ignore these. Their varied achievement can be experienced in country houses throughout Britain, and everyone with an interest in the future of these must hope that the Washington exhibition will encourage a wider American public to visit them. It is gratifying therefore that Christie's, which has for over two centuries made its contribution to the evolution of collecting, has now set up a company that will arrange specialized tours of country houses and their collections for visitors from overseas.

Pictures

CLAUDE JOSEPH VERNET
French 1714–89
*Night: a moonlit Coastal
Landscape with Fisherfolk by a
Fire on a Quay, a Man-o'-War
beyond*
Signed and dated 1767
Oil on canvas
$32\frac{1}{2} \times 40\frac{3}{4}$ in.
(82.5 × 103.5 cm.)
Sold 5.7.85 in London for
£259,200 ($336,960)
One of a pair commissioned
from the artist by Henry
Hoare of Stourhead in 1766

'The Adoration of the Magi' by Andrea Mantegna

R.W. LIGHTBOWN

Mantegna's *Adoration of the Magi*, now so suddenly famous, was until lately a little-known picture, familiar to scholars only in photograph and consequently often doubted. But in the early 16th century it was a well-known and much copied work, though none of the copies suggest its real quality. Its inclusion in the Splendours of the Gonzaga exhibition, held at the Victoria and Albert Museum in 1981, first revealed it as a masterpiece by the hand of one of the greatest artists of the Italian Renaissance, a rare master moreover, for very few autograph paintings by Mantegna have survived the hazards of the centuries. The *Adoration* was in fact one of the last paintings by him still in private hands.

It was painted *c.*1500, during Mantegna's last years, when he seems to have reverted to some of the types of composition and pictorial devices with which he had experimented during his youth in Padua, where he worked until 1460. It had been his ambition in that humanistic city to revive the glories of classical Greek and Roman painting, to be the modern Apelles in fact, and he even signalled his ambition to be regarded as the modern rival of the great ancient Greek master by signing one of his pictures, a *St. Sebastian* painted *c.*1458–60 now in Vienna, in Greek. During the 15th century little was known in reality of Greek and Roman painting, but some artists, Mantegna amongst them, thought that a clear idea of what it must have looked like could be obtained from studying ancient sculptures, which survived in some quantity. He seems to have believed that antique pictures had the simplicity of many antique reliefs, and like them had only summary indications of setting. As a result his outline has always a sculptural strength of definition, his drapery a sculptural rigidity of folds. Indeed his first master Squarcione, on seeing his frescos of the story of St. James in the Ovetari chapel, uttered the famous reproach that 'they were not good, because he had imitated antique things of marble', rather than Nature. The first surviving painting in which Mantegna reproduces something of the effect of an antique relief is the beautiful *Presentation of Christ*, now in Berlin, painted between *c.*1454 and *c.*1460. Here the composition is enclosed in a window frame, within which the figures are shown half-length and in two planes against a plain black ground which concentrates the eye upon their action. So far as we know, pictures of this kind were not painted again by Mantegna for many years after his departure for Mantua in 1460. But during the period from 1490 to 1506 he took to them again, and many of his pictures from these last years were once more conceived almost as coloured sculptures, quietly vitalized into paintings by the artist's mastery of spatial composition, by his precision and delicacy of form and modelling, by his strong accentuation of passages of colour, especially of his favourite yellow and coral red, and by his graphic skill in rendering the texture and patterning of costume.

All of these characteristic stylistic features can be admired in the *Adoration*, which like the early *Presentation* is a composition of half-length figures in a window frame. The Adoration of the Magi was a theme over which 15th-century painters loved to scatter rich pageantry, and Mantegna had painted *c.*1462 just such a splendidly processional *Adoration of the Magi* for his

ANDREA MANTEGNA
Italian 1431–1506
The Adoration of the Magi
Tempera and oil on linen laid down on canvas
21½ × 27⅜ in. (54.6 × 69.2 cm.)
Sold 18.4.85 in London for £8,100,000 ($10,449,000)
From the collection of The Marquess of Northampton, D.L.
Record auction price for any picture

great patron Lodovico Gonzaga, Marquis of Mantua. In this he put out all his virtuosity of invention and technique in order to amaze and dazzle the eye, not only in the principal action, but also in a rich variety of accessory figures and a carefully devised picturesque setting of rocks, hilly slopes and meadowland. In the late *Adoration* all this has gone to make room for a quiet concentration on the principal figures and their interrelationships. We see only the Holy Family, Joseph, the Virgin holding the Child, and the three Kings, Caspar, the oldest King, in the foreground, Melchior and the Moorish King Balthasar in the background. They are carefully contrasted studies in age: Caspar is bald-headed and white-bearded, Melchior a man of grave maturity, and Balthasar a young man. Far from enticing the eye to roam over a rich and various landscape, the six figures are arranged on a dark ground in two planes, like those of a classical relief, so that we consider only their actions and emotions. And by cutting off the figures half-length Mantegna leaves it to our imagination to fill out what he has omitted, if we so wish, whilst claiming our exclusive attention for the three Kings who render Adoration and for the Christ Child who receives it, attended by his parents.

The composition is classically static; it does not prompt us to figure another action that is to follow. Yet as always in Mantegna we see on closer contemplation that the poses of some of the figures imply preceding actions. Caspar has knelt in homage, and taken off the silver cover of a bowl which contains the gold that is his offering. The child gazes downwards at the bowl clasping his white swaddling cloth with a child-like simplicity, while Melchior and Balthasar fix their eyes upon him, Melchior ardently but calmly, Balthasar with youthful *naïveté* of eagerness. The Virgin's eyes are modestly downcast, while Joseph gazes with grave interest at the three Kings. It is characteristic of Mantegna that all these figures are so essentially self-contained that their eyes never really meet. The consequence is a still and dignified serenity which nevertheless is suffused with quiet human warmth. Although the splendour of costume and accessories usual in Adorations of the Magi has been subordinated to the expression of feeling, Mantegna has not neglected these traditional features. But he has introduced them with a discreet richness that in a fashion typical of his art only appears on deeper consideration. Caspar is clothed in a rich heavy robe of watered silk lined with a broad collar of spotted fur, a garment such as only princes wore in the late 15th century. Melchior also wears a fur-trimmed robe and an oriental hat, a kerchief wound round a high cap (a *kufiya*), and Balthasar has a similar hat, a cap of rich spotted fur, also with a kerchief. In addition Balthasar wears long exotic earrings, such as Mantegna must have seen Moors and Africans wearing on the quays of Venice. We know that he made many drawings of such exotic oriental figures from the life, just as Pisanello had done before him, because they are depicted with close and accurate observation in his earlier *Adoration* of *c.*1462. The offerings made by the Kings are also rich and exotically oriental. Caspar holds a blue-and-white bowl, either a piece of Chinese porcelain or a Persian imitation of it, but in either case a highly prized object in a century when porcelain was still a fit present from a Sultan to a Doge. The thick gold ring set with rubies he wears on his upper thumb is a characteristic motif in its quiet suggestion of royal state. Melchior carries a censer containing his offering of Frankincense: it has been identified as Turkish Tombak ware, mounted in gold. Finally Balthasar holds a covered vase of agate, beautifully marked and beautifully shaped, a costly masterpiece of the difficult art of hardstone carving.

Although the colouring is subdued by the ground, it too exploits quiet contrasts between passages of intense vividness of colour, like the beautiful yellow of the Virgin's veil, and delicate passages in its restraint, heralding the High Renaissance in its simplicity and concentration of feeling, and in its subordination of ornament to expression. For whom was it painted? Mantegna was allowed only to work for the Gonzaga, and could paint for others only by their licence. The probability then is that it was painted for a Gonzaga, and indeed the subject, representing the adoration of Christ surrounded by kings, is a fully suitable one for a devotional picture painted for a prince. Quite possibly it was intended for an oratory or chapel in one of the many country palaces of the Gonzaga surrounding Mantua. Unfortunately we have no early record of it, but the Gonzaga inventory of 1627 does list 'a small picture of Our Lord who is visited by the Magi with a black frame', with no artist's name. This picture was kept in a cupboard in the library of the Castello. Did this picture come to England when the Mantuan pictures were sold to Charles I? Certainly Charles owned what his inventory-maker called a *Nativity* attributed to Mantegna that corresponds to no recorded picture by the artist.

PAOLO CALIARI, IL VERONESE
Italian 1528–88
A Youth at a Curtain with an elegantly dressed Boy and a Greyhound
Oil on canvas transferred from panel
87 × 41 in. (205 × 104 cm.)
Sold 18.4.85 in London for £216,000 ($278,640)
This and a companion were parted in the 1570s into two door panels and may be compared to the illusionistic frescos in the Villa Lambert alla longa

Opposite:
GIOVAN BATTISTA MORONI
Italian 1525–78
Portrait of a Gentleman in a green Doublet and a chain-mail Shirt, behind a Ledge
Oil on canvas
23¾ × 20¾ in. (60.4 × 52.7 cm.)
Sold 5.7.85 in London for £345,600 ($449,280)
This exceptionally well-preserved portrait by Moroni, last recorded in the 18th century, is datable *c.*1565

GIOVANNI ANTONIO CANAL, IL CANALETTO
Italian 1697–1768
A Capriccio of Roman Ruins with a Renaissance Church, the Colleoni Monument, Peasants and other Figures
Signed
Oil on canvas
28 × 53 in. (71 × 135 cm.)
Sold 18.4.85 in London for £432,000 ($557,280)
An early work datable *c.* 1723

GIOVANNI ANTONIO CANAL, IL CANALETTO
Italian 1697–1768
The Grand Canal, Venice, looking north-west, from the Palazzo Corner to the Palazzo Contarini dagli Scrigni, with Cà Grande and the Palazzo Pisani, the Campanile of the Carità beyond
Oil on canvas
$24\frac{1}{8} \times 38\frac{1}{8}$ in. (61.3 × 96.9 cm.)
Sold 5.7.85 in London for £388,800 ($505,440)
This picture dates from about 1738–40 and was engraved by Antonio Visentini in *Prospectus Magni Canalis Venetiarum* of 1742. It and the companion view of the Grand Canal with the Rialto Bridge were probably owned by Canaletto's leading English patron, Consul Joseph Smith.

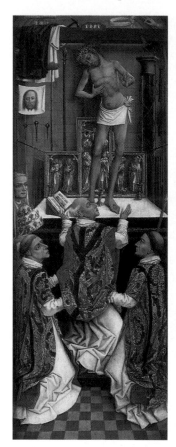

THE MASTER OF THE LEGEND OF SAINT CATHERINE

A Triptych: central panel, *The Madonna and Child seated at a Window with Saint Barbara and Saint Catherine, and music-making Angels beyond*; left wing, *The Mass of Saint Gregory*; right wing, *Saint Ildefonso being invested with a Chasuble by the Virgin, with a kneeling male Donor*; on the outside of the wings, *The Annunciation* (grisaille)

Oil on panel

Central panel $33\frac{1}{2} \times 28$ in. (85×71 cm.); wings $34\frac{1}{4} \times 12\frac{1}{2}$ in. (87×32 cm.)

Sold 11.12.84 in London for £102,600 ($124,146)

JAN BRUEGHEL THE ELDER
Flemish 1568–1625
A Village Market
Signed and dated 1615, and with indistinct inventory number
Oil on copper
$10\frac{1}{8} \times 14\frac{1}{2}$ in. (25.7 × 36.9 cm.)
Sold 18.4.85 in London for £486,000 ($626,940)
From the collection of Lord Margadale of Islay, T.D.
This characteristic work by Brueghel was sold previously by Christie's, 4 June 1864, lot 6, for 110 gns. and subsequently acquired
by Alfred Morrison of Fonthill, ancestor of the vendor

SIR PETER PAUL RUBENS
Flemish 1577–1640
The Virgin and Child enthroned with Angels (a sketch for the crowning section of an altar frame)
Inscribed AVE MARIA
Oil on panel
$17\frac{1}{2} \times 25\frac{1}{2}$ in. (44.5 × 64.8 cm.)
Sold 11.12.84 in London for £194,400 ($235,224)

Opposite:
GERRIT VAN HONTHORST
Dutch 1590–1656
The Adoration of the Shepherds
Signed and dated 1632
Oil on canvas
$48 \times 39\frac{3}{4}$ in. (122 × 101 cm.)
Sold 19.4.85 in London for £167,400 ($217,620)
A preparatory drawing for this picture is in the
Kupferstichkabinett, Berlin Print Room

NICOLAES MAES
Dutch 1632–93
An Old Woman making Lace in a Kitchen
Signed
Oil on panel
14¾ × 13¾ in. (37.5 × 35 cm.)
Sold 18.4.85 in London for £410,400 ($529,416)
Datable *c.*1655

EMANUEL DE WITTE
Dutch 1617–92
The Interior of the Oude Kerk, Amsterdam, with numerous Figures listening to a Sermon
Signed and indistinctly dated
Oil on canvas
$26\frac{1}{2} \times 29$ in. (67.3 × 73.7 cm.)
Sold 19.4.85 in London for £129,600 ($168,480)

SALOMON VAN RUYSDAEL
Dutch 1600–70
A River Landscape with Figures in Boats and Buildings in the distance
Signed with initials and dated 1645
Oil on canvas
38½ × 52 in. (97.8 × 132.2 cm.)
Sold 15.1.85 in New York for $418,000 (£366,666)

SALOMON VAN RUYSDAEL
Dutch 1600–70
The Maas near Gorkum, with a Ferry, a Yacht bearing the Coat-of-Arms of the City of Amsterdam and Travellers in a Waggon by a Monastery
Indistinctly signed and dated 1647
Oil on canvas
38 × 52½ in. (96.5 × 133 cm.)
Sold 21.5.85 in Amsterdam for D.fl.1,083,000 (£246,136)
Record auction price for a work of art sold in the Netherlands
From the collection of Jonkheer P.H. van de Wall Repelaer van Puttershoek, Puttershoek
In the distance is the Groote or St. Maartenskerk, Gorkum: the view is taken from just upstream of the junction of the Waal and
the Maas; the monastery on the right is a fanciful substitute for Slot Loevestein

AELBERT CUYP
Dutch 1620–91
A River Landscape with Sailing Vessels, a Rowing Boat and Sportsmen on a Jetty in the foreground, a Town beyond
Signed
Oil on panel
$17\frac{1}{2} \times 29\frac{3}{4}$ in. (44.5 × 75.5 cm.)
Sold 18.4.85 in London for £237,600 ($306,504)
An early work, to be dated *c.*1644

JAN VAN DE CAPPELLE
Dutch 1624–79
The Visit of the Stadtholder, Prince Frederik Hendrik, to the Fleet of the States General at Dordrecht in 1646
Signed
Oil on panel
30 × 40½ in. (76.2 × 102.8 cm.)
Sold 9.5.85 in New York for $1,650,000 (£1,341,463)
Record auction price for a work by the artist

LUDOLF BAKHUYSEN
Dutch 1631–1708
Dutch Merchantmen driven on to a rocky Coast in a Storm
Signed and dated 1667
Oil on canvas
44 × 65 in. (111.8 × 165.1 cm.)
Sold 19.4.85 in London for £118,800 ($154,440)
Formerly in the collection of the Earl of Onslow

JACOB VAN WALSCAPELLE
Dutch 1644–1727
A Still Life of Flowers
Signed and dated 1681
Oil on canvas
$40\frac{1}{2} \times 35$ in. (102.5 × 89 cm.)
Sold 21.5.85 in Amsterdam for
D.fl.934,800 (£212,454)

OSIAS BEERT
Flemish 1622–78
A Still Life
Oil on panel
21½ × 32¾ in. (54.5 × 83 cm.)
Sold 15.1.85 in New York for $209,000 (£183,333)

JAN DAVIDSZ. DE HEEM
Dutch 1606–84
A Still Life
Signed and dated 1653
Oil on panel
13 × 20 in. (33 × 51 cm.)
Sold 5.6.85 in New York for $220,000 (£169,230)
By order of the Estate of Gerald Oliven

SIR ANTHONY VAN DYCK
Flemish 1599–1641
Portrait of Anne Carr, Countess of Bedford (1617–84), aged 22, holding a Rose
Oil on canvas
39¾ × 32½ in.
(101 × 82.5 cm.)
Sold 23.11.84 in London for £162,000 ($200,880)
This portrait, previously known from early copies, was owned by Philip, 4th Lord Wharton, who commissioned a major series of portraits by Van Dyck, many of which are now in the Hermitage. The sitter was the daughter of Albert Carr, Earl of Somerset, who married William, 5th Earl, subsequently 1st Duke of Bedford, in 1637.

JOHAN ZOFFANY, R.A.
British 1733–1810
A Scene from 'Love in a Village' by Isaac Bickerstaffe, Act 1, Scene 2, with Edward Shuter as Justice Woodcock, John Beard as Hawthorn, and John Dunstall as Hodge
Oil on canvas
51¼ × 65 in. (130.2 × 165.1 cm.)
Sold 26.4.85 in London for £345,600 ($435,456)
From the collection of John Garle, Esq.
Edward Shuter (1728–76) first appeared on stage at Richmond in 1744. He played with Garrick and created many important parts, making his final appearance at the Haymarket in September 1776. John Beard (1716–91) acted mainly at Drury Lane but became actor-manager at Covent Garden in 1761; he was also the most famous male singer in England in the mid-18th century. John Dunstall (1717–78) spent all his acting career at Covent Garden. Isaac Bickerstaffe (1735–1812) wrote about 20 plays and operas, of which *Love in a Village* is the most successful and popular. It was first produced at Covent Garden on 8 December 1762, with the actors shown in the present picture. The music was a mixture of old airs by Thomas Arne, famous opera tunes, new songs and an overture by Karl Abel. In 1772 Bickerstaffe had to flee the country and died abroad in poverty in 1812.
At least two other versions of the picture are known. One is in the Detroit Institute of Arts, where the picture behind the actors is the same as the one in the present picture, *The Judgment of Solomon*; it measures 40 × 50 in. (101.6 × 127 cm.). The other version is in the Somerset Maugham Collection of theatrical paintings at the National Theatre; here the picture behind the actors is the portrait of Charles I's children by Van Dyck in the Royal Collection.

Joseph Wright's Portraits of Mr and Mrs Coltman and Colonel Heathcote

DAVID FRASER

Though major works by the British 18th-century painter Joseph Wright of Derby, A.R.A. (1734–97), have rarely appeared at auctions in recent years, three exceptionally fine portraits have been sold since autumn 1984, including the portraits of Mr and Mrs Coltman and of Colonel Charles Heathcote.

Both portraits date c. 1770–2 and belong to the most innovative and exciting phase of Wright's career. Trained in the London studio of fashionable portrait-painter Thomas Hudson in the 1750s, Wright had already established himself in Derby by the early 1760s with a string of local portrait commissions. From 1765 to 1773 he exhibited at the Society of Artists portraits and exceptional subject-paintings featuring both the dramatic effects of light and shadow for which he was well known, and the unusual scenes of scientific and industrial activities which were unique in British 18th-century painting. Portraits featured in Wright's output throughout his career, and he was primarily a painter of the middle classes – professional people, businessmen, industrialists, and landed gentry. In the standard work on the artist, Benedict Nicolson's *Joseph Wright of Derby* (1968), the author says that the years 1769–71 marked a peak in Wright's career as a portrait painter, and the Coltman and Heathcote portraits of 1770–2 support this opinion.

The double portrait of Mr and Mrs Coltman appears in Wright's account book among pictures of 1770–1 as 'Mr & Mrs Coltman in a Conversation 63'. Against this entry is the note 'pd. 100', and the extra money may have included the frame and possibly payment for some of the other Wrights owned by Coltman. The portrait may well have been the 'small Conversation' exhibited by Wright at the Society of Artists in 1772. It depicts the full-length figures of the artist's friend Thomas Coltman and his wife Mary in a landscape setting, about to go riding; Mrs Coltman is already on horseback and a groom fetches her husband's horse while he stands at her side, apparently discussing something with her to which he is pointing.

This painting can be interpreted as a celebration of Coltman's inheritance of the family estate and his marriage, both happening a year or two before it was painted. Thomas Coltman (1746–1826) came from a wealthy family who had acquired in 1715/16 an estate at Hagnaby Priory, north of Boston in Lincolnshire, as well as owning land in Derbyshire. Though Thomas was only the second surviving son of his father John (died 1763), his eldest brother died in 1768 and Thomas was left as head of the family. He married Mary Barlow in 1769 at Astbury, Cheshire (north of Stoke-on-Trent), where her father lived.

According to Coltman's marriage licence, his Derby residence was somewhere in the parish of St. Werburgh, only a few minutes' walk from Wright's home. Judging from the artist's correspondence, the two men were extremely good friends, and Coltman owned several other pictures by Wright, including single charcoal portraits of himself and Mrs Coltman, two artificial-light subjects of the late 1760s, and a self-portrait by Wright in the manner of Rembrandt that has on the reverse a study for the Tate Gallery's *Experiment on a Bird in the Air Pump* (1768).

JOSEPH WRIGHT OF DERBY, A.R.A.
British 1734–97
Double Portrait of Mr and Mrs
Thomas Coltman about to set out
on a Ride
Oil on canvas
50 × 40 in. (127 × 101.6 cm.)
Sold 23.11.04 in London for
£1,404,000 ($1,740,960)
Record auction price for a
work by the artist

It is an intriguing possibility that Mr and Mrs Coltman appear in the finished version of the latter, one of the most celebrated of Wright's scientific paintings; the elegantly dressed couple standing on the left of the picture bear similarities of colouring and facial features (especially the woman's nose!) to the Coltmans as they appear in both the oil portrait and the single charcoal portaits mentioned above. The couples even have the same psychological and pictorial relationship to each other in the *Air Pump* and oil portrait, the lady gazing intently at the man, whose attention is otherwise engaged looking elsewhere. The *Air Pump* picture was finished for exhibition in 1768 and presumably the Coltmans were courting at this time, which gives the prominent relationship between the couple on the left amorous significance. Memoirs by Wright's niece and his contemporary the architect Gandon mention Wright using his friends and acquaintances as models in his subject-pictures, so the suggestion that the Coltmans appear in the Tate Gallery picture is by no means unreasonable.

Coltman continued to patronize Wright in the early 1770s, giving the artist several hundred pounds as the latter left for Italy in 1773, though Coltman seems not to have acquired any more of Wright's pictures, and by 1780 had returned to Lincolnshire.

Wright's best portraits are undoubtedly those of his friends, not surprisingly, because he would know their personalities and circumstances better and could thus paint them with greater depth of character and sense of their social standing. Thomas Coltman's casual pose and bearing in the double portrait is that of the wealthy landowner surveying his estate, though it must be admitted that the location and building in the painting have not at this stage been identified. He leans on his wife's leg, pointing out to her something in the countryside beyond our range of vision, while she looks down at him. Coltman's later correspondence with Sir Joseph Banks in the 1790s confirms Wright's image of him as the country gentleman of leisure who loved riding: in one letter Coltman says, 'I propose to go out with the Hounds in the Morning wch. I can do more easily than write a letter. No uncommon thing with a Sportsman.'

The portraits of Mr and Mrs Coltman, and that of Colonel Heathcote, mark two significant developments in Wright's art in the early 1770s. Firstly, apart from a few portraits of the 1760s showing children in landscape settings, Wright did not generally depict his sitters as full-length figures until this time. The Coltman portrait format of full-length standing figures in a landscape, smaller in relation to the picture size than previous figures, enabled Wright to suggest more of the sitters' environment (here, the landowner's estate is suggested). He could also make more of the sitters' informal, relaxed poses, as if he had just caught them on their way out for a ride, comparatively private and unaware of the painter's presence, especially as they look away from the artist. Even Mrs Coltman's horse and the dog at its feet are relating to each other rather than to the artist or spectator, thus breaking down formality even further.

Secondly, Wright was beginning at this time to take an interest in landscape for its own sake, producing one or two landscapes before going abroad in 1773. The scenery in the Coltman portrait displays a significant move toward a naturalistic representation of the countryside and away from the stylized, abstract backdrops of foliage, sky and scenery that passed for outdoor settings in previous portraits. The sky itself is full of movement, the white tops of the clouds creating a bright diagonal band across the upper part of the picture. Bold contrasts of light and shadow are seen on the second horse, his groom, and the adjacent brick wall, and the artist darkened the lower sky near the horizon to a heavier blue-grey to accentuate the sunlit end wall of the tall building on the right and the pale-green hill beyond, in the distance. Overall, this impression of a particular type of weather and light anticipates the naturalism of Wright's later landscape paintings.

Opposite:
JOSEPH WRIGHT OF DERBY, A.R.A.
British 1734–97
Portrait of Colonel Charles Heathcote, in the Uniform of the 35th Foot (later Royal Sussex) Regiment
Oil on canvas
50 × 40 in. (127 × 101.6 cm.)
Sold 26.4.85 in London for £410,400 ($517,104)
Heathcote, who joined the army in 1745, was gazetted Lieutenant-Colonel of the 35th Foot in 1769. This portrait, which dates from the early 1770s, cost 30 gns., as Wright's account book establishes.

The portrait of Colonel Charles Heathcote is of the same date and format as the Coltman portrait and appears in Wright's accounts as 'Coll. Heathcote a small full length £31. 10'. It was probably one of the two portraits of officers that Wright exhibited at the Society of Artists in 1772. The artist produced at least six other military portraits in the early 1770s, and though not all are full-length figures their uniforms display the same superb drapery painting that he achieved in the Coltman portrait. Colonel Heathcote (1730–1803) had entered the Army as an Ensign in 1745, progressing to seniority in various regiments; in 1769 he became a Lieutenant-Colonel of the 35th Foot (Royal Sussex) Regiment and served in America with them. It is in the uniform of this Regiment that Wright painted him, and the number 35 of his Regiment appears on one of his buttons. In a letter to his brother from Italy, Wright sends his compliments to 'Col. Heathcote, his lady &c.' and was obviously on friendly terms with the sitter and his family, better equipping him to convey the sitter's character. He painted Heathcote under a tree, like Mr and Mrs Coltman, but Heathcote generally has a more upright bearing of authority, as befits a senior officer in uniform, and Heathcote's tenser, outstretched arm and pointing finger convey a sense of military precision and alertness.

Opposite:
JOSEPH WRIGHT OF DERBY, A.R.A.
British 1734–97
Portrait of John Whetham of Kirklington, with a Newfoundland Dog beside him
Oil on canvas
50 × 40 in. (127 × 101.6 cm.)
Sold 19.7.85 in London for £410,400 ($554,040)
From the collection of the Boddam-Whetham family

THOMAS GAINSBOROUGH, R.A.

British 1727–88

A Wooded Landscape in Suffolk with Cows and a Herdsman, a Village beyond

Dated *c*.1746–7

Oil on canvas

19¼ × 25¾ in. (49 × 65.5 cm.)

Sold 26.4.85 in London for £183,600 ($231,336)

The pendant to this picture sold in the same sale for £43,200 ($54,432)

Payments are recorded in Gainsborough's accounts from the Solly family for two amounts, namely £27. 13s. 0d. received on 7 February 1743, and £19. 12s. 4d. received on 19 July 1743, which must relate to these two pictures

JOHN CONSTABLE, R.A.
British 1776–1837
Sunset through the Trees: A View on Hampstead Heath
Oil on paper laid down on canvas
10 × 11½ in. (25.5 × 29.2 cm.)
Sold 26.4.85 in London for £108,000 ($136,080)
This and other sketches now in the Mellon Collection are probably those mentioned in a letter from Constable to Archdeacon Fisher dated Hampstead 3 November 1821, which reads, 'The last day of October was indeed lovely so much that I could not paint for looking – my wife was walking with me all the middle of the day on the beautiful heath. I made two evening effects. The panorama of this place include what I have named – and has the addition of the finest foreground – in roads, heath, trees, ponds etc., and every description of moveable both dead and alive.'

JOHN FREDERICK HERRING, SEN.
British 1795–1865
The Meet of the East Suffolk hounds at Chippenham Park, with George Mure of Herringswell, M.F.H., and William Rose, huntsman
Signed and dated 1839
Oil on canvas
41 × 62 in. (104.2 × 157.5 cm.)
Sold 19.7.85 in London for £237,600 ($320,760)
George Mure was one of the pioneers of the Suffolk Hunt, of which he was Master in 1825–45. The hounds were kennelled at Herringswell; the huntsman was William Rose and the whip Sam Hibbs.

JOHN E. FERNELEY, SEN.
British 1781–1860
Sir James Boswell, Bt. of Auchenleck, on Mr Little Gilmour's 'Plunder', a bay Hunter, with Huntsmen and Hounds beyond
Signed and dated Melton Mowbray 1829
Oil on canvas
$33\frac{1}{2} \times 41\frac{1}{2}$ in. (85.2 × 105.4 cm.)
Sold 23.11.84 in London for £118,800 ($147,312)
This picture was commissioned in 1829 by W. Little Gilmour, a major patron of Ferneley, and cost 20 gns.

SAMUEL HENRY ALKEN
British 1810–94
The Finish of the Derby in 1868 (detail)
Signed
Oil on canvas
16½ × 39 in. (41.9 × 99 cm.)
Sold 19.7.85 in London for £113,400 ($153,090)
The Derby of 1868 was won by a half-length by Sir Joseph Hawley's 'Blue Gown', ridden by John Wells at 7 to 2, with Baron Rothschild's 'King Alfred' (with Norman up) second, the Duke of Newcastle's 'Speculum' (with Kenyon up) third, and Mr Chaplin's 'St. Ronan' (with Jeffery up) fourth. Sir Joseph, who had three horses in the race, was convinced that another of them, 'Rosicrucian', would win, and did not bet on 'Blue Gown'. Sir Joseph won the Derby four times in all, with 'Teddington' in 1851, with 'Beadsman' in 1858, with 'Musjid' in 1859, and with 'Blue Gown', who was by 'Beadsman', in 1868.

JOHN FREDERICK HERRING, SEN., AND JAMES POLLARD
British 1795–1865; British 1792–1867
Preparing to start for the Emperor of Russia's Cup at Ascot, 1845
Signed, inscribed and dated 1845; signed again and inscribed 'N.B. not to be engraved' on the reverse
Oil on canvas
18¾ × 28½ in. (47.6 × 72.5 cm.)
Sold 26.4.85 in London for £216,000 ($272,160)
There are several instances of Herring and Pollard working in collaboration, Herring painting the horses and Pollard the background, notably *The Doncaster Gold Cup of 1838* from the Joel Collection, sold at Christie's on 23 November 1984 for £777,600 ($1,010,880)

JOHN FREDERICK HERRING, SEN.
British 1795–1865
The Stableyard
Oil on canvas
Signed and dated 1855–6
$39\frac{1}{4} \times 49\frac{1}{4}$ in. (99.6 × 125 cm.)
Sold 23.11.84 in London for £172,800 ($214,272)
It has been suggested that the girl is the artist's daughter, Jenny

JACQUES LOUIS DAVID
French 1748–1825
Vestale couronnée de fleurs
Signed
Oil on canvas
32 × 25¾ in.
(81.3 × 65.4 cm.)
Sold 24.5.85 in New
York for $858,000
(£680,950)
Record auction price
for a work by the artist

LOUIS LÉOPOLD BOILLY
French 1761–1865
*A young Lady with a
Child and a Dog in an
Interior*
Oil on canvas
32 × 26 in.
(81 × 66 cm.)
Sold 30.11.84 in
London for £54,000
($69,660)

ÉMILE JEAN HORACE VERNET
French 1789–1863
La Bataille du Pont d'Arcole
Signed and dated 1826
Oil on canvas
77 × 103 in. (195.5 × 261 cm.)
Sold 8.5.85 in London for £324,000 ($398,520)
Record auction price for a work by the artist
From the Calvin Bullock Collection of Napoleon and Nelson Memorabilia (see page 474)
The battle depicted took place on 17 November 1796. Arcole is a small village in Italy on the Alpone river. Bonaparte, holding the tricolour, urges on his grenadiers and carries the Bridge of Arcole, thus bringing victory over the Austrians.

SIR JOHN EVERETT MILLAIS, BT.,
P.R.A.
British 1829–96
*Portrait of Beatrice Caird,
wearing a white Dress with a blue
Sash*
Signed with monogram and
dated 1879
Oil on canvas
21½ × 17 in.
(54.6 × 43.2 cm.)
Sold 30.11.84 in London for
£97,200 ($125,388)
From the collection of Sir
Ralph Millais, Bt., grandson
of the artist
The sitter was the daughter
of Lady Sophie Caird,
who was the artist's
sister-in-law

Opposite:
JEAN FRANÇOIS MILLET
French 1814–79
*Antoinette Hebert looking in the
Mirror*
Oil on canvas
Signed
39¾ × 32 in. (101 × 81.3 cm.)
Sold 24.5.85 in New York for
$605,000 (£472,660)

FREDERIC, LORD LEIGHTON, P.R.A.
British 1830–96
Greek Girl dancing (Spanish dancing Girl: Cadiz in the old times)
Oil on canvas
35 × 46½ in. (89 × 118 cm.)
Sold 22.3.85 in London for £140,400 ($168,480)
One of a number of major works executed in the mid-1860s in which Leighton first treated classical themes in a manner explicitly inspired by Greek statuary.

JOHN WILLIAM WATERHOUSE
British 1849–1917
Danaïdes
Signed and dated 1904
Oil on canvas
60¾ × 43¾ in.
(154.3 × 111.1 cm.)
Sold 15.2.85 in New York
for $264,000 (£237,837)
Record auction price for a
work by the artist

JAMES JOSEPH TISSOT
French 1836–1902
Portrait of Mrs Kathleen Newton (Mavourneen)
Signed and dated 1877
Oil on canvas
35½ × 20 in. (90 × 51 cm.)
Sold 30.11.84 in London for £162,000 ($196,020)

MAX LIEBERMANN
German 1847–1935
Going to Church in Laren
Signed and dated 99
Oil on canvas
27 ¾ × 39 ⅝ in. (70.5 × 100.2 cm.)
Sold 24.5.85 in New York for $143,000 (£111,720)
By order of the Estate of Gerald Oliven

BAREND CORNELIS KOEKKOEK
Dutch 1803–62
A frozen Waterway with Skaters near a Bridge
Signed and dated 1836
Oil on panel
14½ × 18½ in. (37 × 46 cm.)
Sold 23.4.85 in Amsterdam for D.fl.171,000 (£38,863)

The Rediscovery of 19th Century Scandinavian Painting

PHILIP HOOK

In recent years the eyes of the international art market have been opened to the quality and appeal of Scandinavian painters of the 19th century; the Scandinavians, too, may have been agreeably surprised by how highly their major masters are now rated in relation to other European painters of the period. Gone are the days when people's lists of famous Nordic artists began and ended with Edvard Munch. The merits of a large range of 'new' names are now appreciated by the international collector, and prices have increased dramatically, creating new stars of the saleroom out of men like Eckersberg, Zorn, Thaulow, and Hammershøi.

There was little painting of significance produced in any Scandinavian country prior to 1800, so the 19th century was their coming of age artistically. It was a challenging and stimulating time, when attitudes veered from entranced devotion to foreign schools and their teachings to fierce independence, prompting stern dissertations like that of the Dane N. Høyen in 1844, *On the Conditions for Development of a National Scandinavian Art*. In fact it was often a combination of these two elements – susceptibility to stimulation from abroad, without losing a strong sense of national identity – which produced some of the best and most distinctive work of the period.

Artists who looked abroad tended to turn to Germany and France, with German teaching markedly in the ascendant in the first half of the century, and Paris taking over as the dominant influence in the second half. Johan Christian Dahl, for instance, the Norwegian landscape painter, was a leading follower of Caspar David Friedrich and provides a link between his native Norway and Dresden (he also worked in Copenhagen). Then there was the Düsseldorf connection, forged by a succession of genre painters like the Norwegian Adolf Tidemand and the Swede Bengt Nordenburg, who studied and worked in that city, painting peasant interiors as grim and turgid as anything the natives could produce.

But fortunately there were also the Danes, who in the first half of the 19th century enjoyed what is fittingly termed their Golden Age in painting. Those who saw the recent exhibitions in London and Paris have had the chance to relish the charm of these painters who represent an extraordinary self-contained and original flowering of landscape and genre which owed almost nothing to outside influence. They have been described as 'the first independent naturalists, and their work consists largely of carefully observed, straightforward slices of life, presented with a refreshing lack of sentimentality. In this they reaped the benefits of a certain degree of isolationism: the Danes avoided – through ignorance – the perils of a Greuze-inspired pursuit of *sensibilité* and the dangers inherent in an over-developed sense of *gemütlichkeit*, that coyness which beset the southern Germans. Painters like Eckersberg and Købke are now being given internationally the credit which they deserve. Købke particularly is understood to be, at his best, on a par with anyone else in Europe in his lifetime, and museum directors are today falling over each other to secure the rare examples of his work which may come on the market.

By the 1870s and 1880s Paris had become the major attraction for a generation of Norwegian, Swedish, Danish and Finnish artists. It is hard to think of any important late 19th-century Scandinavian who did not spend part of his formative years in or around the French capital. For landscape painters like the Finn Halmar Munsterhjelm, the Barbizon School provided a new stimulus, while others, notably the Norwegian Frits Thaulow, operated on the fringes of Impressionism. Thaulow's performance at auction over the past five years is a dramatic illustration of the way an artist's prices can spiral upon discovery by the international art market. At the end of the 1970s the highest price paid at auction for his work was £8,487. A sharp rise followed, helped by the fact that a number of exceptional examples of his work were offered at Christie's. In 1982, for instance, his early view of the Oslo Royal Palace made £43,200; a year later his *Les Eaux bleus* reached £81,000; and in the past year his beautiful *La Laïta à Quimperlé* achieved an extraordinary £151,200. Thaulow was an endearing character who seems to have enjoyed life – the late Sir William Rothenstein described him as 'a huge Norwegian, bearded, genial, a great trencherman, he dispensed hospitality to all and sundry'.

If one man was the idol of the Scandinavians who congregated in Paris it was Jules Bastien-Lepage. Indeed, for a few brief years in the 1880s he was probably the most admired painter in France, perhaps in the world. His brand of photographic realism seemed to most people the ultimate in realism, and his influence was felt across Europe, where many different artists imitated his technique, an integral part of which was painting *en plein air*. This was a practice whose appeal was understood by many Scandinavians, from the Swedes Anders Zorn and Carl Larsson, to Peder Severin Krøyer and Michael Ancher in Denmark, and Erik Werenskjold and Harriet Bakker in Norway, as well as a painter like Albert Edelfelt, a Finn who was also based in Paris. Their best pictures, while owing an initial debt to Bastien-Lepage, succeed in creating something new and distinctively Scandinavian.

The Skagen School is a case in point. This was a group of mainly Danish painters whose Parisian experience led them to congregate in the little fishing village of Skagen to paint the locals *en plein air* bathed in the beautiful light of the Scandinavian summer. There are certain parallels with the English Newlyn School, another group of *plein air* painters who based themselves in a fishing village. Krøyer, the leading light, was the Stanhope Forbes of the colony, although undoubtedly an artist of greater range. Perhaps Michael Ancher was the Skagen Walter Langley, with his penchant for interminable oilskinned worthies. Skagen also puts Newlyn in the shade when it comes to lurid romance: Krøyer's wife Marie, who was the subject of many of his best pictures, ran away with a Swedish composer, a blow from which the artist never recovered. A tragic love life does no harm to an artist at auction today, and Krøyer's prices are well into the six-figure bracket.

'The land of shame-faced prudery' was how Richard Muther described Denmark in 1907, incongruous words to us 80 years later. Muther was trying to account for the lack of ideal nude painting there in the 19th century. This absence is significant, and characteristic of most Scandinavian painting. After Thorwaldsen classicism dies, and Scandinavian painters strive after realism, sometimes fantasy, but rarely the ideal. Nudity is treated, but without the hypocritical cover of a classical or oriental setting. So a painter like Anders Zorn flourished with his endless open-air nudes, at his best the poet of Swedish landscape and womanhood with the same free handling of paint of a Sargent or Sorolla, and at his repetitive worst no more than the chronicler of the nudist camp.

The trends of the late 19th and early 20th century in Scandinavia were a continuing interest in 'hard-edge' realism – an artist like the Dane L.A. Ring has been compared revealingly with Andrew Wyeth – and an increasing feeling for symbolism, as exemplified by a number of artists including Vilhelm Hammershøi. Hammershøi is a beguiling mixture of Whistler, Vermeer

FRITS THAULOW
Norwegian 1847–1906
La Laïta à Quimperlé
Signed
Oil on canvas
28¾ × 36¾ in. (73 × 93 cm.)
Sold 30.11.84 in London for £151,200 ($182,952)
Record auction price for a work by the artist

LAURITS ANDERSEN RING
Danish 1854–1935
June: Girl blowing Dandelion Seeds, Frederiksvaerk, 1899
Signed and dated 1899
Oil on canvas
$34\frac{1}{2} \times 48\frac{1}{2}$ in. (87.5 × 123.5 cm.)
Sold 30.11.84 in London for £30,240 ($36,590)
Now in the National Gallery, Oslo

and Khnopff, with something else as well. His grey mysterious interiors suggest a spirit not at ease with itself, a condition which a recent native critic diagnoses rather severely as an endemic Danish complaint called 'corroding provincialism'. Exposure to a wider international public indicates that Hammershøi none the less strikes chords in the metropolitan imagination as well, and in March Christie's sold his marvellous *Interior with a Woman seated on a white Chair* for £108,000.

Significantly this picture fetched £2,593 when offered at auction in Denmark less than 10 years ago. What has happened in between? The answer is that the increased level of activity in Scandinavia of an international auction house like Christie's has introduced painters such as Hammershoi to the international collector. No longer are Scandinavian pictures being offered merely to the internal market, but Americans, Japanese and other Europeans have all been enabled to compete for the work of Thaulow, Larsson, and the rest. So prices have spiralled. And Scandinavians may take justifiable pride in the way the quality of their major 19th-century masters is now being appreciated and sought-after by a world-wide public.

VILHELM HAMMERSHØI
Danish 1864–1916
Interior with a Woman seated on a white Chair
Signed with initials
Oil on canvas
22½ × 19 in. (57 × 49 cm.)
Sold 22.3.85 in London for £108,000 ($129,600)
Record auction price for a work by the artist
Painted in 1900 in the artist's apartment, Strandgade 30

CARL LARSSON
Swedish 1853–1919
Alma
Signed with initials, inscribed
and dated 1887
Pastel
22½ × 17½ in.
(57.2 × 44.5 cm.)
Sold 20.6.85 in London for
£54,000 ($69,660)
In 1885 the artist left Grez-
sur-Loing, France, with his
family and returned to
Sweden, but for a number of
years the influence of
contemporary French
painting persisted, as the
present pastel illustrates. In
particular he was intrigued
by the fashion for Japanese
decorative art, an interest
which had an abiding effect
on his work. By 1887 he was
in the forefront of the
Swedish modern movement,
and was beginning his
decoration of the Furstenberg
Gallery in Gothenburg.

JEAN FRANÇOIS MILLET
French 1814–75
Path with Chestnut Trees near Cusset
Signed
Pastel on blue paper
16¾ × 21 in. (42.5 × 53.3 cm.)
Sold 25.10.84 in New York for $176,000 (£141,935)

CHARLES ROBERTSON, A.R.W.S
British 1844–91
Carpet Bazaar, Cairo
Signed and dated 1887
Watercolour heightened with white
30 × 52 in. (77 × 132 cm.)
Sold 30.11.84 in London for £75,600 ($91,476)

WINSLOW HOMER
American 1836–1910
Fresh Eggs
Signed and dated 1874
Watercolour and bodycolour
on paper
9¾ × 8⅝ in.
(23.8 × 19.5 cm.)
Sold 31.5.85 in New York for
$352,000 (£270,769)

WINSLOW HOMER
American 1836–1910
Houses on a Hill
Signed and dated 1879
Oil on canvas
15⅞ × 22⅝ in. (40.3 × 57.5 cm.)
Sold 31.5.85 in New York for $660,000 (£507,692)

WINSLOW HOMER
American 1836–1910
The Guide
Signed and dated 1895
Watercolour on paper
laid down on board
16¼ × 14 in.
(41.2 × 35.6 cm.)
Sold 7.12.84 in New
York for $231,000
(£189,344)

FREDERICK CHILDE HASSAM
American 1859–1935
White Church, Provincetown
Signed and dated 1900
Oil on canvas
20¼ × 13⅝ in. (51.3 × 34.5 cm.)
Sold 15.3.85 in New York for $132,000
(£120,000)

JASPER FRANCIS CROPSEY
American 1823–1900
The Isle of Capri
Signed and dated 1893
Oil on canvas
28 × 44¼ in. (71 × 112.3 cm.)
Sold 7.12.84 in New York for
$187,000 (£153,278)

GRANT WOOD
American 1892–1942
Parson Weems' Fable
Signed and dated 1939
Charcoal, pencil and chalk on paper
38¼ × 50 in. (97.2 × 127 cm.)
Sold 31.5.84 in New York for
$297,000 (£228,461)
Parson Weems fabricated the
popular tale of George Washington
and the cherry tree. The drawing for
the painting of the same title depicts
Wood's fascination with the
romance of folklore as represented in
this story.

GEORGIA O'KEEFE
American b.1887
Out Back of Marie's
Signed with initials OK in star device, dated 30 and inscribed with title on reverse
Oil on canvas
20 × 24 in. (49.9 × 61 cm.)
Sold 7.12.84 in New York for $297,000 (£243,442)

AMMI PHILLIPS
American 1787–1865
Portrait of a Girl in a Red Dress
Oil on canvas
32 × 27 in.
(81.3 × 68.6 cm.)
Sold 26.1.85 in New York for $682,000
(£598,245)
Record auction price for a work by the artist and for any American folk painting

WILLIAM RUSH
American 1756–1833
Andrew Jackson
Painted terracotta bust
19⅞ in. (50.5 cm.) high
Sold 31.5.85 in New
York for $250,000
(£192,310)
Record auction price for
a work by the artist

Above:
FREDERICK WILLIAM MACMONNIES
American 1863–1937
The Horse Tamers
Pair of bronze equestrian groups
Inscribed 'First Proof' and 'Mac-Monnies Scult.' and 'Leblanc-Barbedienne Fondeur'
38 in. (96.5 cm.) and 40 in. (101.6 cm.) high
Sold 31.5.85 in New York for $352,000 (£270,772)
Record auction price for a work by the artist

Right:
FRÉDÉRIC-AUGUSTE BARTHOLDI
French 1834–1904
Liberty Enlightening the World
Metal model of the Statue of Liberty
Inscribed '4th July 1776' and 'Registered in Washington 31 Aout 1876
A Bartholdi 1875 No 9939' and 'A Avoiron Paris 223'
50½ in. (128.3 cm.) high
Sold 31.5.85 in New York for $121,000 (£93,080)
Record auction price for a work by the artist
From the collection of the Fowler Museum, Los Angeles, California

RUFINO TAMAYO
Mexican b.1900
Retrato de Olga
Signed and dated 0.48
Oil on masonite
48 × 36 in.
(122 × 91.5 cm.)
Sold 30.5.85 in New
York for $170,500
(£131,150)

DIEGO RIVERA
Mexican 1886–1957
Diana Cazadora
Signed and dated 1941
Oil on canvas
77 × 47 in. (195.5 × 119.4 cm.)
Sold 28.11.84 in New York for $132,000
(£108,197)

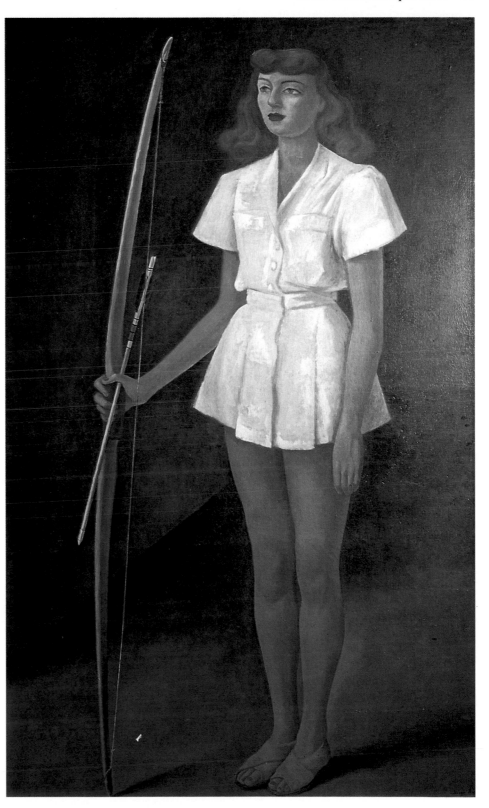

Above:
CAPTAIN THOMAS DAVIES
British *c.* 1737–1812
A South View of the City of New York in North America, taken from the Governors Island
Signed, inscribed and dated 1760
Watercolour
12 × 40½ in. (30.5 × 103 cm.)
Sold 4.6.85 in London for £110,000 ($141,900)

CONRAD MARTENS
British d. 1878
Balmoral looking towards Sydney Heads
Signed
Watercolour heightened with white
17¼ × 25¼ in. (44 × 64 cm.)
Sold 13.9.84 in Sydney for $A100,000 (£64,516)
From the Dr John L. Raven Collection

Modern Pictures and Sculpture

AUGUSTE RODIN
French 1840–1917
Eve
Signed
White marble
30½ in. (80 cm.) high
Executed in 1899–1900
Sold 3.12.84 in London for
£156,600 ($187,920)

EUGÈNE BOUDIN
French 1824–98
La Plage de Trouville à l'heure du bain
Signed and dated 68
Oil on panel
8½ × 13¾ in. (21.5 × 35 cm.)
Sold 3.12.84 in London for £129,600 ($155,520)

CLAUDE MONET
French 1840–1926
La Promenade (Argenteuil)
Signed
Oil on canvas
25⅝ × 31½ in. (60 × 80 cm.)
Painted in 1875
Sold 13.11.84 in New York for $2,090,000 (£1,607,692)
From the collection of The Hon. Walter Annenberg
It is likely that the subjects are the artist's wife, Camille, his son Jean, and the infant's nurse. At Argenteuil, Monet enjoyed his first
garden and the company of Manet and Renoir, who worked nearby.
There are four versions of this landscape, differing according to times of the year. Only one distant figure appears in each of the
other versions, two of which are in private collections and one, *Peupliers près d'Argenteuil*, is in the Museum of Fine Arts, Boston.

PIERRE AUGUSTE RENOIR
French 1841–1919
Vase de fleurs
Signed and dated 71
Oil on canvas
31¾ × 25½ in.
(80.7 × 64.8 cm.)
Sold 15.5.85 in New York for
$1,210,000 (£937,984)
This was probably painted
while Renoir was living in the
Paris suburb of Saint-Cloud
in the summer of 1871 after
the bloody defeat of the
Commune. Renoir's
friendship with the collector
and art critic Theodore Duret
(who was also a patron of
Manet) furthered his
fascination with Japanese art
and artifacts. The vase in this
work, probably French-made
with an oriental motif, is very
similar to one that appears,
holding dried grasses and a
Japanese fan, in *Nature morte
avec bouquet* (The Museum of
Fine Arts, Houston).

Opposite:
PAUL CÉZANNE
French 1839–1906
La Maison et l'arbre
Signed
Oil on canvas
26 × 21½ in. (66 × 55.5 cm.)
Painted *c.* 1873–4
Sold 13.11.84 in New York
for $1,760,000 (£1,353,846)
Camille Pissarro, with whom
Cézanne was particularly
close at that time, also
painted the same view in
1874.

Opposite:
VINCENT VAN GOGH
Dutch 1853–90
Allée des Alyscamps
Oil on canvas
36¼ × 29 in. (92 × 73.5 cm.)
Sold 15.5.85 in New York for
$2,420,000 (£1,875,969)
This work was painted
towards the end of October
1888 in Arles. Les Alyscamps
(The Elysian Fields) is an
avenue at Arles lined with
poplar trees and stone tombs
which date from the time of
the Roman occupation of
Gaul. Van Gogh made four
paintings of Les Alyscamps,
two horizontal and two
vertical. Professor Pickvance
indicates that the vertical
paintings were probably
painted first, on rough canvas
with a thick weave, and the
horizontal ones later, on
canvas newly purchased by
Gauguin, who himself
painted this same subject
twice. It is commonly
supposed that they worked at
the same time, but Mark
Roskill maintains that this is
unlikely and that Gauguin
probably did not start on his
canvases until a few weeks
later, although he may well
have made some notes while
Van Gogh was working
there.

PAUL GAUGUIN
French 1848–1903
Conversation tropiques (Nègresses causant)
Signed and dated 87
Oil on canvas
24⅛ × 29⅞ in. (61.5 × 76 cm.)
Sold 15.5.85 in New York for $1,870,000 (£1,449,612)
Painted in Martinique as one of the '*douzaine de toiles dont quatre avec des figures bien supéreures à mon époque de Pont-Aven*', as he described his work on a visit to his friend Emile Schuffenecker

MAURICE UTRILLO
French 1883–1955
Rue à Sannois
Signed
Oil on board
19½ × 28½ in. (49.5 × 72.5 cm.)
Painted *c.*1911
Sold 3.12.84 in London for £116,640 ($139,968)
Record auction price for a work by the artist

EDGAR DEGAS
French 1834–1917
Femme en robe blanche assise
Stamped with signature
Pastel on board
28⅜ × 19¼ in. (72 × 49 cm.)
Executed *c.*1888–92
Sold 14.11.84 in New York
for \$286,000 (£220,000)
By order of the Estate of
Kathrin Hochschild

PABLO PICASSO
Spanish/French 1881–1974
Vase de fleurs
Signed
Oil on canvas
$25\frac{5}{8} \times 19\frac{3}{4}$ in. (65 × 50 cm.)
Sold 15.5.85 in New York for
$1,210,000 (£937,984)
Pierre Daix assigns a date of
1901 to this painting, while
Zervos and Palau y Fabre
prefer 1904

Opposite:
ODILON REDON
French 1840–1916
Vase de fleurs bleu
Signed
Pastel on paper mounted at
the edges on board
$33\frac{3}{4} \times 27\frac{1}{8}$ in.
(85.2 × 69 cm.)
Executed *c.* 1905
Sold 15.5.85 in New York for
$330,000 (£255,813)

Picasso's Deceptive Conservatism

ROBERT CUMMING

Picasso often painted the seated female figure, and it is a subject which recurred regularly from the very early *Woman in Blue* of 1901 in the Museo Naçional de Arte Moderne in Madrid to the late portraits of Jacqueline Roque. Some of these paintings were conscious exercises in portraiture, but in other cases the seated female figure was used for purposes which were quite different: the Tate Gallery's Cubist *Seated Nude* of 1909 is a good example of his using the subject as a means of investigating form and picture making; at other times he used the subject as a means of revealing feeling and emotion rather than a likeness.

Femme assise au chapeau (*Seated Woman in a Blue Hat*), painted in 1923, is a marvellous and characteristic example of Picasso's painting style and interests of the early 1920s, and for this reason merits a short discussion. Some writers have seen this phase of Picasso's career as something of a betrayal of his commitment to Modern Art, and therefore aesthetically inferior to those works in which he redefined many of the traditional rules and perceptions governing painting and sculpture. Such criticisms do, I believe, misunderstand both Picasso and the development of 20th-century art. *Seated Woman in a Blue Hat* shows Picasso at the height of his powers, and the deceptive conservatism of the style, technique, and subject should serve to increase rather than diminish our admiration for his creativity. From our viewpoint in the penultimate decade of the 20th century we can see that the development of art in the last 80 odd years has not been just a single-minded progression towards new styles, subjects and attitudes which have sought to break with the art of the past. That may be the dominant strain, and the essence of what Modern Art is, or was, but 20th-century art has an important counter-balance to this movement in which the traditional styles and concerns of Western art have been reinvigorated and made relevant to our own times. One of the qualities that makes Picasso the outstanding figure of 20th-century art is that as well as being the prime mover behind the avant-garde and the new horizons of Modern Art, he was equally a leading figure in showing that the old values must not be neglected or allowed to die. Overall it is impossible to think of any other artist who has brought such inventive vigour and balance to both faces of 20th-century painting and sculpture, and the masterly technique and deep humanity of *Seated Woman in a Blue Hat* owes more than a passing nod to Picasso's great Spanish forbears Velázquez and Goya.

Picasso began to turn away from a consuming interest in Cubism in 1916. That year he first became deeply occupied with the ballet, designing the costumes and set for *Parade* which Diaghilev's Ballet Russe first performed in May 1917 to the music of Erik Satie. This theatrical and musical milieu, rather different to that of the avant-garde painters and sculptors, undoubtedly had an influence on Picasso, and led directly to his first visit to Italy in February 1917. It was in Rome and Naples, at the relatively late age of 36, that Picasso made contact for the first time with the heartland of Western European painting and sculpture. The experience must have been electrifying, and it is tempting to ask if the gods had not already planned that it should be in the same month, February 1917, that he was to meet Olga Koklova. She was a

PABLO PICASSO
Spanish/French
1881–1974
Femme assise au chapeau
Signed
Pastel on unprimed
canvas
51⅛ × 38¼ in.
(130 × 97 cm)
Executed in 1923
Sold 13.11.84 in New
York for $4,290,000
(£3,300,000)
By order of
The Edward James
Foundation

dancer in the corps de ballet of Diaghilev's company. Picasso fell in love with her, and they were married in July 1918.

Seated Woman in a Blue Hat sums up much of the atmosphere of these early happy years of marriage. There was financial and emotional security, new artistic interests via the ballet and Italy, and a new life-style. Picasso and his new wife moved to the fashionable Rue de la Boetie in central Paris away from the Bohemian artists' districts. There was a comfortable apartment separate from the studio. Picasso and Olga were well received in fashionable society. There were smart soirées and gala evenings at the Opéra, and when Picasso visited London for the first time, in May 1919, he wore a bowler hat and took time to go to the best tailors. Most importantly, however, his first child, a son, Paolo, was born on 4 February 1921.

I have described *Seated Woman in a Blue Hat* as a painting, but that description is technically inaccurate. It is a large work of $51\frac{1}{8} \times 38\frac{1}{4}$ in. (130×97 cm.) executed on raw canvas, but the medium is pastel, not oil paint. In other words Picasso has used a technique usually associated with small-scale work for a picture whose conception and scale might more aptly be described as monumental. This technique, together with the work's sketchy quality, is an effective, simple, and brilliant means of giving this large picture a particular tenderness and intimacy. It is also, of course, a tribute to Picasso's outstanding skill as a draughtsman, and an example of his enduring interest in sculpture, for the head is deeply modelled, displaying a sculptor's rather than painter's interest in form.

Picasso painted portraits of Olga seated in a chair on two occasions: an unfinished work of 1917, which also has a natural coloured background; and in 1923, when the face is strongly modelled, especially round the nose and eyes. *Seated Woman in a Blue Hat* is not a portrait of Olga, but it is not difficult to see in it reflections of these two portraits. It also connects with two other works of the summer of 1923, both painted in Antibes. There is the monumental *Pipes of Pan* with two life-size sculptural figures – a work which Picasso himself esteemed very highly – and the tiny and exquisite *Famille au bord de la mer*, in size a mere 6×8 in. (15.2×20.3 cm.), in which a small boy, the age of Paolo, plays with the ear of his sleeping father stretched naked on a beach, whilst his mother, who might be the same figure as *Seated Woman in a Blue Hat*, sits quietly by with an arm stretched towards the child in gentle restraint.

Seated Woman in a Blue Hat was purchased by Edward James in the mid-1930s, at first sight an unlikely acquisition by such a devotee of Surrealism. For 26 years, from 1958 to 1984, his picture hung on loan in the Tate Gallery, where it made an effective foil to the celebrated *Three Dancers* of 1925, in which there was a sudden change to a tense, angular, and anguished style that culminated in *Guernica*. In 1925 Picasso's marriage effectively came to an end in anything but a legal sense and with it the harmony and tenderness and domesticity shown by *Seated Woman in a Blue Hat* disappeared from his painting for ever.

PABLO PICASSO
Spanish/French 1881–1974
Femme à la mandoline
(La Musicienne)
Signed and dated 25
Oil on canvas
$51\frac{5}{8} \times 38\frac{3}{8}$ in.
$(131 \times 97.5$ cm.$)$
Sold 13.11.84 in New York
for $1,925,000 (£1,480,769)
From the collection of The
Hon. Walter Annenberg

AMEDEO MODIGLIANI
Italian 1884–1920
Giovanotto dai capelli rossi
Signed
Oil on canvas
$39\frac{5}{8} \times 24\frac{5}{8}$ in. (100.5 × 65.2 cm.)
Painted in 1919
Sold 13.11.84 in New York for
$1,925,000 (£1,480,769)

AMEDEO MODIGLIANI
Italian 1884–1920
Jeanne Hébuterne
Signed
Oil on canvas
18 × 11½ in. (45.7 × 29.2 cm.)
Painted in 1917–18
Sold 3.12.84 in London for £702,000
($842,400)
This painting was given in 1933 to the
National Galerie, Berlin, by the Italian
government, together with eight other
contemporary Italian pictures, in
exchange for a painting by F.P.
Michetti. It was then removed as
entartete Kunst in 1937 and sold in the
famous sale of pictures from German
museums in Lucerne in June 1939,
when it was bought by the husband of
the consignor to our sale for
Sw.fr.6,600.

ARISTIDE MAILLOL
French 1861–1944
Flore
Signed on the base
Bronze with green patina
63 in. (160 cm.) high
Executed in 1911
Sold 13.11.84 in New York for $528,000
(£406,154)

Opposite:
MARC CHAGALL
Russian/French 1887–1985
Le Clown au cheval blanc
Signed
Gouache on grey paper
24¾ × 18⅞ in. (63 × 48 cm.)
Painted in 1926–7
Sold 16.5.85 in New York for $140,800
(£110,000)
From the collection of Edmund W. Mudge,
Jun.

GEORGE BRAQUE
French 1882–1963
Paysage à l'Estaque
Signed and dated 06
Oil on canvas
23⅝ × 31⅞ in. (60 × 81 cm.)
Sold 13.11.84 in New York for $605,000 (£465,385)

FERDINAND HODLER
Swiss 1853–1918
Herbstschnee im Engadin
Signed and dated 1907
Oil on canvas
25 ⅛ × 33 ⅞ in. (64 × 86 cm.)
Sold 24.6.85 in London for £237,600 ($304,128)
One of only eight pictures of the Engadin in the whole of Hodler's *oeuvre*. These were done during a visit at the end of August and during early September 1907. The surrounding mountains excited him because, as he told his friend and fellow painter Willy Burger, 'I have never yet seen such a light as up here: it is fantastic!' (W. Burger, *Erinnerunger*, in the Hodler exhibition catalogue, Kunsthaus, Zurich, 1964, p. 23). Of the remaining seven pictures, one, *Silvaplanersee im Herbst*, is in the collection of the Kunsthaus, Zurich, and another, *Malojalandschaft*, was sold 5 December 1983, lot 11, also at Christie's, London.

ERNST BARLACH
German 1870–1938
Tod im Leben
Signed and dated 1926
Wood
32⅝ in. (83 cm.) high
(including three-tiered
wooden base)
Sold 24.6.85 in London for
£172,800 ($221,184)
*Record auction price for a
work by the artist*

WILHELM LEHMBRUCK
German 1881–1919
Weiblicher Torso
Signed and stamped
C. Valsuani cire perdue
Bronze with dark brown
patina
46 in. (117 cm.) high
Conceived in Paris in 1910;
cast 1910–14
Sold 24.6.85 in London for
£140,400 ($179,712)
Record auction price for a
work by the artist
The features are those of
Anita, the sculptor's wife,
who was the model for all
Lehmbruck's early nudes

EMIL NOLDE
German 1867–1956
Sonnenblumengarten
Signed
Oil on canvas
26¾ × 35 in. (68 × 89 cm.)
Painted in 1937
Sold 24.6.85 in London for £345,600 ($442,368)
Record auction price for a work by the artist

Opposite:
FRANZ MARC
German 1880–1916
Der Baumträger
Oil on canvas
55½ × 43 in. (141 × 109 cm.)
Painted in 1911
Sold 3.12.84 in London for £210,600 ($252,720)

PAUL KLEE
Swiss 1879–1940
Tief-Ebene
Signed, inscribed with title and S.CI X and dated 1932.9 on the mount
Watercolour on Ingres paper mounted by the artist on board
Image size: 12 × 19 in. (30.5 × 48 cm.)
Mount size: 15¾ × 22¼ in. (40 × 56.5 cm.)
Sold 14.11.84 in New York for $247,500 (£189,062)
From the James Gilvarry Collection

PAUL KLEE
Swiss 1879–1940
Partie aus G
Signed, inscribed with
title and C1 III and
dated 1927 Y.5. on the
mount
Watercolour and oil
transfer on Ingres paper
laid down by the artist
on board
Image size: 12¾ ×
9½ in. (32.5 × 24 cm.)
Mount size: 20 ×
15½ in. (51 × 39.5 cm.)
Sold 14.11.84 in New
York for $242,000
(£189,062)
From the James
Gilvarry Collection

PAUL KLEE
Swiss 1879–1940
Citronen-Ernte
Signed, inscribed and numbered
on the stretcher 37 U 19
Tempera on burlap, laid on
burlap
27½ × 18¼ in. (70 × 46.4 cm.)
Painted in 1937
Sold 3.12.84 in London for
£243,000 ($291,600)

Opposite:
JOAN MIRÓ
Spanish 1893–1983
Femme et chat
Signed and dated 1950 on the
reverse
Oil on partly chiselled board
23⅞ × 19⅜ in. (60.7 × 49.5 cm.)
Sold 3.12.84 in London for
£259,200 ($311,040)

FRANCIS PICABIA
French 1879–1953
Flirt
Signed
Ripolin, toothpicks, straws,
staples and lead wire on
canvas
36¼ × 28¾ in. (92 × 73 cm.)
Painted *c.* 1924–5
Sold 12.11.84 in New York
for $214,500 (£167,578)
Record auction price for a
work by the artist
From the Barnet Hodes
Collection
This was one of the 80 works
which Duchamp offered at
auction at Hôtel Drout on
8 March 1926, for which sale
he wrote the catalogue. 'At
the auction itself, a crowd of
illustrious friends (and former
friends) vied for some of
Picabia's most important
works. Breton went away
with *Procession Seville* and
Catch as Catch Can . . . Léger
purchased *Optophone I* . . .
Tzara got *Flirt* . . . several
examples of the 'monster'
style figured in the auction
. . . those paintings were
accompanied in the catalogue
by two works, *Flirt* and *La
Lecture* . . . which, except for
their added collage elements,
belong to the 'monsters' in
subject and style . . . In fact,
it is impossible to determine if
Picabia initially conceived
Flirt and *La Lecture* in their
present forms or reworked
what had once been 'finished'
paintings in the monster
style.' (W. Camfield, *Francis
Picabia, His Art, Life and
Times*, Princeton, 1979, pp.
217 and 218.)

SALVADOR DALÍ
Spanish b.1904
Figura de cajones
Signed and dated 1937
Pen and black ink on board
29¾ × 22 in. (75.5 × 56 cm.)
Sold 14.11.84 in New York
for $121,000 (£93,077)

ALEXANDER CALDER
American 1898–1976
Untitled
Signed with initials and dated 56
Mobile of painted sheet metal
117¾ in. (310 cm.) span
Sold 25.6.85 in London for £142,560 ($182,480)
The lot included a photocopy of a letter from the artist to the vendor showing how the mobile should be suspended

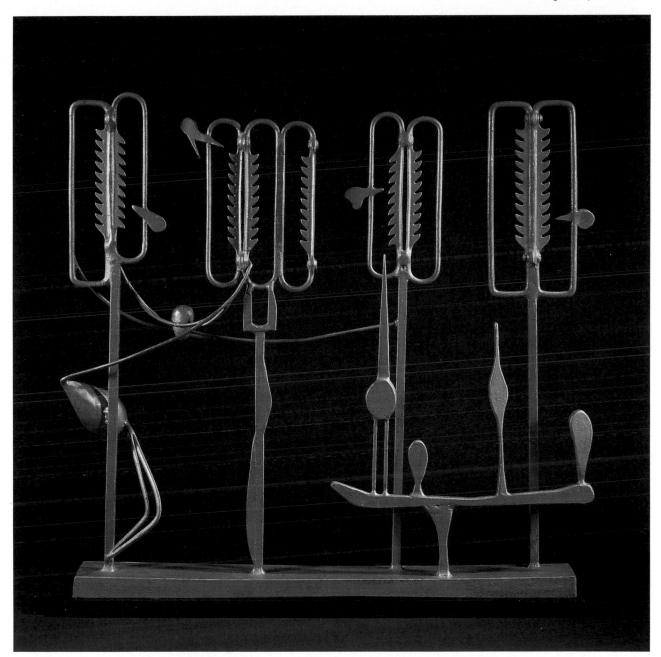

DAVID SMITH
American 1906–65
The Forest
Signed and stamped 1950
Painted and welded steel on wooden base
40 × 38 × 4¾ in. (101.5 × 96.5 × 12 cm.)
Sold 1.5.85 in New York for $264,000 (£207,874)

JACKSON POLLOCK
American 1912–56
The Magic Mirror
Signed and dated 41; signed and
dated again on the reverse
Oil and mixed media on canvas
46 × 32 in. (116.8 × 81.2 cm.)
Sold 1.11.84 in New York for
$374,000 (£301,613)

JEAN-PAUL RIOPELLE
Canadian b.1922
Peinture no. 906
Signed on reverse
Oil on canvas
35 × 45½ in. (89 × 115.5 cm.)
Sold 25.6.85 in London for £48,600 ($62,690)

WILLEM DE KOONING
American/Dutch b.1904
Two Women
Signed
Oil on paper mounted on canvas
21⅞ × 28½ in. (55.7 × 72 cm.)
Sold 1.11.84 in New York for $1,980,000 (£1,596,774)
Record auction price for a contemporary work of art and for any work by a living artist

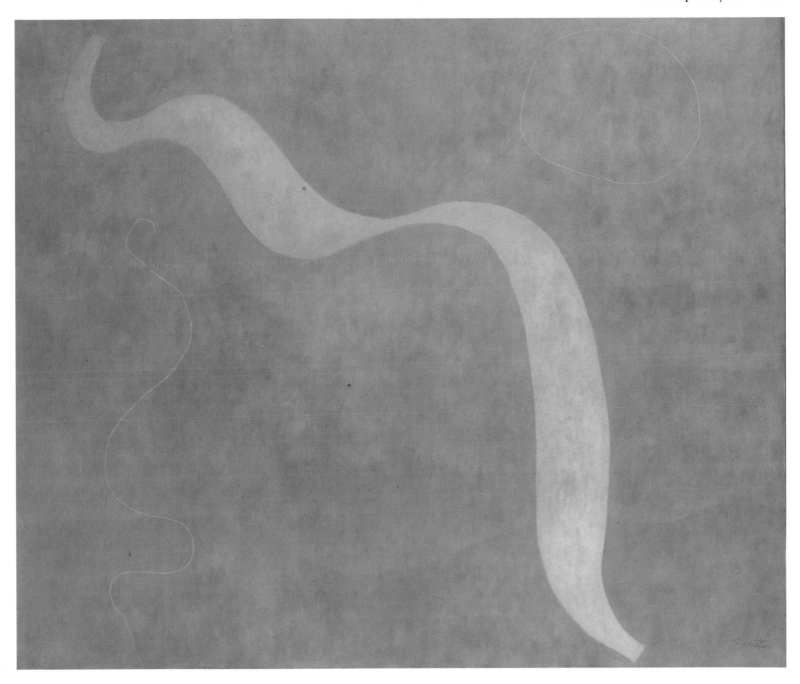

WILLIAM BAZIOTES
American 1912–63
Serpentine
Signed; signed again, inscribed with title and dated 1961 on the reverse
Oil on canvas
66⅛ × 77⅞ in. (168 × 198 cm.)
Sold 1.5.85 in New York for $209,000 (£164,566)
Record auction price for a work by the artist

FRANZ KLINE
American 1910–62
Untitled
Signed and dated 60 on the reverse
Oil on canvas, unframed
$116\frac{1}{4} \times 79$ in. (295.2 × 200.5 cm.)
Sold 1.5.85 in New York for $880,000 (£692,913)
By order of the Estate of Robert Bollt
Record auction price for a work by the artist

HANS HOFMANN
American/German 1880–1966
Ave Maria
Signed and dated 65; signed
again, inscribed with title and
dated 1965 on the reverse
Oil on canvas
72 × 48 in. (182.9 × 121.9 cm.)
Sold 1.5.85 in New York for
$275,000 (£216,535)

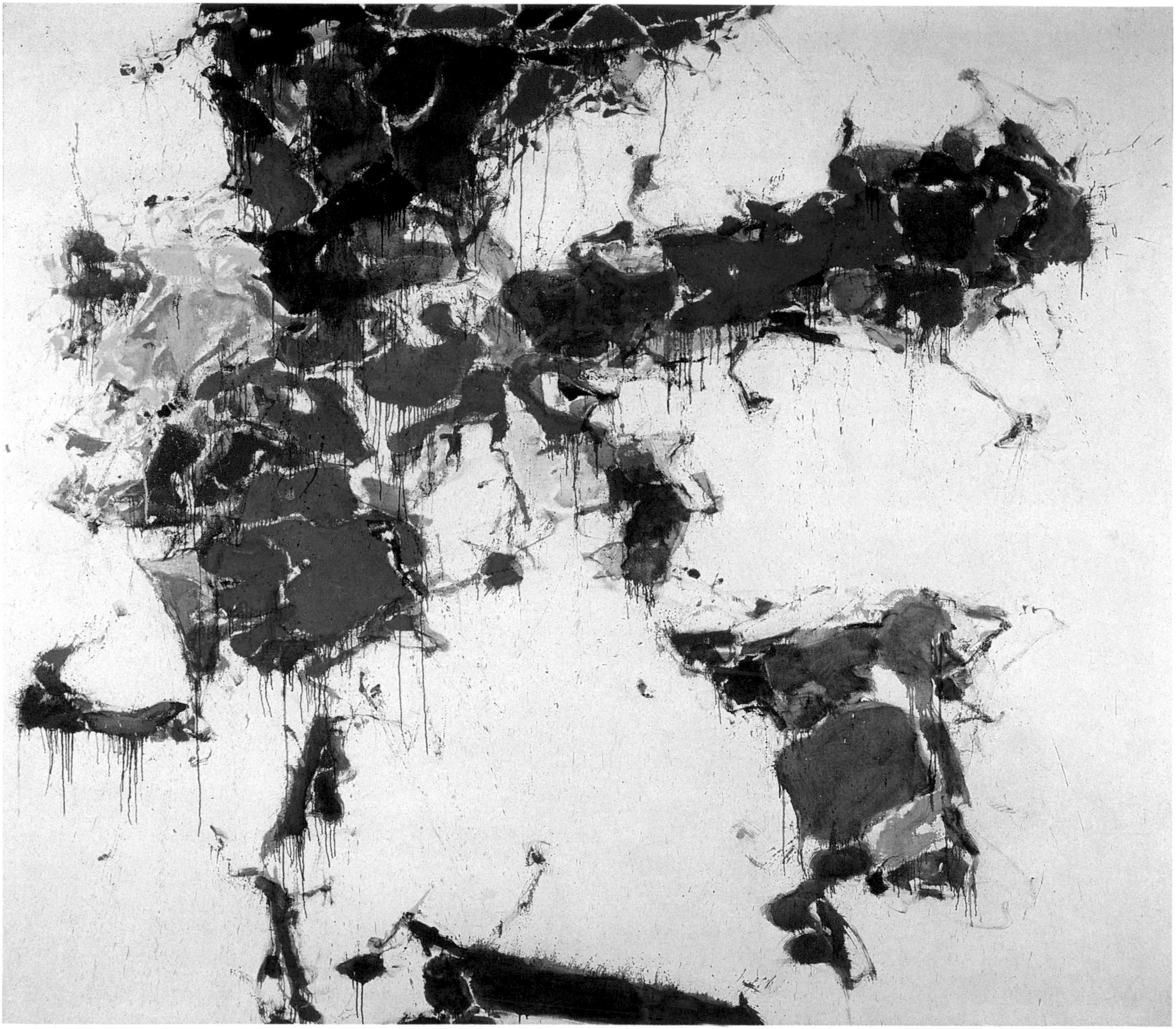

SAM FRANCIS
American b.1923
Towards Disappearance
Oil on canvas
$116\frac{1}{2} \times 126$ in. (296 × 320 cm.)
Sold 1.11.84 in New York for $770,000 (£620,968)
Record auction price for a work by the artist

ADOLPH GOTTLIEB
American b.1903
Apaquogue
Signed, inscribed with title and dated 1961 on the reverse
Oil on canvas
72 × 90 in. (183 × 228.5 cm.)
Sold 1.11.84 in New York for $242,000 (£195,161)
Record auction price for a work by the artist
From the collection of Mrs Albert D. Lasker

KAREL APPEL
Dutch b.1921
Black Animal with Dying Bird
Signed and dated 58
Oil on canvas
51¼ × 76¾ in. (130 × 195 cm.)
Sold 25.6.85 in London for £41,040 ($52,120)

A New Spirit in Contemporary Art

MARINA VAIZEY

We are in the middle of a noisy, cheerful, and excitingly active revival of interest in contemporary painting and sculpture. And, although the British are not famous now as patrons of the contemporary, albeit British patronage of art both of the past and of the present was amongst the strongest in the world until the First World War, the new debate about contemporary art has much of its roots in an exhibition, heavily criticized, that took place in London in January 1981 at the Royal Academy, A New Spirit in Painting.

This was, indeed, the first major exhibition of contemporary art on an international scale to take place in London since the famous '54–64' exhibition at the Tate Gallery in 1964. The early 1970s had seen the critical ascendancy in Europe of conceptual art, in the main from America. But what seems to have happened since A New Spirit is a change in the tone of the debate. From weary voices chorusing that Modernism was over, and that Modernism had failed, another view adapted the term Post-Impressionism by declaring that we were all in the new phase of Post-Modernism. There is a spirit of energy, optimism, and internationalism. New labels have been invented: for the Italians, 'Trans-avant-garde', meaning among others the three Cs, Sandro Chia, Francesco Clemente, and Enzo Cucchi. For the Germans, 'new wild' has been used, and international reputations have been made by such painters as Georg Baselitz, Sigmar Polke, A.R. Penck, Markus Lupertz, to name but few; Anselm Kiefer is widely regarded as one of the most interesting, dramatic, and impressive painters working today, and Joseph Beuys, who has described himself as a sculptor of society, remains one of the most controversial post-war artists. In America, young painters make headlines and very high prices: when Julian Schnabel simply changed galleries, the move made news not just in art magazines but in the *New York Times*. Art and young artists attract attention in a way that has not happened since Andy Warhol started to use the media as an art-form, and Christo involved the media as part of the whole process of his major environmental installations.

The new internationalism and the increasing fascination with contemporary art is a phenomenon of the 1980s. By the end of 1981, the *New Yorker* was saying, only slightly tongue in cheek, that 'Contemporary art is no longer a New York exclusive' and that the heyday of Abstract Expressionism as the dominant international style was not only well and truly over but seen to be over. Indeed, in the mid-1980s Mark Rothko is perceived as a modern old master, and the Rothko Foundation is ensuring that there are significant holdings of his paintings in major museums throughout the world.

There are more dealers, more places to show, more museums, and more – and, I believe, better and even more interesting – artists at work than at any time this century since the period before the First World War (of which the 1920s can be seen as an extension for these purposes). It is true that all the 'isms' beginning with Impressionism, which expanded subject-matter dramatically – the Impressionists were the first group of artists to take the suburbs seriously – opened up in unprecedented fashion the possibilities for art. Minimalism and conceptual art

GEORG BASELITZ
German b.1938
Adler
Signed with initials and dated 26.1.82; signed again, inscribed with title and dated on the reverse
Oil on canvas
$78\frac{1}{2} \times 98\frac{1}{4}$ in. (199.5 × 249.5 cm.)
Sold 25.6.85 in London for £54,000 ($68,580)

could be seen in the 1970s as a purist reaction to all those overwhelming possibilities, and by returning to the building blocks of art – line, form, colour – reacting to the incessant bombardment on our senses of all the visual media. Now in the 1980s all possibilities are being embraced.

The 'new spirit' in painting acknowledges masters such as Picasso, Balthus, Max Beckmann, and Francis Bacon, whose major summer retrospective (1985) at the Tate confirms his stature as among the greatest and most disturbing of 20th-century painters. In major exhibition after major exhibition from Westkunst in Cologne in 1981, which looked at European and American art as a series of reconstructed gallery shows from 1939 to the present, to La Grande Parade at Amsterdam's Stedilijk Museum in December 1984, which looked at European and American painting since 1940, the period is continually under review. But it is the interest in the present that is revitalizing the retrieval of the recent past. West Berlin's Zeitgeist of 1982 seemed a portentously named survey of the current work, but in the event was fully justified, building on the excitement generated by A New Spirit. Contemporary German art has toured American museums, the 'New Art' was shown at the Tate in 1983 (the gallery's Patrons of New Art is a small collectors' organization dedicated to these aims), and the Tate's controversial Turner Prize, inaugurated in 1984, was awarded to the British painter Malcolm Morley, long resident in New York. Los Angeles opened its Temporary Contemporary, the first museum dedicated exclusively to contemporary art in Los Angeles, in 1983, with the showing of nine private collections. The Los Angeles Museum of Contemporary Art has since purchased much of the collection of Count Panza, an Italian industrialist who has made a particularly adventurous collection of American art. New York's Museum of Modern Art opened its newly expanded building in May 1984, and hosted an enormous International Survey of Recent Painting and Sculpture, signalling an involvement with absolutely contemporary art that had been lacking over the past several decades; meanwhile the Metropolitan Museum with its new curator of 20th-century art, William Liebermann, announced ambitious plans for a new wing entirely devoted to 20th-century and contemporary art, which even involves a vast roof-top sculpture garden (carpeted with Astroturf). In the past year, new contemporary museum projects have been announced from Fort Lauderdale, Florida, to Houston, Texas, from Frankfurt, Germany, to Turin, Italy. This evolving and expanding institutional development matters, for this is where most of us see art.

But the institutions are dependent on the private collector, and it is the growing diversity and strength there, fed by more galleries and specialized auction sales, that is the best sign of health for the creation and sale of contemporary art in an atmosphere where to a certain extent cut-backs in public expenditure are affecting, primarily through contracting higher education, some support systems for artists.

What many commentators feel is the most surprisingly beautiful new showing place for contemporary art is in a central London suburb, St. John's Wood: in a disused industrial paint factory, magnificently converted to prime viewing space, the public has been invited, free, to see some of the work from the largest collection of contemporary art being made, now, anywhere – the Saatchi Collection. Mr and Mrs Charles Saatchi (he is English, she American, and the London based Saatchi & Saatchi advertising agency is among the world's biggest) have collected several score artists in depth and breadth. The opening installation mixed minimal, conceptual, and painterly work, showing holdings of Andy Warhol, Cy Twombly, Brice Marden, Donald Judd, Richard Serra and Bruce Nauman. The collection is highly personal, and deeply committed, but reflects also the Post-Modernist eclectic pluralism that is typifying the new energy in both making and evaluating contemporary art. Painting and sculpture are the ingredients;

but the painting, for example, embraces the huge mixed-media work of Julian Schnabel and the fervent engagement with the drama of history by Anselm Kiefer, as well as the highly personal and emotionally charged London landscapes and portraits of Leon Kossoff. Expressionist and Minimalist are two polarities in a collection which is as much predicated by the emotional richness of figurative painting as by works which through severe yet opulent simplicity concentrate on the articulation of space.

There is also a new lightheartedness in contemporary art, a kind of wacky humour, and a much greater willingness to involve the public. Christo has been working in this way since the late 1960s, and this autumn he plans to wrap up Paris's Pont Neuf. But an artist like the painter Bruce McLean, winner of the first prize in the 1984 Liverpool John Moores exhibition, began as a performance artist, a member of the Nice Style Pose Band, and appeared at the Tate as King for the Day in a mad spoof of practically every art style that could be conjured up, and then some, and he still performs at galleries and museums. But he is also a marvellously enthusiastic painter. The artists of the landscape in Britain, such as Richard Long and Hamish Fulton, also have international reputations (Richard Long will have a retrospective at New York's Guggenheim in 1986) and could perhaps be described as performing in landscape: Fulton records his walks through photographs; Long will actually make sculptures *in situ* from found stones or wood, and also makes wall-hanging map pieces, books, and paintings using mud prints of his own body.

There is a new school of British sculpture, too, which is already well established on the international map of art. Some of these sculptors – Tony Cragg, Bill Woodrow – use found material, the rubbish of the streets. Others such as Julian Opie concentrate on the ephemera of domesticity, and in Opie's case operate in a borderland between painting and sculpture. Barry Flanagan has, in bronze, an anarchic wit, with a prancing, boxing, dandified hare as the creature most commonly portrayed; and Flanagan is currently undertaking a major public commission in New York.

Humour, alternating between the dead pan and the ferocious, is one aspect of art now, from the graffiti and street-wise imagery of New York to the solemn cornucopias of plastic fruit constructed by the young British artist Edward Allington. But also surfacing in new and beautiful modes is a return to tradition, and specifically a romantic involvement with the past. The young British painters Therese Oulton and Christopher Le Brun create richly evocative turbulences, reminiscent of vast and dramatic landscape. The American Susan Rothenberg concentrates on linear depictions of animals against ruffled white backgrounds, which somehow remind the spectator of the sense of ancient ritual and ceremony, of some archaic simplicity and symbol. And there is the elaborate, savage, and beautiful social comment of Gilbert & George, the realism of the nudes of Philip Pearlstein, the extraordinary involvement with a kind of painted photography of Chuck Close – photography, of course, is another story.

Rarely can the field have been more richly inviting, open, and full of unexpected possibilities for collectors in contemporary art, for the apparent monopoly of New York in the making of significant art since the war has long since been challenged by a dazzling diversity, supported by a growing number of institutional, corporate, and private collectors.

KONRAD KLAPHECK
German b.1935
Der Harem
Signed and dated 68 on the
reverse
Oil on canvas
45 × 39 in. (114.2 × 99 cm.)
Sold 25.6.85 in London for
£12,960 ($16,459)

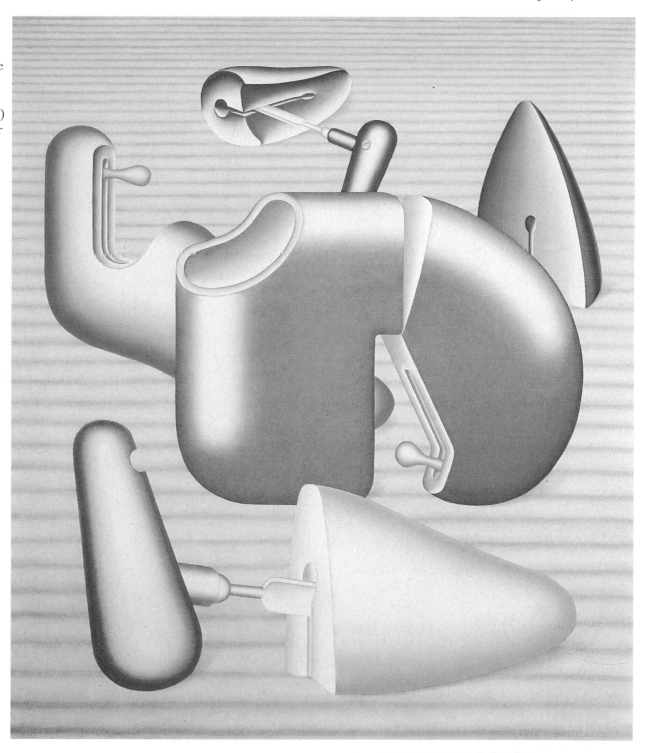

SIR JOHN LAVERY, R.A., R.S.A., R.H.A.
British 1856–1941
Girl in a Red Dress reading by a Swimming Pool
Signed
Oil on board
24 × 20 in. (61 × 51 cm.)
Painted in 1936
Sold 7.6.85 in London for £39,960 ($51,948)

Opposite:

FRANK WRIGHT BOURDILLON
British 1851–1924
The Jubilee Hat
Signed and dated 1887
Oil on canvas
$36\frac{1}{2} \times 27\frac{1}{2}$ in. (92.7 × 70 cm.)
Sold 15.3.85 in London for £43,200
($46,656)
Record auction price for a work by the
artist
F.W. Bourdillon is remarkable for an
artist of his merit in having only practised
as a painter for 12 years. The son of an
Indian Civil Servant (his name is of
Huguenot origin), he started life as a
coffee planter and amateur ornithologist,
and it was his paintings of birds which led
him to be encouraged to become a painter.
He studied at the Slade and then in Paris
in 1883–4 after which he moved to
Oxford. His first visit to Cornwall
occurred in 1886 when he stayed at
Polperro, and in 1887 he came to Newlyn
where he stayed until 1892, sharing digs
with Stanhope Forbes. He was particularly
friendly with Forbes and Norman Garstin.
Bourdillon specialized in interior and
history scenes. Early in 1892 he was
converted to a deep Christian conviction
and gave up painting to become a
missionary in India, where he married
another missionary. He later returned to
Ramsgate, where he lived out the rest of
his life as a curate.

RICHARD THOMAS MOYNAN, R.H.A.
British 1856–1906
An Invitation to go Haymaking
Signed and dated 1899
Oil on canvas
20 × 30 in. (51 × 76 cm.)
Sold 15.3.85 in London for £21,600 ($23,328)
Record auction price for a work by the artist

EDWARD ARTHUR WALTON, R.S.A.
British 1860–1922
Grandfather's Garden
Signed and dated 1884
Watercolour
22½ × 21 in. (57 × 53.5 cm.)
Sold 13.12.84 in Glasgow for £18,360 ($22,399)
Record auction price for a work by the artist

SAMUEL JOHN PEPLOE, R.S.A.
British 1871–1935
The Coffee Pot
Signed
Oil on canvas
25 × 33¼ in. (63.5 × 84.5 cm.)
Painted *c.* 1905
Sold 25.4.85 in Glasgow for £84,240 ($106,142)
Record auction price for a work by the artist

Opposite:
CHARLES GINNER, R.A.
British 1878–1952
Plymouth Pier from the Hoe
Signed
Oil on canvas
30 × 24 in. (76 × 61 cm.)
Painted in 1923
Sold 7.6.85 in London for £31,320
($40,716)
From the collection of Sir Gavin Lyle, Bt.

SPENCER GORE
British 1878–1914
Blue and Green Bottles and
Oranges
With the studio stamp
Oil on canvas
20 × 16 in. (51 × 40.5 cm.)
Painted in 1914 at the
artist's house,
6 Cambrian Road,
Richmond, shortly before
he died
Sold 9.11.84 in London
for £43,200 ($55,296)
Record auction price for
a work by the artist

SIR WILLIAM NICHOLSON
British 1872–1949
Welsh Bread
Signed
Oil on canvas
20 × 24 in. (51 × 61 cm.)
Painted in 1924
Sold 7.6.85 in London for £23,760 ($30,888)
Record auction price for a work by the artist
From the collection of Sir Gavin Lyle, Bt.

TRISTRAM HILLIER, R.A.
British 1905–84
The Anchor
Signed
Oil on panel
28½ × 24 in.
(72.5 × 61 cm.)
Sold 7.6.85 in London
for £18,360 ($23,868)

ARTHUR BOYD
Australian b.1920
White Cockatoo, Wimmera
Signed
Tempera on board
23 × 29¾ in. (58.5 × 75.5 cm.)
Painted *c.*1948–52
Sold 15.3.85 in London for £25,920 ($27,994)

SIR ALFRED MUNNINGS, P.R.A.
British 1878–1959
A Park Meeting, The Eclipse Stakes, Sandown Park
Signed
Oil on board
20 × 26 in. (51 × 66 cm.)
Sold 7.6.85 in New York for $242,000 (£186,153)

SIR WILLIAM LLEWELLYN, P.R.A.
British 1858–1941
The Goose Girl
Signed, dedicated and dated '87 To my friend F. Short'
Oil on canvas
20 × 30 in. (51 × 76 cm.)
Sold 15.3.85 in London for £25,920 ($27,994)
Record auction price for a work by the artist

Women Artists: a Rare and Mostly Unseen Legacy

REBECCA JOHN

I have never found that artists are either unpractical or difficult to get on with, or particularly dirty. Some are, but they are very rarely the best ones. If they wear beards, why shouldn't they? If they like to have strange hats, why shouldn't they? If you will ignore this and remember that they are probably just as intelligent and just as hard-working and just as anxious to have a happy life as you are, you will probably find them very much easier to get on with. My experience has always been that they are infinitely more adjustable than businessmen.

These astonishing words form part of an introduction to a book entitled *Young Artists of Promise*, a publication designed to attract the attention of potential buyers to the work of 120 artists (30 female), all of whom were working in Britain in 1957. There is worse to come: something about girl students giving up art training because of marriage and babies, 'just as it should be', because these are the 'future patrons'. The book is best forgotten, but such crude remarks do at least compel the reader to think back on the changing prejudices that have surrounded the artist as a member of society throughout the history of painting.

What exactly are the images that come to mind at the mention of the term 'Women Artists', beardless, straw-hatted and otherwise? Readers of the many recent books on the subject, the majority of which were published in the United States in the late 1970s, will have formed a very different picture of the part they played from any connected with living memory. Even considering that feminist writing becomes charged with emotion from time to time, emphasizing women's difficulties and often overlooking the fact that it was not always easy for men either, it is still a moving story about a rare, mostly unseen legacy.

By the 17th century, long after the work of the medieval illuminators had unconsciously signalled the beginning of the history of women painters, it was considered perfectly suitable for a lady to take up painting – as a toil-less hobby. But as if to confound social respectability the 17th century threw up the Italians Artemesia Gentileschi and Elisabetta Sirani, and in Holland Judith Leyster, Rachel Ruysch, and Clara Peeters, together with a number of other brilliant still-life painters scattered around Europe. With the exception of Sofonisba Anguissola, Caterina van Hemessen, and Lavinia Fontana in the 16th century, these were the first female artists of calibre to emerge following the 'vacuum' of the Renaissance. It was not until graphic materials became widely available in the 18th century, coinciding with the establishment of the Academies, that competition began to step up and women in numbers began to long for independence and recognition in the face of whatever restrictions existed in the culture of their time. By the 19th century some wished to travel and were often allowed to do so; by 1900 it was not unusual for a girl wanting to study painting and drawing to make her way to Paris, the centre of the art world, enrol at one of the Academies, and take lodgings as an 'art student'.

Having once separated the work of painters according to their sex, the tendency to categorize subject-matter reveals some false assumptions. The lazy temptation to couple women artists

ELISABETTA SIRANI
Italian 1638–65
Porcia wounding her Thigh
Signed and dated 1664
Oil on canvas
39¾ × 54¾ in.
(100 × 139 cm.)
Sold 11.12.84 in London for
£19,440 ($23,328)

with the 'feminine world' becomes a nonsense when one considers that themes such as the love between a mother and child and domestic elegance have been subjected to intense male scrutiny throughout the history of painting. But does the female hand, guided by a more intuitive mind, impart a warmer, compassionate mood to these shared themes? One has only to look again at the children of Renoir and Cassatt ('hatless' or 'with hats' as categorized in the Witt Library) to understand at once that it is futile to 'read in' degrees of male or female handling. Brutal, hesitant, or just plain talented techniques are universal. Flowers, the one subject that was generally felt to be for ladies, and is still customarily linked with the female hand, have been closely studied by male artists as far apart as Dürer and Epstein. Georgia O'Keefe's close-ups of lilies and Elizabeth Blackadder's isolated beauties of recent years, Rachel Ruysch's celebrations and Ann Vallayer-Coster's single twig of orange blossom are random examples of dignified handling of a subject which, due in part perhaps to a flirtation with oriental techniques, is too often and easily committed to paper with a few limp trails of watercolour.

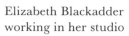
Elizabeth Blackadder
working in her studio

Long before those relatively free individuals who were able to extend their talents into the field of design, such as the Russians Popova, Exter and Goncharova (theatre), Sonia Delaunay (textiles), the Dublin portraitist Sarah Purser (stained glass), Vanessa Bell (ceramics and furniture), there existed a category of female artists quite separate in time and circumstance. These were the daughters of painting fathers. Maria Robousti 'La Tintoretta', Ann Louise de Deyster, Clara Peeters, Jane Nasmyth, and Goya's protégé Rosaria Weiss all collaborated on their father's canvases, and so close was this working relationship that there have apparently been some doubtful attributions, usually one-sided and to the credit of the father. It could seem that a good 200 years of the history of women and art is made up of devoted collaborators and emulators, which has therefore given birth to a history of exceptions we cling to for evidence of female genius. Artemesia Gentileschi, Angelica Kauffmann, and Rosa Bonheur triumphed where their fathers trod. And then there are those daughters who neither emulated their father's work or took the art world by storm, but developed their own private style, such as Orovida Pissarro and Vivien John.

It is tempting to continue categorizing women artists as if they are mere satellites circulating giant planets, and ask those proud loners to stand up in the imagination and take a bow. Giovanna Garzoni, Mary Cassatt, Cecelia Beaux, Rosa Bonheur, and Romaine Brooks all preferred work to marriage. Conviction and tenacity, coupled with the required skills to portray a personal vision, are a rare combination of qualities. Scientific direction, the dedication to the improvement of technical skills, could be said to be the most testing attribute of a great artist. It is

OROVIDA PISSARRO
French b.1893
Tiger leaping on a Spearman
Signed and dated 1929
Tempera on linen
48¼ × 32¼ in.
(122.5 × 82 cm.)
Sold 15.3.85 in London for
£6,480 ($7,760)

now evident that it is present in the work of Gwen John, as it is in the exquisite still-life painting of Fede Galizia, Maria van Oosterwijk, Louise Moillon, and Giovanna Garzoni, all artists
working in 17th-century Europe. Shells, dishes of fruit, scattered food, flowers, a sort of feminine
inconography that litters the rooms of so many present-day middle-class homes, provided vital
subject-matter for the obsessively detailed investigation of these artists.

Giovanna Garzoni has become famous for one work, her *Dish of Broad Beans*; or perhaps the
beans are more famous than her name, like Meret Oppenheim's fur cup and saucer, *Déjeuner
en fourrure*, created in 1936. It seems that simplicity will never fail to appeal, and it is warming
to think that so much unpretentious work hangs in private houses, where a small painting or
drawing can impart a certain magic to a room – I remember Carrington's works on silver paper
creating just such an effect at home. It is also gratifying to think that the majority of work has
escaped commercial exploitation, and the dreadful fate of shoddy reproduction in cheap art books.

A light, investigative approach seems to characterize some of the better contemporary work,
present for example in Elizabeth Blackadder's elegant studies of *Orientalia*, and although Susan
Hiller's work is weighted with profound questions mainly about the categorization of art – she
is an intellectual artist – her work is light on the eye and always delicately presented. Having
worked for some 16 years, using different media for each of her main pieces, her video work
Belshazzar's Feast was last year acquired by the Tate Gallery.

Should an educated but inexpert eye be confronted with 200 paintings muddled together from
four centuries, would it be possible to single out all those executed by the female hand? It seems
unlikely, although were any narrative paintings included, they would almost certainly be the
work of male artists, since this is a genre hardly touched by women. The definition 'woman
artist' is likely to tell us more about the artist than the art, and the memory of the conditions
in which they worked – whether read about or experienced first hand – tends to remain inseparable
from personal familiarity with their work. I can't help remembering here the cold northern
light and smell of Gauloises which permeated Elizabeth Frink's studio in the 1950s, a harsh
environment splattered with plaster.

I can think of quite a few women artists who would spurn the label and shudder at the thought
of being referred to as a member of such a group. Would Elizabeth Lutyens have called herself
a woman composer? It is somehow not very becoming and, besides, excellence transcends gender
distinction.

Drawings, Watercolours and Prints

EDWARD LEAR
British 1812–88
A Walk on a windy Day: an Album of Nonsense Drawings
The first drawing signed with monogram and dated 26 December 1860, each
subsequent drawing numbered and inscribed, and one dated 2 June 1860
Pen and brown ink
10 drawings laid down on the leaves of the album
$8\frac{1}{2} \times 11\frac{3}{4}$ in. (21.5 × 29.2 cm.) overall
Sold 9.7.85 in London for £15,120 ($19,656)

JACOPO NEGRETTI, PALMA IL GIOVANE
Italian 1555–1628
The Deposition
Inscribed 'Tintoretti'
Brown and cream oil paint
10½ × 16 in. (26.9 × 40.8 cm.)
Sold 2.7.85 in London for £43,200 ($55,728)
By order of the Trustees of the Harewood Charitable Trust
Owned in the 18th century by Robert Houlditch, this formed part of the notable collection assembled by the 6th Earl of Harewood.
Formerly attributed to Domenico Tintoretto, it was recognized at Christie's as one of the rare oil *modelli* executed by Palma in the
1610s; no corresponding picture has been traced.

GIOVANNI BATTISTA PIAZZETTA
Italian 1682–1754
A nude Youth sprawled on his Back, upon a Bank, lying on a Standard
Inscribed 'Gio: Batta: Piazzetta'
Black and white chalk on grey paper
$19^3/_4 \times 15$ in.
(50.4 × 38.3 cm.)
Sold 13.12.84 in London for £75,600 ($91,476)
This and three other academy figures sold at the same time are notable additions to Piazzetta's graphic *oeuvre*. Evidently drawn from the life, this study served as the model for the smaller version in the Kress album, now in the Pierpont Morgan Library, which was in turn used for the *Studj di Pittura gia Dissegnati da Giambatista Piazzetta ed ora con l'intaglio di Marco Pitteri* published by Giovanni Battista Albrizzi in 1760.

GIOVANNI DOMENICO TIEPOLO
Italian 1712–1804
Punchinellos in a 'Malvasia'
Signed on the edge of a table 'Do: Tiepolo f.'
Black chalk, pen and brown ink, two shades of brown wash,
watermark GAF
15 × 18¼ in. (38.2 × 46.6 cm.)
Sold 13.12.84 in London for £73,440 ($88,862)
This drawing which shows a Malvasia, named after the wine
from Monemvasia sold in the city, belongs to the celebrated
series of 103 Punchinello drawings which date from the late
1790s

Opposite:
ANTONIO CANAL, IL CANALETTO
Italian 1697–1768
The Church of the Gesuiti, Venice
Inscribed 'Giesuiti in Venezia' below the pen borderline
Pen and brown ink, grey and light brown wash
12¼ × 10¼ in. (31.2 × 25.8 cm.)
Sold 13.12.84 in London for £50,760 ($61,420)
This drawing, which was owned by the great French
connoisseur P.J. Mariette and is first recorded in the catalogue
of his sale in 1775, was sold previously at Christie's with the
collection of William Esdaile in 1840 for £3. 18s. It is related
to the central section of Canaletto's *Campo dei Gesuiti*, formerly
in the Harvey collection at Langley Park.

Giesulti in Venezia

Opposite:
ROSALBA CARRIERA
Italian 1675–1757
A young Lady with a Parrot
Pastel
23 × 18¾ in. (58 × 48 cm.)
Sold 13.12.84 in London for £145,800 ($176,418)
Record auction price for a pastel by the artist
From the collection of Mrs Donald S. Stralem
This exceptional pastel is evidently of the 1730s when Rosalba
was at the zenith of her career. It may be compared with the
celebrated pastel of the dancer Barberina Campani at Dresden
and the characterization perhaps suggests that the unidentified
subject of the present work was also an actress or dancer.
Rosalba was much admired in France and this and a second
pastel by her has complemented the notable collection of French
18th-century drawings assembled by Casimir Stralem and
sold on the instructions of Mrs Donald S. Stralem of New York.

NICOLAS LANCRET
French 1690–1743
Studies of two Men
Red chalk
7⁷⁄₁₆ × 9¹⁵⁄₁₆ in. (18.6 × 25.3 cm.)
Sold 13.12.84 in London for £45,360 ($54,886)
Record auction price for a drawing by the artist
From the collection of Mrs Donald S. Stralem
This is a study for *Le Déjeuner de jambon* which, with its
companion *Le Déjeuner d'huitres* by Jean François de Troy, was
commissioned by Louis XV in 1735 for the dining-room of the
Petits-Appartements at Versailles. Both pictures are now in
the Musée Condé, Chantilly. Lancret later painted a second
version which is now at Boston (Forsyth Wickes Collection).

JEAN HONORÉ FRAGONARD
French 1732–1806
A Bull entering a Stall
Black chalk, brown and grey wash, watermark grapes
$10\frac{1}{16} \times 15\frac{7}{8}$ in. (25.6 × 40.4 cm.)
In a Louis XVI frame
Sold 13.12.84 in London for £113,400 ($137,214)
From the collection of Mrs Donald S. Stralem
Bulls provided the subject for some of Fragonard's most celebrated drawings. This brilliant study has been compared with *Le Char à boeuf*, which Fragonard drew in Naples in 1774.

FRANÇOIS BOUCHER
French 1703–70
A sleeping Girl
Red, black and white chalk on blue paper
$8\frac{3}{4} \times 12\frac{1}{2}$ in. (22.3 × 31.7 cm.)
Sold 13.12.84 in London for £75,600 ($91,476)
Record auction price for a drawing by the artist
From the collection of Mrs Donald S. Stralem
This figure was used for Diana in *Diana and Callisto*, dated 1745, at the California Palace of the Legion of Honor, San Francisco, which is one of a set of five paintings commissioned by Madame de Pompadour for the Château de Bellevue

JEAN MICHEL MOREAU, MOREAU
LE JEUNE
French 1744–1814
N'ayez pas peur, ma bonne amie
Signed 'JM. moreau le jeune.
1775'
Pen and brown ink, brown
wash
$10^{3}/_{4} \times 8^{1}/_{2}$ in. (27 × 21.9 cm.)
Sold 10.4.85 in London for
£97,200 ($119,556)
From the collection of Mr
and Mrs Deane F. Johnson,
New York City
This drawing was engraved
for the series *Monument du
Costume*, more fully entitled
*Estampes pour servir à l'histoire
des modes du costume en France
dans le dix-huitième siècle*. This
illustrates the life of *une femme
de bon ton* and was intended to
represent fashionable life of
the time; as a result furniture
and costume are described
with close precision.

JEAN AUGUSTE DOMINIQUE INGRES
French 1780–1867
Portrait of Henri Joseph Rutxhiel, Sculptor
Signed and dated 'a Rome 1809'
Pencil
6⅞ in. (17.5 cm.) diameter
Sold 25.10.84 in New York for $165,000 (£133,064)
The Belgian sculptor H.J. Rutxhiel (1775–1837) arrived in Rome in 1809, having won a Grand Prix in the previous year for his relief of *Icarus and Daedalus*. He returned to Paris in 1811.

WOLF HÜBER
German 1490–1553
The Angel appearing to Joachim (?)
Dated 1531 and with added
monogram AD
Pen and black ink
7¼ × 5 in. (18.3 × 12.9 cm.)
Sold 10.4.85 in London for
£140,400 ($172,692)
From the De Mestral de Saint
Saphorin Collection

PIETER MOLIJN
Dutch 1595–1661
A Scene on the Ice with Skaters and Waggons
Signed 'PM (monogram) olyn./-1655.'
Black chalk, grey wash
$5\frac{3}{4} \times 7\frac{1}{2}$ in. (14.6 × 19.2 cm.)
Sold 26.11.84 in Amsterdam for D.fl.148,200 (£35,454)
An exceptional example of Molijn, formerly in the Llanover Album compiled in the 18th century and acquired in 1945 by Baron Paul Hatvany

HENDRICK VAN STEENWIJCK THE YOUNGER
Flemish 1580–1649
The Crypt of a Church with two Men sleeping
Signed
Pen and brown ink, brown wash heightened with white on blue-grey paper
$5 \times 6\frac{1}{2}$ in. (12.4 × 16.8 cm.)
Sold 26.11.84 in Amsterdam for D.fl.205,200 (£49,090)
One of the few known drawings by Steenwijck, whose pictures of church interiors are so numerous

EDWARD HASSELL
British 1777–1852
The Library, Binfield, Berkshire
Pencil, pen and grey ink and
watercolour heightened with white
$13\frac{3}{8} \times 18\frac{1}{4}$ in. (34 × 46 cm.)
Sold 13.12.84 in London for £12,960
($15,682)
This drawing of the Library at Binfield
was executed shortly after the death of
Margaret, Lady Walsh, in 1836. The
decoration is characteristic of the
period. Some of the furniture such as
the Grecian couch and bobbin-turned
chair are comparable with examples in
Gillows' catalogues of the 1820s. Other
details include the copy of the *Nautical
Almanack* for 1836 on the table in the
foreground.

FILIPPO JUVARRA
Italian 1676–1736
*A terraced Garden with Statuary and Boscage
below a Palace: Project for the Stage*
Inscribed 'deliziosa'
Black chalk, pen and brown ink, grey
wash
$7\frac{3}{4} \times 7\frac{1}{2}$ in. (19.9 × 19.1 cm.)
Sold 13.12.84 in London for £19,440
($23,522)
A design for Scene VI of the 1714
production of *Tito e Bernice* at the Teatro
Capranica, Rome

JOHANN HEINRICH FUSELI, R.A.
Swiss/British 1741–1825
*Portrait Study of a Woman,
probably Mrs Fuseli, her Head
inclined to the left*
Black chalk heightened with
white, the verso with a study
of legs in pencil, watermark
Strasburg lily
$12\frac{1}{2} \times 12\frac{1}{8}$ in.
(31.75 × 30.5 cm.)
Sold 9.7.85 in London for
£113,400 ($156,492)
Formerly in the collection of
Randall Davies, F.S.A.
This exceptional drawing
probably dates from the close
of the artist's most creative
decade in England,
1790–1800. Sophia Rawlins,
whom Fuseli married in
1788, was the subject of the
majority of his most brilliant
portrait studies.

JOHN ROBERT COZENS
British 1752–97
Pays de Valais, near Geneva
Signed on the original mount
Watercolour
19⅜ × 26¾ in. (49.8 × 67.8 cm.)
Sold 9.7.85 in London for
£28,080 ($38,750)
One of a number of watercolours
deriving from a sketch made by
the artist on 30 August 1776 in
the course of his first Italian tour.
Formerly in the collections of Sir
Frederick Eden, for whom Cozens
painted it, and Norman D. Newall.

FRANCIS TOWNE
British 1740–1816
*Keswick Lake, looking towards Lodore
Fall*
Signed and dated 1805; signed and
inscribed on the back of the
mount: 'A View of Keswick Lake
Looking toward Lowdore fall
drawn on the spot 1786 & finished
Nov 25th 1805 by Francis Towne'
Pen and brown ink and watercolour
8⅜ × 13¼ in. (21.6 × 33.5 cm.)
Sold 20.11.84 in London for
£14,040 ($17,690)
From the collection formed by the
late Sir William Worsley, 4th Bt.,
of Hovingham Hall, Yorkshire.
Fourteen watercolours from this
collection, one of the finest to be
built up after Towne's rediscovery
in the early years of this century,
were included in the sale.
Towne's tour of the Lake District
in 1786, made with his friends
James White and John Merivale,
was his last extensive foray
outside his native Exeter. This
watercolour is an excellent
example of the artist's practice of
working up a drawing from a
sketch done many years before,
and may be connected with
Towne's only exhibition of his
works, held in London in 1805.

THOMAS GAINSBOROUGH, R.A.
British 1727–88
An Ox-Cart by the Banks of a navigable River
Pencil and black chalk
$10\frac{3}{4} \times 14\frac{7}{8}$ in. (27 × 35.8 cm.)
Sold 20.11.84 in London for
£25,920 ($32,659)
One of several sheets by the artist dating from the late 1750s which were probably intended for translation into prints.
Formerly in the collection of Gerald Robinson, and previously sold at Christie's, 30 June 1906, for 11 gns.

JOHN CONSTABLE, R.A.
British 1776–1837
Fishing Boats on a Beach, probably at Brighton
Dated 25 Sep 1824
Pencil, pen and brown ink, grey-brown wash
$7 \times 10\frac{1}{4}$ in. (17.7 × 25.6 cm.)
Sold 19.3.85 in London for
£27,000 ($30,240)
A previously unknown drawing, belonging to a group of similar sketches made at Brighton and Worthing in the summer and early autumn of 1824, while the artist was staying there with his ailing wife Maria.
Formerly in the collection of the artist's son, Charles Golding Constable.

WILLIAM PARS, A.R.A.
British 1742–82
Strawberry Hill, Middlesex, from the Garden
Pencil, pen and grey ink and watercolour with touches of white heightening
14$\frac{3}{4}$ × 21 in. (37 × 53.3 cm.)
Sold 19.3.85 in London for £14,040 ($15,725)
Record auction price for a work by the artist
From the collection of Lord O'Hagan
Pars's beautiful drawings of Horace Walpole's Gothick extravaganza, made just after his return from Ireland in 1772, earned him
a warm recommendation from his patron to Horace Mann, British Minister at Florence

JOHN RUSKIN
British 1819–1900
Portrait Study of Lily Armstrong
Signed
Pencil and watercolour
heightened with white
14 × 9¾ in. (35.5 × 25 cm.)
Sold 9.7.85 in London for
£14,040 ($19,375)
By order of the Trustees of the
Harewood Charitable Trust
A rare and characteristically
sensitive portrait study of the girl
who, after Rose la Touche,
occupied the strongest place in
Ruskin's affections during the
1860s. He later described her as
'the most beautiful creature in
face and form I ever saw
anywhere'.

DAVID COX
British 1783–1859
Windermere during the Regatta
Signed and dated 1832 and inscribed as title on the artist's label attached to the backboard
Pencil and watercolour
17 ¾ × 23 ¾ in. (44.8 × 60.1 cm.)
Sold 9.7.85 in London for £11,880 ($16,394)
Formerly in the collection of Sir Daniel Cooper, Bt., and sold previously at Christie's, 14 January 1944, for 155 gns.

FRANÇOIS LOUIS THOMAS FRANCIA
French 1772–1839
A Kaag going to windward in a Squall
Signed and dated (18)35 on the
reverse
Watercolour
$6\frac{3}{8} \times 10\frac{1}{8}$ in. (16.4 × 25.6 cm.)
Sold 9.7.85 in London for £8,100
($11,178)
Francia returned to Calais in
1817 at the end of a 22 year
sojourn in England, and for the
rest of his life took his subjects
from the vicinity of his birthplace

JOHN SCARLETT DAVIS
British 1804–44
*The River Wye with Chepstow Castle
in the distance*
Signed and dated 1834
Pencil and watercolour
heightened with gum arabic
$7\frac{7}{8} \times 13$ in. (20.2 × 33 cm.)
Sold 9.7.85 in London for £7,020
($9,687)

WILLIAM CALLOW
British 1812–1908
The Grand Canal, Venice, looking towards the Salute
Signed and dated 1859
Pencil and watercolour
$10\frac{5}{8} \times 14\frac{5}{8}$ in. (27 × 35.6 cm.)
Sold 9.7.85 in London for £19,440 ($26,827)
Based on a sketch made on the artist's honeymoon in Venice, August 1846

ALBERT GOODWIN
British 1845–1932
St. Leonards
Signed, inscribed and dated 1908
Watercolour
17½ × 22 in. (44.4 × 55.8 cm.)
Sold 18.12.84 in London for £9,720
($11,956)

ARCHIBALD THORBURN
British 1860–1935
Duck on icy Marshland
Signed and dated January 1907
Watercolour heightened with bodycolour
21⅝ × 30⅜ in. (53.4 × 77.5 cm.)
Sold 14.5.85 in London for £12,960
($16,200)
By order of the Executors of the late Lady
Colman
Record auction price for a watercolour by the
artist

DANTE GABRIEL ROSSETTI
British 1828–82
Portrait of Elizabeth Siddal, in profile to the right
Watercolour
$7\frac{1}{8} \times 6\frac{3}{8}$ in.
(17.8 × 15.3 cm.)
Sold 14.5.85 in London for £25,920 ($32,400)
From the collection of John Street, Esq.
One of only two recorded watercolour portraits by Rossetti of his favourite model who became, briefly, his wife from 1860 until her death only two years later

ARTHUR RACKHAM
British 1867–1939
*Alice's Adventures in Wonderland:
At this the whole Pack rose up into
the Air, and came flying down upon
her!*
Signed and dated 07
Pen and black ink and
watercolour heightened with
white
$11\frac{1}{8} \times 7\frac{1}{8}$ in. (28.3 × 18.2 cm.)
Sold 24.5.85 in New York for
$30,600 (£23,538)
Reproduced in L. Carroll,
Alice's Adventures in Wonderland,
London, William Heinemann,
1907

WILLIAM JAMES BENNETT
British 1787–1844
Niagara Falls: View of the American Fall, taken from Goat Island
Watercolour on paper laid down on board
$17^{1}/_{4} \times 20^{1}/_{2}$ in. (43.4 × 52 cm.)
Sold 21.9.84 in New York for $41,800 (£33,440)

Opposite:
EDMUND DULAC
British 1882–1953
The Snow Queen
Signed and dated 10, and inscribed (on background) 'Many a winter's night she flies through the streets (The Snow Queen)'
Watercolour, bodycolour, pen and black ink
$12^{3}/_{8} \times 9^{3}/_{4}$ in. (31.4 × 24.7 cm.)
Sold 15.2.85 in New York for $73,700 (£66,396)

ALBRECHT DÜRER
German 1471–1528
The Abduction of Proserpine
(Bartsch 72; Meder, Hollstein 67)
Etching on iron, a fine Meder I impression before the rust
spots
P. 12⅛ × 8⅜ in. (30.8 × 21.3 cm.)
Sold 7.5.85 in New York for $37,400 (£30,406)
From the estate of George and Marianne Khuner

ALBRECHT DÜRER
German 1471–1528
The Sea Monster
(Bartsch 71; Meder, Hollstein 66)
Engraving, a fine, rich Meder a-b impression
S. 9⅞ × 7⅜ in. (25.1 × 18.8 cm.)
Sold 7.5.85 in New York for $19,800 (£16,100)
From the estate of George and Marianne Khuner

Far right:
CAMILLO PROCACCINI
Italian 1546–1629
The Transfiguration
(Bartsch 4)
P. $22\frac{1}{2} \times 13\frac{5}{8}$ in.
(57 × 34.5 cm.)
Sold 26.6.85 in London for
£17,280 ($22,291)
Record auction price for a
print by the artist

Right:
FRANCESCO MAZZOLA, IL
PARMIGIANINO
Italian 1503–40
The Entombment
(Bartsch 5)
Etching, first state (of two)
S. $12\frac{1}{4} \times 9\frac{3}{8}$ in.
(31.2 × 23.7 cm.)
Sold 26.6.85 in London for
£8,100 ($10,449)
Record auction price for a
print by the artist

Far right:
HENDRIK GOLTZIUS
Flemish 1558–1617
Apollo
(Bartsch 141; Hirschmann 131)
Engraving
P. $13\frac{7}{8} \times 10\frac{3}{8}$ in.
(43.2 × 30.5 cm.)
Sold 26.6.85 in London for
£14,040 ($17,970)

Right:
HENDRIK GOLTZIUS
Flemish 1558–1617
Proserpine
(Bartsch 236; Hirschmann 370)
Chiaroscuro woodcut printed
in black, ochre and brown
Oval, S. $13\frac{3}{4} \times 10\frac{1}{8}$ in.
(34.8 × 25.8 cm.)
Sold 26.6.85 in London for
£15,120 ($19,320)
Record auction price for a
print by the artist

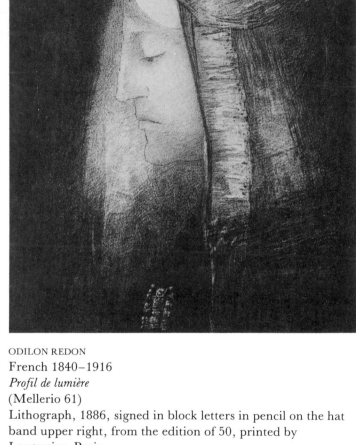

RODOLPHE BRESDIN
French 1825–85
Le Bon Samaritain
(Van Gelder 100)
Lithograph, 1861, a fine, early impression printed with exceptional clarity, from the third printing, 1867
L. 22¼ × 17½ in. (56.6 × 44.5 cm.)
Sold 7.5.85 in New York for $27,500 (£22,360)
Record auction price for a print by the artist

ODILON REDON
French 1840–1916
Profil de lumière
(Mellerio 61)
Lithograph, 1886, signed in block letters in pencil on the hat band upper right, from the edition of 50, printed by Lemercier, Paris
L. 13⅜ × 9½ in. (34.2 × 24.2 cm.)
Sold 6.12.84 in London for £28,080 ($33,977)

Opposite:
PAUL GAUGUIN
French 1848–1903
Projet d'assiette
(Guérin, Agustoni and Lari 1)
Lithograph handcoloured with watercolour and bodycolour, 1889, signed in pencil and inscribed 'Dessins Lithographiques'
L. 8¾ × 8¼ in. (22.2 × 21 cm.)
Sold 7.11.84 in New York for $44,000 (£33,846)

PAUL GAUGUIN
French 1848–1903
Noa Noa (Embaumé embaumé)
(Guérin, Agustoni and Lari 17)
Woodcut printed in colours, 1894–5, from
the edition of about 30 impressions printed
by L. Roy
L. 14 × 8 in. (37.8 × 22.5 cm.)
Sold 6.12.84 in London for £30,240
($36,590)

EDVARD MUNCH
Norwegian 1863–1944
Frauen am Meeresufer
(Schiefler 117 a2)
Woodcut printed in colours with the promontory of the shore handcoloured to tone in with the green of the ground, 1898, signed in pencil
L. 17¾ × 20⅛ in. (45 × 51.1 cm.)
Sold 7.11.84 in New York for $101,200 (£77,846)

EDVARD MUNCH
Norwegian 1863–1944
Madonna, liebendes Weib
(Schiefler 33 AIa)
Lithograph, 1895, on
stiff, pale green-grey
wove paper, signed in
pencil, rare, with the
embryo border
L. $23\frac{1}{2} \times 17\frac{1}{4}$ in.
$(60 \times 44.1$ cm.)
Sold 6.12.84 in London
for £41,040 ($49,658)

Above:
MAX ERNST
German 1891–1976
Composition (Battle of the Fish)
Woodcut with extensive handcolouring in watercolour,
1917, signed and dated in black ink
L. 7½ × 13¼ in. (19.1 × 33.8 cm.)
Sold 7.11.84 in New York for $17,600 (£13,538)
This previously unrecorded woodcut was probably made
while Ernst was on leave during the First World War

Left:
MAX ERNST
German 1891–1976
Ohne Titel (Mutter mit badenden Kindern)
(Spies, Leppien 2)
Linocut printed in burgundy, blue and two shades of
green, 1911, first state (of two), signed in pencil, the
colours applied by hand to the block in the manner of a
monotype, probably unique in this state
L. 4¾ × 5 in. (12 × 12.9 cm.)
Sold 6.12.84 in London for £17,280 ($20,909)
Record auction price for a print by the artist

PAUL KLEE
Swiss 1879–1940
Jungfrau im Baum Inv. 3, Jungfrau (träumend)
(Kornfeld 4 b)
Etching, 1903, signed, titled and dated in
pencil, inscribed with the worknumber '2',
numbered 18/30
P. $9\frac{3}{8} \times 11\frac{13}{16}$ in. (23.8 × 30 cm.)
Sold 7.11.84 in New York for $26,400
(£20,308)
From the collection of the late James
Gilvarry

EMIL NOLDE
German 1867–1956
Tänzerinnen
(Schiefler–Mösel 132)
Woodcut, 1917, signed in pencil, from the
edition of about 12
L. $9\frac{1}{8} \times 12\frac{1}{4}$ in. (23.2. × 31 cm.)
Sold 7.5.85 in New York for $15,950
(£12,970)

Opposite:
JACQUES VILLON
French 1875–1963
Comédie de société
(Auberty and Perusseux 43; Ginester and
Pouillon E75)
Etching with aquatint printed in colours,
1902, second (final) state, signed and dated
in pencil, numbered 38/50
P. $19\frac{5}{8} \times 16\frac{1}{2}$ in. (50 × 41.8 cm.)
Sold 27.6.85 in London for £35,640
($45,975)

EL LISSITZKY
Russian 1890–1941
Chad Gadya (The Tale of a Goat)
(Karshan 1–11)
Lithographs printed in colours, 1919, lithographed title page and set of 11 plates, one of only a few
surviving copies, from the edition published in 1919, with the rare lithograph executed as a dustcover
for this edition (unrecorded by Karshan)
S. 11½ × 8 in. (29 × 20.5 cm.)
Sold 27.6.85 in London for £56,160 ($72,446)

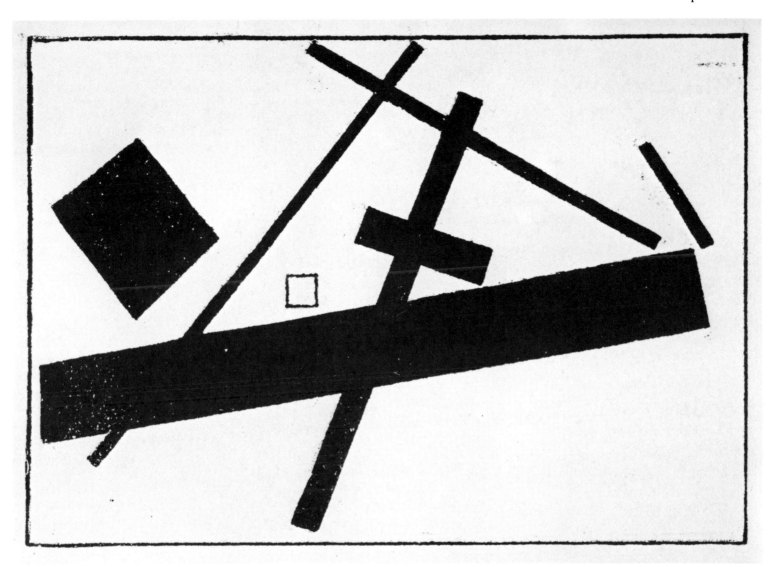

KASIMIR MALEVICH
Russian 1878–1935
Suprematizm 34 Risunka (Suprematism, 34 drawings)
(Karshan 37–71; Andersen pp. 129–64)
Lithographs, 1920, lithographed title, four sides of lithographically printed handwritten text and 34 plates, one of only
about five known copies, printed at the Vitebsk Art Workshops, probably under the direction of El Lissitzky, published
by Unovis (Affirmation of New Art), Vitebsk, 1920
S. 8⅝ × 7 in. (22 × 18 cm.)
Sold 6.12.84 in London for £49,680 ($60,113)

MAURITS CORNELIS ESCHER
Dutch 1898–1972
Three Spheres II
(Bool and Locher 339)
Lithograph, 1946, signed in
pencil, numbered 'No 12/40'
L. $10\frac{1}{8} \times 18\frac{1}{4}$ in.
(26 × 46.6 cm.)
Sold 27.6.85 in London for
£11,880 ($15,325)

LYONEL FEININGER
German 1871–1956
The Old Locomotive Windspiel
(Prasse L2)
Lithograph, 1906, signed in
black ink, one of six known
impressions
L. $6\frac{1}{4} \times 12\frac{3}{4}$ in.
(15.9 × 32.4 cm.)
Sold 7.11.84 in New York for
$10,450 (£8,038)

STUART DAVIS
American 1894–1964
Barber Shop Chord
(Cole 18)
Lithograph, 1931, signed in pencil,
numbered 20/25
L. 14 × 19 in. (35.5 × 48.3 cm.)
Sold 13.10.84 in New York for $18,700
(£12,064)
Record auction price for a print by the
artist

WINSLOW HOMER
American 1836–1910
Yachting Girl
(Museum of Fine Arts, Houston,
cat. L9)
Lithograph with white heightening,
1880, trimmed to the subject and
mounted on card, initialled in white,
signed again in pencil on the mount,
one of four known impressions
L. 7⅞ × 12⅝ in. (20 × 32 cm.)
Sold 16.3.85 in New York for $42,900
(£39,000)
Record auction price for a print by the
artist

JOHN NASH
British 1752–1835
The Royal Pavilion at Brighton
(Abbey, Scenery, 62)
Coloured aquatints and
uncoloured line etchings, title and
set of 31 aquatints and 26 from
the set of 27 line etchings,
published by J. Nash,
London, 1826
S. 21⅛ × 16⅝ in.
(53.7 × 42.3 cm.)
Sold 5.3.85 in London for
£10,260 ($10,876)

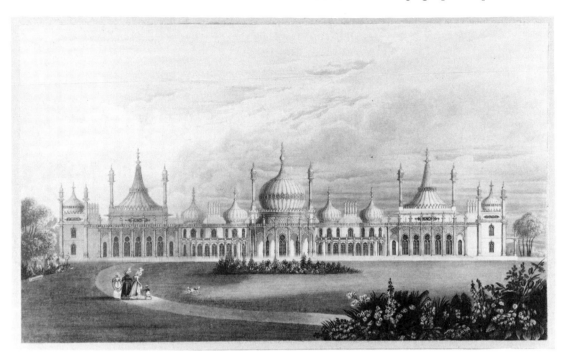

THOMAS GAINSBOROUGH
British 1727–88
*Wooded Landscape with two Country
Carts and Figures*
(Hayes 9)
Soft-ground etching, 1779–80,
the very rare first state (of two)
with the trial printed text lower
right, printed by the artist himself
P. 11⅝ × 15¼ in. (29.7 × 39 cm.)
Sold 5.3.85 in London for
£11,340 ($12,020)
Record auction price for a print
by the artist

Opposite:
JASPER JOHNS
American b.1930
Color Numerals: Figure 7
(Field 111; Geelhaar 123)
Lithograph printed in colours,
1968–9, signed and dated in
pencil, numbered 38/40, with the
Gemini G.E.L. blindstamp
S. 38 × 31 in. (96.5 × 78.7 cm.)
Sold 7.11.84 in New York for
$20,900 (£16,077)

A Passion for Paper and Stones: Tatyana Grosman and Universal Limited Art Editions

JUDITH GOLDMAN

In 1955, when Tatyana Grosman's husband Maurice had a heart attack, Mrs Grosman realized she had to make a living. She was 51 years old. 'What shall I do?' she told an interviewer. 'I hadn't learned anything. I had no craft. So I said to myself, "I have to start something. Probably it will be something I will do for the rest of my life, so it has to be worthwhile . . . Whatever I start, I have to put into it everything, all my life experience, all that I love, all that I am interested in . . ." I decided to publish, to combine words and images, but only words and images that I love.'

In 1957 Mrs Grosman published her first edition *Stones*, a book of poems by Frank O'Hara and lithographs by Larry Rivers. Twenty-seven years later in 1982 at the time of her death at 78, the publishing firm Mrs Grosman founded, Universal Limited Art Editions, had issued over 700 etchings, lithographs, woodcuts, and illustrated books. And not only that, there was at the time and always had been general agreement that prints bearing the embossed imprint of ULAE, issued in eccentrically numbered editions of 23, 37 or 41, were among the best in the world. That they set the standard for quality in printed art.

What distinguished these prints? Why did so many people consider them of another, a different, and a higher order? What exactly did people mean when they said that ULAE prints had a look about them? Even the studio's detractors said that. What was that look? The prints appeared both immediate and considered. They had dense surfaces, and images never sat awkwardly on those surfaces. Image and paper invariably matched, melding so perfectly that the image seemed to be literally part of the paper. ULAE prints never seemed new. It was as if they had always existed. Looking at a ULAE print, what one noticed was its authenticity. What one saw was art.

Two passions of Tatyana Grosman's distinguished ULAE prints: her love of paper and belief in the power of stones. To Mrs Grosman, paper was an active not a passive element. Paper represented the stuff of printmaking. It was essential, the fabric of a print. What stone was to the sculptor, words to the writer, notes to the musician, paper was to the printmaker. Talking about paper Mrs Grosman could sound rhapsodic. She believed paper could inspire. And she constantly searched for paper, purchasing it in exotic places; returning from trips to France, Italy, and Switzerland, she invariably carried paper.

From the start, she had paper specially made and watermarked with the names of her artists. For her first publication, *Stones*, she commissioned paper from Douglass Howell of Wesbury, Long Island. And she had him make special wrappers out of blue jeans for *Stones'* unbound sheets for the simple reason that the book's creators Larry Rivers and Frank O'Hara both wore blue jeans.

In Tanya, Douglass Howell had met his match and vice versa. Howell, who had a sense of time only equalled by that of Tanya, who had none, could only produce a few sheets of paper a day and then only if it did not rain. Howell's pace added more than a year to the project,

JASPER JOHNS
American b.1930
Working Proof for 'Decoy'
(Field 134; Geelhaar 11.1-5)
Lithograph extensively
handcoloured with oil paint,
black wash, coloured chalks,
and collage, 1967–71,
working proof A/D, signed
and dated in blue ink and
white crayon, inscribed 'For
Tanya with love' and
'Working Proof (Litho with
Additions)', with the ULAE
blindstamp
S. $41\frac{3}{8} \times 30$ in.
(105.1 × 76.2 cm.)
Sold 18.4.85 in New York for
$176,000 (£136,430)
Record auction price for a
print by the artist
From the collection of the late
Tatyana Grosman

but Mrs Grosman didn't care. At ULAE, there was always all the time in the world. The right paper was worth the wait. The wrong paper could imbalance an otherwise perfect image.

That Mrs Grosman's first publication was titled *Stones* is appropriate, for she felt as passionate about stones as she did about paper. On the subject of stones, she sounded as mystical as a participant at a seance. She liked the sensuality of stones, their soft, skin-like surfaces. She was aware of stones. Acknowledging their presence, when she walked through the small lithography studio next to her house, she smiled and nodded at stones; and she touched the stones, gently resting a hand on them, in a reassuring, protective gesture, the way an adult places a hand on the head of a small child.

'The stone itself', she said, 'inspires, imposes, limits. The grain is always slightly different. One is rough. One is gentle. Some stones are grey, like granite. Some more sand coloured. One has beaten edges. Another smooth. No two stones are alike.' The physical attributes of stones – their colour, shape, stoneness, surface. Mrs Grosman believed in their power, that every characteristic mattered. A smooth pale grey surface might lead an artist in one direction. An uneven edge might alter his course entirely.

A story that is so often told that it has become part of the myth of ULAE is how in the studio's early days Mrs Grosman, in order to entice artists to try their hand at lithography, would have the heavy limestones carried up steep loft staircases to artists' studios. She thought the ambiance where artists worked was important. In fact, she believed in ambiance quite the way she believed in stones and was convinced that an artist would be more comfortable working in familiar surroundings than commuting to her Long Island studio.

She was also counting on something taking place between the artist and the stone. She wanted her artists to develop a feeling for the stone, to be seduced. The romance took. The love affair with stones was not Tanya's alone. A striking characteristic of ULAE lithographs is the part the shape of stones play in defining compositions. Artists who have incorporated the shape of the stone into compositions include Barnett Newman, Helen Frankenthaler, Jasper Johns, Robert Motherwell, Larry Rivers, Edwin Schlossberg, Robert Rauschenberg, Lee Bontecou. As the titles of lithographs attest, Tatyana Grosman's infatuation with stones was contagious. Larry Rivers was not the only artist to title lithographs after *Stones*. Robert Motherwell called a lithograph *Celtic Stone*, another *Black Douglas Stone*. And Helen Frankenthaler printed a lithograph on a grey paper the colour of clay and titled it *A Slice of the Stone Itself*. Frankenthaler called her maiden lithograph *First Stone*, as did Lee Bontecou, who, with a few exceptions, titles all her lithographs after *Stones*. Sam Francis added the superlative 'very' to his first lithographic foray, calling it *Very First Stone*. Not only was Francis distinguishing his first stone from those of Frankenthaler and Bontecou, his title held an ironic comment, for in the time that passed between 1959, the year Francis drew his stone, and 1968, the year it was printed, he had completed many other lithographs.

It was Barnett Newman who best expressed Mrs Grosman's feeling for stones. In the text accompanying his 1963–4 series of colour lithographs *Cantos*, Newman wrote: 'as in all interpretive arts, so in lithography, creation joined with the playing; in this case not of a bow and string, but of a stone and press. The definition of a lithograph is that it is writing on stone. But, unlike Gertrude Stein's rose, the Stone is not a stone. The stone is a piece of paper.' The perfect merging of elements. That was the genius of a ULAE print. 'The stone is a piece of paper' sounds like something Mrs Grosman might have said. 'Everything that comes out of ULAE', her friend Jasper Johns once said, 'is somehow stamped with Tanya's personality.'

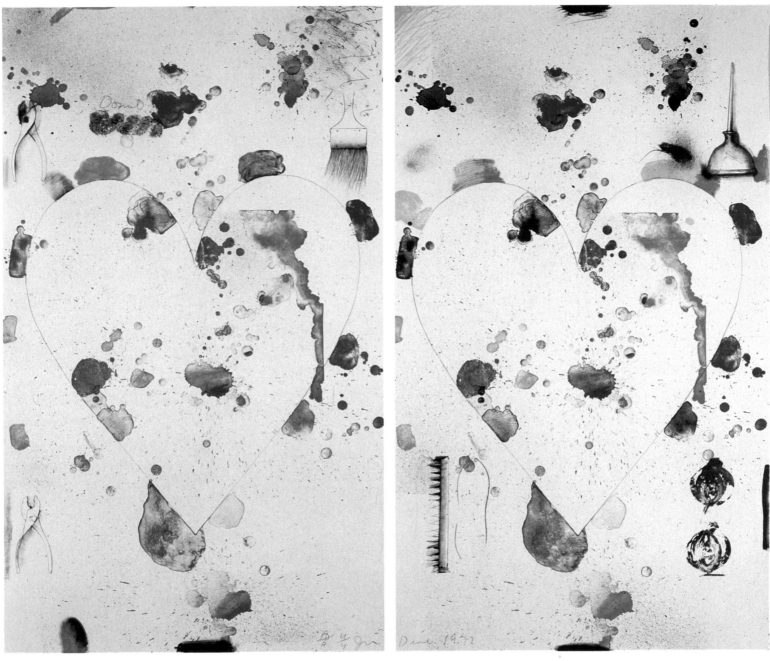

JIM DINE
American b. 1935
2 Hearts (the Donut)
Lithograph printed in colours, 1972, on two sheets, signed and dated in pencil, numbered 4/4 and inscribed 'A/p'
(the edition of 17), with the ULAE blindstamp
S. 55 × 32¼ in. (140 × 82 cm.)
Sold 18.4.85 in New York for $24,200 (£18,760)
Record auction price for a print by the artist
From the collection of the late Tatyana Grosman

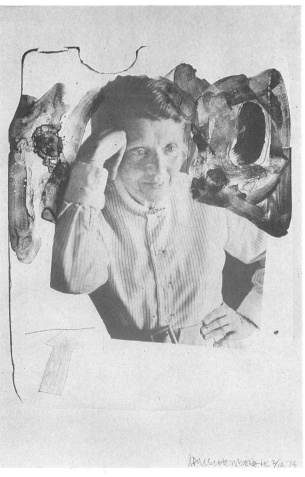

Above:
LARRY RIVERS AND FRANK
O'HARA
American b.1923;
American 1926–66
Stones
West Islip, Universal Limited
Art Editions, 1957–9
(UCLA 14)
Lithographs, title, letterpress
colophon and set of 12 plates
in-texte, all signed and dated
by Rivers, copy VIII of XXV
(there were also five artist's
proofs)
S. $21\frac{1}{4} \times 25\frac{3}{8}$ in.
(54 × 64.8 cm.)
Sold 18.4.85 in New York for
$9,350 (£7,248)
From the collection of the late
Tatyana Grosman

Right:
ROBERT RAUSCHENBERG
American b.1925
Tanya
Lithograph and blind embossing,
1974, signed and dated in brown
crayon, numbered 2/18 and
inscribed 'HC' (the edition 50), with
the ULAE blindstamp
S. $23 \times 15\frac{3}{8}$ in. (58.5 × 39 cm.)
Sold 18.4.85 in New York for $6,050
(£4,690)
From the collection of the late
Tatyana Grosman

Books and Manuscripts

EVELYN WAUGH
Vile Bodies
Autograph manuscript, signed, of his second
novel, with a presentation inscription to
Bryan and Diana Guinness, and inscribed
proof of the design for the dust-jacket
Sold 27.3.85 in London for £59,400
($73,062)
From the collection of The Hon. Jonathan
Guinness

BOOK OF HOURS
Illuminated manuscript with 20 large miniatures produced for Claude de Toulongeon, chamberlain to Philippe le Bon, Duke of Burgundy
Probably Bruges *c.*1480
Sold 13.12.84 in London for £91,800 ($111,078)

ANGLO-SAXON GOSPEL
LECTIONARY
Two leaves with three
full-page illuminated
miniatures
Canterbury *c.* 1000
Sold 13.12.84 in
London for £367,200
($444,312)
An important example
of Anglo-Saxon
illumination, the scene
illustrated shows the
episode of Christ
instructing St. Peter at
Capernaum on the
tribute money (Gospel
of St. Matthew XVII
24–7)

FESTUS CORIN
The Childes first Tutor
Original calf binding, 16mo
London 1664
Sold 27.3.85 in London for £8,100
($9,963)
A hitherto unrecorded primer for
children

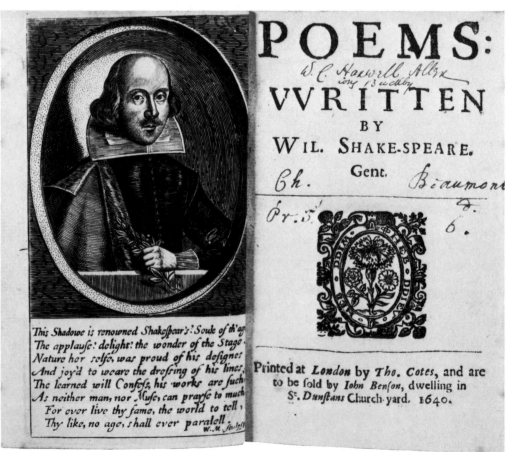

WILLIAM SHAKESPEARE
Poems
First collected edition
Later calf binding, small 8vo
1640
Sold 16.11.84 in New York for $31,900
(£24,920)

WILLEM AND JAN BLAEU & OTHERS
Composite Atlas
386 large engraved 17th-century maps, mostly Dutch, a few with outline colouring
Contemporary calf binding, folio
Sold 14.11.84 in London for £21,600 ($27,216)

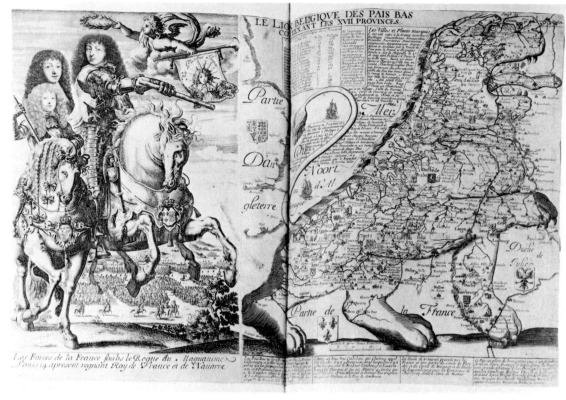

Right:
JOHN DEE
General and Rare Memorials pertayning to the Perfect Arte of Navigation
First edition
Contemporary limp vellum binding, folio
London 1577
Sold 19.9.84 in London for £11,880 ($14,731)
One of the great Tudor navigational works, only 100 copies were printed

Far right:
GALILEO GALILEI
Discorsi e dimostrazioni matematiche
Small 4to
Leiden 1638
Sold 13.12.84 in London for £3,024 ($3,659)
The first edition of the first modern textbook on physics

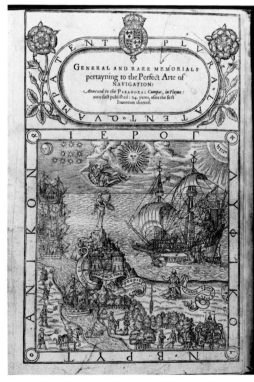

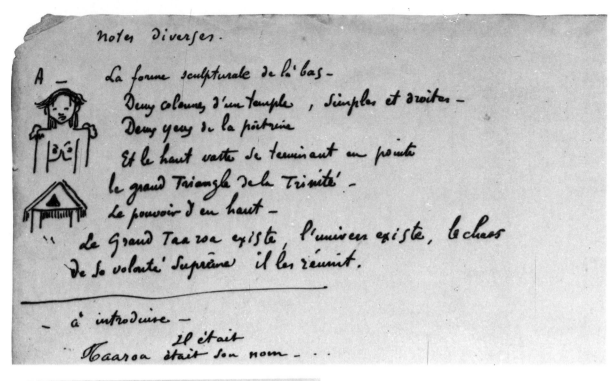

Above:
PAUL GAUGUIN
Noa Noa
Autograph manuscript of the original version
of his Tahitian journal, with four small
sketches in the text
Sold 14.12.84 in New York for $132,000
(£108,196)
Record auction price for a manuscript by a
modern artist

Left:
SIR EDWARD BURNE-JONES
Collection of 75 autograph letters, signed, to
his daughter, including approximately 60 pen
and ink sketches
1873–96
Sold 19.9.84 in London for £11,880 ($14,731)

JOHANNES BRAHMS
Alte Liebe
Autograph manuscript, signed, of the first of the *Five Songs*, opus 72, scored
for voice and piano, in G minor
Sold 27.3.85 in London for £48,600 ($59,778)

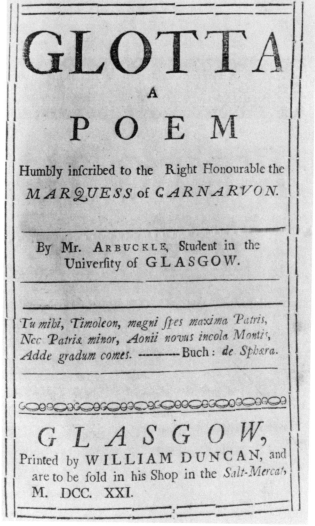

JAMES ARBUCKLE
Glotta
A poem, 22 pages, containing the earliest description
in verse of the game of golf
Glasgow 1721
Sold 27.3.85 in London for £5,400 ($6,642)

Plate 613

A ZUÑI GIRL

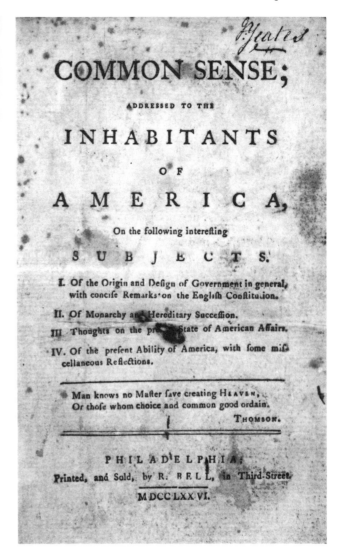

SIGNERS OF THE DECLARATION OF INDEPENDENCE
Complete set of 56 autograph letters, documents and other items, including
48 full autograph letters signed
Sold 14.12.84 in New York for $192,000 (£157,786)
From the collection of Donald and Robert Sang
Illustrated here is a war letter from Thomas Jefferson to Major-General
Nathanael Greene, Richmond, 18 February 1781

Opposite:
EDWARD S. CURTIS
The North American Indian
40 volumes, 723 large photogravures, one of only 272 sets
Large folio
New York 1907–30
Sold 14.5.85 in New York for $99,000 (£76,744)
From the collection of Margaret Z. Van Beuren

THOMAS PAINE
Common Sense; addressed to the inhabitants of America
First edition, first issue
Philadelphia 1776
Sold 16.11.84 in New York for $28,600 (£22,343)
The first public appeal for an independent American
Republic

DAVID ROBERTS
The Holy Land, Syria, Idumea,
Arabia, Egypt and Nubia
Six volumes, 241
lithographed plates, finely
hand-coloured and mounted
on card, by L. Hague after
D. Roberts
Large folio
London, F.G. Moon 1842–9
Sold 17.7.85 in London for
£75,600 ($98,280)

Le Perroquet Jaune écaillé de rouge. Pl. 137.

FRANÇOIS LEVAILLANT
Histoire naturelle des perroquets
Two volumes, large paper copy, 145 colour-printed plates, finished by hand, uncut as issued
Folio
Paris 1801–5
Sold 19.9.84 in London for £21,600 ($26,784)

CACCABIS RUBRA.

Bouquet de Camélias Narcisses et Pensées.

P . J Redouté .

Victor

Collection of 520 books from the library of Marie-Louise, Empress of France,
later Duchess of Parma, assembled by her from the time she became the wife of
Napoleon in 1810 to her death at Parma in 1847
Mostly bound in red morocco with her monogram
Sold 8.5.85 in London for £81,000 ($97,200)
From the Calvin Bullock Collection (see page 474)

VIRGIL
Les Bucoliques
Translated by Paul Valéry
Lithographs by Jacques Villon
Bound by Creuzevault in green box-calf, onlays of white, light
green and violet, dart-shaped decoration, with gilt filets, 4to
Paris 1953
Sold 12.5.85 in Geneva for Sw.fr.52,800 (£16,150)

COMTESSE DE NOAILLES
Les Climats
Coloured woodcut illustrations by F.L. Schmied
Bound by Paul Bonet in green morocco, sides decorated with
large gilt radiating design, 4to
Paris 1924
Sold 12.5.85 in Geneva for Sw.fr.52,800 (£16,150)

JOSEPH-CHARLES MARDRUS
Histoire charmante de l'adolescente sucre d'amour
Woodcut illustrations by F.L. Schmied
Bound by Paul Bonet in green crushed morocco, with pointillé decoration of palladium, morocco *doublures* with gold circular design enclosing red and gold discs, 4to
Paris 1927
Sold 12.5.85 in Geneva for Sw.fr.99,000 (£30,280)

FIODOR DOSTOÏEWSKI
Les Frères Karamazov
Three volumes, 100 lithographs by Alexandre Alexeieff
Bound by Paul Bonet in green morocco, with grey, black and yellow geometric onlays, gilt filets, large circular pontillé design of palladium, each volume in variant binding, 4to
Paris 1929
Sold 12.5.85 in Geneva for Sw.fr.242,000 (£74,000)

Modern Fine Bookbinding in France and Britain

JEFF CLEMENTS

The craft of fine bookbinding has undergone a considerable transformation in the last 50 years or so. Until the end of the 19th century it was easily categorized as an applied art-form concerned essentially with the decorative aspects of design and of more interest to bibliophiles and interior designers than to serious collectors in other graphic arts fields such as printmaking. Even the now obsolete word for the subject 'Bibliopegy' conveys the sense of dark antiquarian bookshops or well-screened and rarely moved lines of leather bindings on country house bookshelves.

During the early part of the 20th century there emerged a generation of artist craftsmen who were concerned not only with bookbinding as a traditional skill, with a long and little-changing technical heritage, but also with fine bookbinding as a means of expression. Designs were produced with some relationship to the text and more significantly the styles were a direct reflection of the artistic developments of the day. Thus we are left with something of a dilemma. Is a finely bound 20th-century book, individually designed and produced as a means of creative expression, an artefact properly belonging to the world of libraries, bibliography and book collecting? Or should these intriguing works be seen as a highly significant contribution to the Modern Art movement echoing, or playing an active role in, the changing styles of art nouveau, art deco, the abstract art of the late 1930s through to the post-war period, culminating in the recent revived interest in figurative painting much in evidence today?

There can be little doubt that this difficulty in placing modern fine bookbindings in an easily defined category has resulted in this fertile source of inspiration for designers and craftsmen (particularly in France, Belgium, Germany and Great Britain) remaining an undervalued and largely unappreciated art-form. No doubt as time passes the historical work of the 1920s and 1930s will be reassessed and compared with other art objects of the same period, and indeed this is now evident with the sale this year of the three-volume binding of *Les Frères Karamazov* by Fiodor Dostoïewsky from the atelier of Paul Bonet, probably the most eminent French book-binding designer of the period and certainly the most well known (see page 218).

It is worth considering these three Bonet bookbindings of 1929 in some detail as they show how beautifully the traditional bookbinding techniques can be used to interpret in a fresh and original way the very essence of the art deco movement of the 1930s. Tooling in palladium and gold on morocco goatskin contrasts with the delicate use of finely pared coloured leather onlays, and the designs show a direct relationship with the paintings of such well-known 20th-century figures as Wassily Kandinsky and El Lissitzky. The three bindings, although using the same basic design material, are really quite different, providing a 'theme and variations' effect on the symbolic images of the male signs. It was at this time that Paul Bonet was particularly interested in the build-up of dynamic forms using the simplest of motifs, and the large circular units which appear six times, twice on each book, show a fascinating method of designing with single dots to convey both tension and form. One curious feature is the horizontal

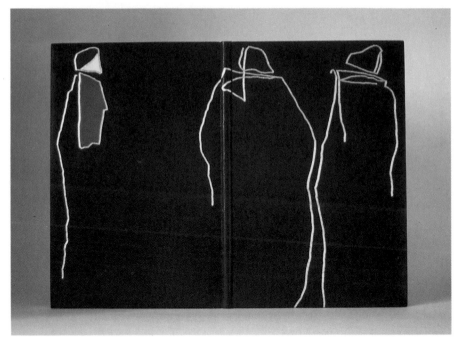

1

2

row of gold dots which appears on each volume and is not placed in the same position relative to the top edge of each book as one might expect. It is very important to notice in these bindings that the materials and techniques are in keeping with the design concept, a wholly natural and unaffected response to the title without the artificial striving after effect evident in later French bindings.

It is useful to contrast these bindings with the two-volume edition of *Histoire charmante de l'adolescente sucre d'amour* by Joseph-Charles Mardrus, printed in 1927 and bound to designs by Bonet in 1930. This set uses a counter-change of texture and colour between the richly gilt spines (notice the mirror images) and foredge strips contrasting with the linear dotted forms traversing the upper and lower covers, very much in the spirit of the time but providing an original response to the medium (see page 218). Some 10 years later Bonet was able to build up very rich and effective radiating designs from traditional tools by the simple but striking use of geometric measurement, often using only gold on morocco leather. His binding for *Les Climats* by the Comtesse de Noailles illustrates the work of this period to very good effect, the skill of the craftsmen contributing largely to the success of the design, elegant and timeless in its simplicity (see page 217).

Many post-war French bookbindings are of smooth calf, and the wide colour range available makes this a very useful if somewhat bland and inorganic material. The binding of *Les Bucoliques* by Virgil, designed by Henri Creuzevault during the 1950s, shows how the decorative aspects of the art deco period continued to be applied some 20 years later (see page 217). In fact the all-pervading influence of the French bookbinders such as Bonet, Creuzevault and Pierre Legrain was so strong that this approach to bookbinding design continued for a much longer period than with other applied art-forms, the technical virtuosity of the craftsmen specializing in this

1. *An Answer to the Satyr on Mankind*
Binding designed and bound by Ivor Robinson, 1983
Black morocco goat onlaid black, white and ochre calf, gold tooling
12 1/2 × 4 1/4 in. (32 × 10.5 cm.)
In the collection of Nicholas Fisher

2. Tennyson: *In Memoriam*
Binding designed and bound by James Brockman, 1985
Metal, single hinge binding, painted white, grey, tan, dark brown and black with leather-covered studs in the same colours
15 × 11 1/2 in. (38 × 29 cm.)

3

4

3. Haberman: *The Furtive Wall*
Binding and box designed and made by Jenni Grey, 1984
Grey sirocco goat with onlaid leather wedges and blind tooled. The box built up with hand-made and dyed paper
The book $9\frac{3}{4} \times 6$ in. $(25 \times 15$ cm.)

4. The Essays of Ralph Waldo Emerson
Binding designed and bound by Jeff Clements, 1985
Blue oasis morocco goat inlaid beige, red, brown and black morocco, blind linear tooling
$13\frac{3}{4} \times 9\frac{1}{2}$ in. $(35 \times 24.2$ cm.)

area tending to overshadow the genuine creative thinking of the period. Some of this work, although fascinating for its combination of technique and superficial effect, adds little to the development of fine bookbinding as a means of artistic expression. Exceptions must include talented artists such as Rose Adler and Pierre Lucien Martin who retained much individuality in their work and an appreciation of the creative philosophies then being explored.

It is interesting to compare the emergence of fine bookbinding in Great Britain at this time, for it was during the early part of the 1950s that the Guild of Contemporary Bookbinders was formed, later named Designer Bookbinders. Unlike their counterparts in France, who divide the production of a fine binding between designer, binder and *doreur*, British bookbinders usually produce 'one off' fine bindings, carrying out the designs and most of the bookbinding techniques themselves. In some cases gilt edges are entrusted to a specialist, but otherwise all the operations including sewing, edge trimming, headbanding, covering, and carrying out the cover design and titling are the responsibility of one person. It can easily be appreciated that the opportunity to adjust and modify the design concept during the various binding stages and the personal choice and selection of materials can have a significant effect on the final outcome of the binding. For those reasons, until some 10 years ago, the technical virtuosity of the French craftsmen tended to make some British bookbindings appear rather heavy by comparison, although more practical and stimulating.

As in France the number of really talented designer craftsmen is very small and although Designer Bookbinders has a total membership of over 600 only some 20 or so are exhibiting fellows with an international reputation. Modern British bookbindings are now to be seen in all the major collections in the world and numerous university libraries and private collections, many of them in the USA.

The exciting variety of designs produced by fine bookbinders in this country has been matched by extraordinary use of materials and techniques. Some designer bookbinders such as Ivor Robinson and Bernard Middleton rely on traditional techniques, but use them in an entirely fresh and original way. Robinson for example uses dark, often black, morocco, punctuated by only one or two onlays and containing linear gold elements built up with short lengths tooled individually. This gives a strong nervous energy to the cover design. Although often appearing to be abstract his designs usually contain references to the human form or apparel such as helmets (see fig. 1).

Some bookbinders work in a range of materials not often associated with fine bookbinding, such as sandpaper, slate, wood, photographs and various metals, which are incorporated into the making of the bookcovers in conjunction with traditional materials, calf, morocco and vellum. Angela James and Lou Smith are noted for their distinctive use of unusual materials and James Brockman has produced work which questions the whole concept of traditional binding techniques. His recent binding for Tennyson's *In Memoriam*, for example, consists of two brass plates drilled with holes and joined by a large single hinge at the spine. The metal surface is paint-sprayed and the leather-covered bosses are slotted into the holes, providing a very satisfying visual and tactile surface (see fig. 2).

Some designer bookbinders have become more concerned with the book as part of a complex sculptural unit, the complete assemblage bearing a direct relationship to the text. These are now known as 'bookwork', and as with other design philosophies there is a considerable variety of approach. Philip Smith has produced 'book walls' using volumes placed flat within a large rectangular framework which provides a continuous design surface extending across the front covers of a number of books. He and others have also made 'containers' and detachable units which fit on to parts of the covers. Other serious bookbinders active in this field include Dee Odell Foster, David Sellars and Jenni Grey, whose binding and container for *The Furtive Wall* beautifully illustrates how this combination can be seen both as a free-standing sculpture and a protection for the book (see fig. 3).

In complete contrast to the 'bookwork' approach, a number of designer craftsmen have sought to achieve highly personal but absolute statements by producing distinctive bindings of apparent simplicity, relevant to the text but not allowing complex techniques to destroy the physical qualities of the book. Also, by careful selection and use, basic materials such as paper and dyed leather can be used to convey the natural beauty and innate characteristics. Bookbinders such as Romilly Saumarez Smith, Elizabeth Marples and Trevor Jones produce highly significant work by this means. This is well illustrated by the bindings for the Essays of Ralph Waldo Emerson, showing how a dramatic and powerful effect can be achieved by using only inlaid morocco leather and blind tooling (see fig. 4).

In recent years there has been better communication and a much stronger interaction between British and Continental bookbinders, so that throughout Europe recent work now shows more confidence in technique, experiment and a vigorous range of design philosophies. There is no doubt that because of the difficulty in 'placing' modern fine bookbinding it is still an undervalued and largely unappreciated art-form awaiting discovery. However, as we now recognize the significant and original contribution made by the bindings of the 1920s and 1930s to the art of the period, so must there be a greater appreciation of present-day fine bookbinding with its variety, vigour, and challenging methods of presentation.

Furniture

Regency ormolu and cut-glass vase
Inscribed 'Publish'd April 23rd 1824 by W. Collins. 227 Strand London'
22 in. (56 cm.) high; 19 in. (48 cm.) diameter
Sold 27.6.85 in London for £11,340 ($14,630)
Collins supplied metal work for Bath House, Piccadilly, the Royal Pavilion, Brighton, and for Stowe House

One of a set of six George II
giltwood side chairs
27 in. (69 cm.) wide; 42 in.
(107 cm.) high
Sold 27.6.85 in London for
£124,200 ($160,222)
Originally from Ditchley
Park, Oxfordshire

One of a pair of George III mahogany armchairs
*c.*1770–5
Attributed to Thomas Chippendale
Sold 20.4.85 in New York for $82,500 (£62,500)
In his introduction to the catalogue of the 1979 Chippendale
exhibition at the Leeds Art Galleries at Temple Newsam House,
Christopher Gilbert referred to this pair of chairs as 'the most
illustrious newly discovered chairs corresponding to one of the
firm's [Chippendale & Haig's] standard design types of
*c.*1770–5 . . .' They are part of a suite of seat furniture, originally
comprising two sofas, two card tables and at least 12 armchairs,
supplied to Dingley Hall, a Northamptonshire house owned by
the Hungerfords for a century, from 1770, and which was
purchased along with its contents by the 8th Viscount Downe in
1883.

Queen Anne walnut wing armchair
36½ in. (93 cm.) wide; 46½ in. (118 cm.) high
Sold 11.4.85 in London for £36,720 ($46,634)

George III green-painted and
gilded wine-cooler made for
Henry Frederick, Duke of
Cumberland, for
Cumberland House,
Pall Mall
After a design by
Robert Adam
36 in. (91.5 cm.) wide;
19¾ in. (50 cm.) high;
24½ in. (62 cm.) deep
Sold 27.6.85 in London for
£37,800 ($48,760)

Photograph reproduced courtesy of the Sir John Soane Museum

Robert Adam's design for this wine-cooler (together with a sideboard and a pair of urns) is dated
28 October 1780. It has not previously been certain if this furniture was executed, but the evidence of
the Duke of Cumberland's sale (Christie's, 25 February 1793 and eight days following) is conclusive
on this point. Lots 59–61 of the 7th day correspond exactly with the furniture shown in the drawing.
The 'elegant cistern' (lot 61) was sold for £3. 17s. to 'Bernard', who also purchased the table and urns.
The subsequent history of this suite is unknown.
Henry Frederick, Duke of Cumberland (1745–90), a younger brother of George III, took up residence
at 86 Pall Mall, built in 1761–3 for Edward Duke of York, in 1768. He commissioned Adam to
redecorate the interior between 1780 and 1788 and the furniture designs date from 1780–2.

One of a pair of George III mahogany stools
Branded VR BP N22224 1866
23½ in. (59.5 cm.) wide
Sold 27.6.85 in London for £12,960 ($16,720)
Stools of this model appear in the watercolours of the
interiors of Windsor Castle done by Charles Wild and
James Stephanoff for W.H. Pyne's project for *Royal
Residences*, 1819. They are shown throughout the King's
suite, appearing in the watercolours of the King's Closet,
King's State Bedchamber, King's Drawing Room and
King's Eating Room.

Regency giltwood throne armchair
Attributed to Morel & Hughes
Sold 27.6.85 in London for £21,600 ($27,850)
Four armchairs of exactly the same design, except for the toprails, are
shown in a watercolour by C. Wild of the Ante-Chamber to the Throne
Room at Carlton House

One of a pair of George II mahogany hall settees
49 in. (124 cm.) wide; 38½ in. (98 cm.) high; 20½ in. (52 cm.) deep
Sold 11.4.85 in London for £51,840 ($65,837)
A set of six hall settees identical to these are now at Chatsworth but were made for Devonshire House. They appear to derive from a design of c. 1758–60 by John Linnell, who may in turn have been influenced by a design by William Kent published in 1744.

One of a pair of William and Mary scarlet and gold lacquer X-frame open armchairs
26½ in. (67 cm.) wide; 39½ in. (100 cm.) high
Sold 11.4.85 in London for £32,400 ($41,148)

One of a pair of George III mahogany library armchairs
Sold 11.4.85 in London for £28,080 ($35,662)

One of a pair of George II giltwood pier-tables, with D-shaped white marble top inlaid in the manner of Bossi
35½ in. (90.5 cm.) wide; 35 in. (89 cm.) high; 17 in. (43 cm.) deep
Sold 27.6.85 in London for £118,800 ($153,250)
Originally from Lowther Castle, Cumbria

George II giltwood chandelier
60 in. (153 cm.) diameter; 58 in. (147.5 cm.) high
Sold 29.11.84 in London for £32,400 ($39,204)
A chandelier of the same design hangs in the Saloon at Woburn Abbey and is identified with a bill rendered on 28 October 1758 by
W. Hollinworth & Co. to John, 4th Duke of Bedford. It cost £86. 0s. 0d.

One of a pair of George II
grey-painted and parcel-gilt
mirrors
68 × 42 in. (173 × 107 cm.)
Sold 27.6.85 in London for
£81,000 ($104,490)
Formerly at Dyrham Park,
Middlesex, and
Wateringbury Place, Kent

Opposite:
One of a pair of early George
III white-painted and gilded
picture frames
Attributed to William Vile
and John Cobb
75 × 59 in. (190.5 × 150 cm.)
Sold 11.4.85 in London for
£32,400 ($41,148)
Originally supplied to the 6th
Earl of Coventry for Croome
Court, Worcester

Charles II walnut and floral marquetry cabinet-on-stand
46½ in. (114 cm.) wide; 67½ in. (172 cm.) high; 20 in. (51 cm.) deep
Sold 29.11.84 in London for £34,560 ($41,818)

George III mahogany
secrétaire
32½ in. (82.5 cm.) wide
Sold 27.6.85 in London for
£32,400 ($41,800)

George III satinwood
and marquetry
serpentine-fronted
library bookcase
*c.*1775
119 in. (302.5 cm.) high;
83 in. (210.5 cm.) wide;
24 in. (61 cm.) deep
Sold 24.10.84 in New
York for $220,000
(£177,419)

One of a pair of George III satinwood commodes
With a label inscribed 'Hon. C. Cavendish Augt 5 1854 No 787'
58 in. (147 cm.) wide; 33½ in. (85 cm.) and 33¼ in. (84.5 cm.) high; 24½ in. (62 cm.) deep
Sold 29.11.84 in London for £59,400 ($71,874)

One of a pair of Regency oak and chinese lacquer side cabinets
49½ in. (126 cm.) wide; 22½ in. (57 cm.) deep; 36¼ in.
(92 cm.) high
Sold 29.11.84 in London for £51,840 ($62,726)

Opposite:
George I green japanned bureau bookcase
Early 18th century
94¾ in. (240.7 cm.) high; 39 in. (99 cm.) wide;
23½ in. (59.5 cm.) deep
Sold 20.4.85 in New York for $143,000 (£108,330)

George III mahogany secrétaire-cabinet
43 in. (109 cm.) wide; 82 in. (208 cm.) high;
25½ in. (65 cm.) deep
Sold 11.4.85 in London for £81,000 ($102,870)

Opposite:
George III satinwood and marquetry cabinet-
on-stand
40½ in. (103 cm.) wide; 20 in. (51 cm.) deep;
84¼ in. (213 cm.) high
Sold 29.11.84 in London for £140,400
($169,884)
Formerly in the collection of the Earl of Craven,
Combe Abbey, Warwickshire
This cabinet was almost certainly made for
William, 6th Baron Craven (1738–91), who
inherited the extensive Craven properties in
Berkshire and Warwickshire from his uncle, the
5th Baron, in 1769.
The interior of the cabinet is elaborately inlaid
in engraved, stained and shaded woods with
classical ruins after Clérisseau on the doors and
the following named buildings on the drawers
and cupboard:

Left:
    Beaumaris Castle
    Comb Abby
    Wenlock Abby
    Dunstable Priory
    Butley Priory

Centre:
    Malmsbury Abby
    Salisbury Cathedral
    Netley Abby

Right:
    Leicester Abby
    Caldecot Castle
    Kennelworth Castle
    Durham Castle
    Tinmoth Monastery *(sic)*

Regency parcel-gilt amboyna centre table
c. 1825
30 in. (76.1 cm.) high; 59¾ in. (152 cm.) diameter
Sold 20.4.85 in New York for $41,800 (£31,670)

Opposite:
Suite of Chinese wallpaper
18th century
Comprising 16 sheets approximately
9 ft. × 4 ft. (274 × 122 cm.);
Sold 27.6.85 in London for £59,400
($76,630)

Pair of Louis XV arrangements of flowers set in Capodimonte (Carlo III) two-handled buckets filled with *tôle peinte* stems and foliage set with about 70 Vincennes or early Sèvres porcelain flowers
1750–60
27½ in. (70 cm.) high
Sold for £91,800 ($119,340)

Louis XV ormolu and Meissen porcelain basket
1750–60
22 in. (56 cm.) high
Sold for £30,240 ($39,312)

Both sold 20.6.85 in London

Louis XIV ormolu mantel clock with striking movement incorporating lunar and terrestrial calendar, with the arms of Léopold Lorraine and Elisabeth-Charlotte of Orléans
By F. Richard A. Lunéville
36 in. (91.5 cm.) high; 24 in. (61 cm.) wide
Sold 20.6.85 in London for £51,940 ($67,520)
François Richard (1678–1759) was born in Charleroi and worked in Nancy from 1708. He was an accomplished *mécanicien* and gained a considerable reputation from the elaborate waterworks he constructed in the gardens of the Château de Lunéville. The latter was burned to the ground in January 1719.
Léopold-Joseph-Charles-Dominique-Agapet-Hyacinthe, Duke of Lorraine, was born at Innsbruck and succeeded his father in 1697. He consolidated his country's strained relationship with France by marriage in 1698 to the niece of Louis XIV, Elisabeth-Charlotte of Orléans (1676–1744), daughter of the king's brother by his second wife, the formidable Charlotte-Elisabeth of Bavaria (Liselotte). The marriage commemorated on this clock initiated a golden age of prosperity in the history of the duchy.

Louis XVI porcelain-mounted tulipwood parquetry guéridon, the top mounted with an oval Sèvres plaque
Stamped RVLC JME, the porcelain with blue interlaced Ls and date letter q for 1769 and with incised number 25 and painter's mark for Guillaume Noël
12¾ in. (32.5 cm.) wide; 30 in. (76 cm.) minimum height; 40 in. (102 cm.) approximate maximum height
Sold 20.6.85 in London for £152,000 ($197,600)
Formerly in the Hillingdon Collection and sold previously at Christie's on 29 June 1972

Opposite:
Empire ormolu and bronze centre table, the circular top inset with watercolour divided panels of summer flowers
The outer watercolours signed E.P.
36½ in. (92.5 cm.) diameter; 30¾ in. (78 cm.) high
Sold 20.6.85 in London for £43,200 ($56,160)

Far left:
One of a pair of ormolu and chinese porcelain vase candelabra, with the coat-of-arms of Captain Fernando de Valdés y Tamón, governor of the Philippines 1735–50
The porcelain early Qianlong, the mounts *c.* 1830
The candelabra 90 in. (229 cm.) high; 36 in. (91.5 cm.) wide
The pedestals 19½ in. (49.5 cm.) high; 32 in. (81 cm.) wide
Sold 15.11.84 in London for £43,200 ($54,864)

Left:
One of a pair of Empire ormolu and cut-glass vases
41½ in. (105 cm.) high; 11½ in. (29 cm.) wide
Sold 20.6.85 in London for £41,040 ($53,350)

Louis XV tulipwood, amaranth and marquetry table à transformations
Attributed to Jean-François Oeben
34 in. (86.5 cm.) wide; 27¾ in. (70.5 cm.) high; 16 in. (41 cm.) deep
Sold 6.12.84 in London for £110,160 ($133,294)
From the collection of the Duke of Abercorn

Louis XVI ormolu-mounted
black Japanese lacquer
secrétaire à abattant
Late 18th century
Stamped M CARLIN JME twice
50 in. (127 cm.) high;
34½ in. (87.6 cm.) wide;
16 in. (40.7 cm.) deep
Sold 9.5.85 in New York for
$220,000 (£178,861)

One of a pair of Louis XVI ebony meubles d'appui
Stamped P. GARNIER
38½ in. (98 cm.) wide; 33½ in. (85 cm.) high; 15 in. (38 cm.) deep
Sold 20.6.85 in London for £75,600 ($98,280)

Louis XVI tulipwood bureau à cylindre
Stamped J.F. LELEU JME
57¾ in. (147 cm.) wide; 45¾ in. (116 cm.) high; 30 in. (76 cm.) deep
Sold 20.6.85 in London for £113,400 ($147,420)

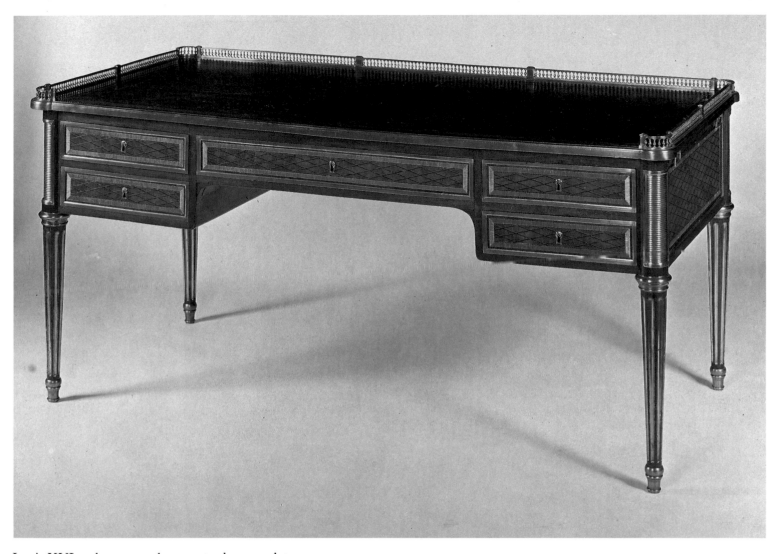

Louis XVI mahogany and parquetry bureau plat
Stamped J.H. RIESENER twice
64 in. (163 cm.) wide; 31½ in. (80 cm.) high; 32 in. (81 cm.) deep
Sold 6.12.84 in London for £86,400 ($104,544)
Formerly in the Hillingdon Collection and sold previously at Christie's on 29 June 1972

Pair of Louis XIV torchères
Attributed to André-Charles
Boulle
13 in. (33 cm.) diameter;
50¾ in. (129 cm.) high
Sold for £172,800 ($224,646)

Louis XIV centre table
Attributed to André-Charles Boulle
45 in. (115 cm.) wide; 31¼ in. (79.5 cm.) high; 29 in. (73.5 cm.) deep
Sold for £264,600 ($343,980)

Both sold 20.6.85 in London
From the collection of Sir Francis Dashwood, Bt.
Purchased by Sir George Dashwood, 5th Bt., *c.*1854–6 following the sale of Halton to the Rothschilds
and placed in the Yellow Saloon at West Wycombe

Louis XIV ebony and polychrome Boulle commode
46 in. (117 cm.) wide; 32½ in. (83 cm.) high; 25¼ in. (64 cm.) deep
Sold 6.12.84 in London for £47,520 ($57,499)

Louis XIV Boulle casket and associated Louis XIV Boulle stand
The stand 29 in. (74 cm.) wide; 34½ in. (87.5 cm.) high; 20¼ in. (51.5 cm.) deep
Sold 20.6.85 in London for £73,440 ($95,470)

Early Louis XV kingwood and parquetry commode
Attributed to Charles Cressent, with a painted inventory number 494
57½ in. (146 cm.) wide; 34½ in. (88 cm.) high; 25 in. (63.5 cm.) deep
Sold 20.6.85 in London for £237,600 ($308,880)

Louis XVI kingwood bureau plat
Attributed to Joseph Baumhauer, called Joseph
74¾ in. (190 cm.) wide; 32 in. (81 cm.) high; 38 in. (96.5 cm.) deep
Sold 20.6.85 in London for £388,880 ($505,440)
From the collection of Edmund de Rothschild, Esq.

Russian satinwood, tulipwood and marquetry games table
*c.*1770
39½ in. (100 cm.) wide; 29¼ in. (74 cm.) high; 19¾ in. (50 cm.) deep
Sold 20.6.85 in London for £140,400 ($182,520)
The form and style of decoration of this table reflect the prevailing fashion in Russia under Catherine the Great for English furniture and design, in particular for the work of John Linnell, whose slick technique and vivid style of marquetry were evidently much admired. A pair of commodes by Linnell at Tsarskoe Selo of *c.*1770 and another commode of *c.*1780 bear witness to his popularity and a number of other pieces of Russian-made furniture in the English style show the degree of dependence on English prototypes.

Biedermeier ormolu-mounted
and parcel-ebonized inlaid
walnut secrétaire à abattant
*c.*1815–20
105$\frac{1}{2}$ in. (268 cm.) high;
37 in. (94 cm.) wide
Sold 21.11.84 in New York
for $154,000 (£114,925)

Roman trumeau
*c.*1730
104½ in. (265 cm.) high;
59 in. (150 cm.) wide
Sold 23.4.85 in Rome for
L.70,000,000 (£26,923)

Milanese ivory inlaid ebony cabinet in the
Renaissance style
Designed and made by the Fratelli Andreoni
59 in. (155 cm.) wide; 127 in. (322 cm.) high;
26½ in. (67 cm.) deep
Sold 28.3.85 in London for £28,080 ($34,260)
The brothers Carlo and Giovanni Andreoni were
leading Milanese cabinet-makers in the late 19th
century. They exhibited at the 1881 Milan
International Exhibition.

Anglo-Indian engraved ivory-inlaid bureau bookcase
Second half 18th century, Vizagapatam
121 in. (302.5 cm.) high;
47½ in. (121 cm.) wide;
27½ in. (70 cm.) deep
Sold 24.10.84 in New York for $104,500 (£84,274)

Opposite:
Gothic Mille-fleurs tapestry fragment
Early 16th century, Franco-Flemish
132½ × 117 in.
(331.2 × 292.5 cm.)
Sold 13.6.85 in New York for $154,000 (£118,461)

Federal inlaid mahogany and
bird's-eye maple dressing
bureau
Attributed to John and
Thomas Seymour, Boston,
1794–1816
75 in. (190.5 cm.) high;
36 in. (91.5 cm.) wide;
21¼ in. (54 cm.) deep
Sold 13.10.84 in New York
for $71,500 (£57,200)

Eyre Family Chippendale
carved mahogany scalloped-
top tea table
Philadelphia, 1760–75
35 in. (89 cm.) diameter of
top; 28$\frac{1}{2}$ in. (72.5 cm.) high
Sold 26.1.85 in New York for
$286,000 (£250,877)
Record auction price for an
American tea table

Queen Anne tiger maple dressing table
Delaware Valley, 1750–70
29¼ in. (74.5 cm.) high; 32⅓ in. (82 cm.) wide; 20 in. (51 cm.) deep
Sold 26.1.85 in New York for $93,500 (£82,017)
By order of the Estate of C. Graham Gibbs

Federal carved mahogany settee
Attributed to Duncan Phyfe, New York, 1800–10
31¼ in. (79.5 cm.) high; 73½ in. (186.5 cm.) wide; 23½ in. (59.5 cm.) deep
Sold 13.10.84 in New York for $77,000 (£61,600)

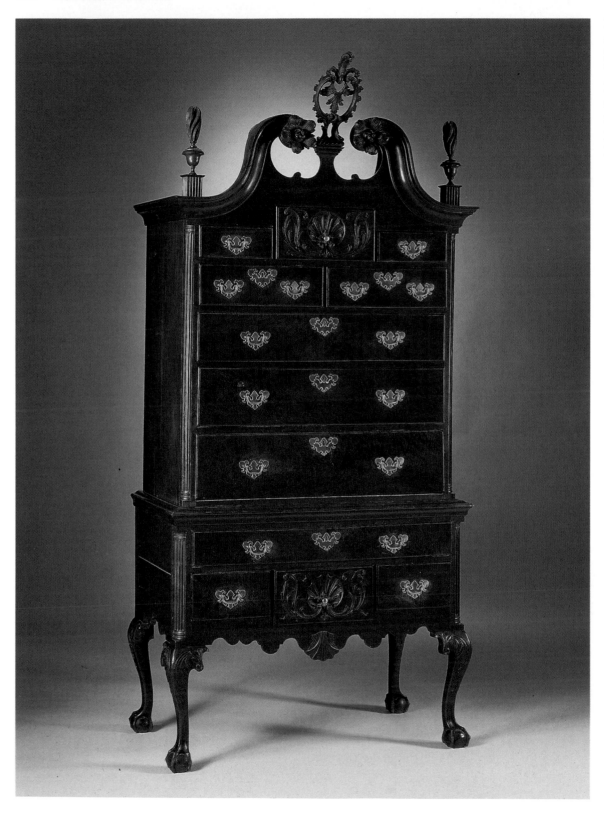

Hollingsworth Family
Chippendale carved walnut
high chest of drawers
Thomas Affleck,
Philadelphia, *c.*1779
Sold 23.5.85 in New York for
$363,000 (£283,590)
From the collection of
Mrs William Maier

Queen Anne inlaid walnut
desk and bookcase
Boston, 1730–50
90½ in. (230 cm.) high;
40 in. (101.5 cm.) wide;
24½ in. (62 cm.) deep
Sold 13.10.84 in New York
for $99,000 (£79,200)

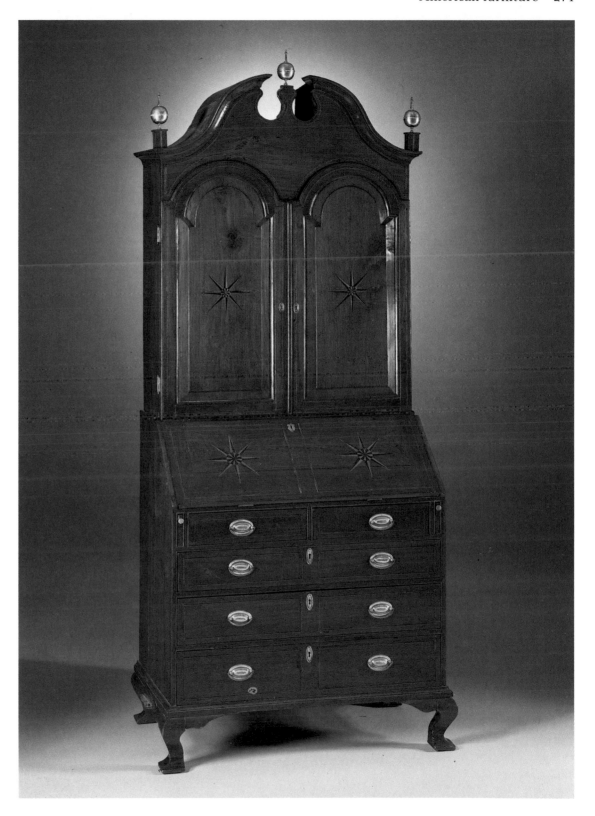

Italian violin
By Domenico
Montagnana
1737
Length of back
$14\frac{1}{16}$ in. (35.8 cm.)
Sold 2.4.85 in London
for £86,400 ($110,940)

Left:
Italian violin
By Antonio Stradivari
*c.*1729–30
Length of back 14 in. (35.5 cm.)
Sold 20.11.84 in London for £167,400 ($210,924)
From the collection of the late Mr Joseph Wechsberg

Right:
Italian violin
By Peter Guarneri of
Mantua
1707
Length of back
13 $\frac{15}{16}$ in. (35.4 cm.)
Sold 2.4.85 in London for
£108,000 ($139,320)

Far right:
Italian violin
By Joseph Guarneri
1706
Length of back
14 in. (35.5 cm.)
Sold 2.4.85 in London for
£135,000 ($174,150)

Italian viola
By Giovanni Paolo
Maggini
c. 1600–10
Length of back
16$\frac{7}{8}$ in. (42.9 cm.)
Sold 20.11.84 in London
for £129,600 ($163,296)

Italian violin
By Antonio Stradivari,
1690
Length of back 14 in. (35.5 cm.)
Sold 31.10.84 in New York at Christie's East for
$308,000 (£248,390)

Italian violin
By Carlo Bergonzi
1739
Length of back 13 $\frac{15}{16}$ in. (35.4 cm.)
Sold 31.10.84 in New York at Christie's East for
$132,000 (£106,450)
Sold in a leather case by W.E. Hill & Sons

Isfahan Serafian carpet
17 ft. 4 in. × 12 ft. (528 × 367 cm.)
Sold 18.4.85 in London for £64,800
($82,296)

Opposite:
Antique silk and metal thread Tabriz
rug
5 ft. 8 in. × 4 ft. 9 in.
(172 × 143 cm.)
Sold 25.10.84 in London for £22,680
($27,670)

Antique Heriz carpet
12 ft. 10 in. × 9 ft. 7 in.
(392 × 290 cm.)
Sold 25.10.84 in London for
£37,800 ($46,116)

Antique 'Star' Kazak
7 ft. 9 in. × 5 ft. 5 in. (236 × 165 cm.)
Sold 25.10.84 in London for £34,560 ($42,163)

Kerman Lavere Palace carpet
Last quarter 19th century
23 ft. × 16 ft. 7 in. (701 × 505 cm.)
Sold 30.10.84 in New York at Christie's East for $45,100 (£36,670)

English pile carpet
Early 19th century
27 ft. × 17 ft. (823 × 518 cm.)
Sold 11.4.85 in London for £34,560 ($43,891)
An almost identical carpet from Herriard Park, Hampshire, is in the Victoria and Albert Museum. The only significant difference
is that the ground of the outer border is the same colour as the main ground, not ivory as on this carpet.

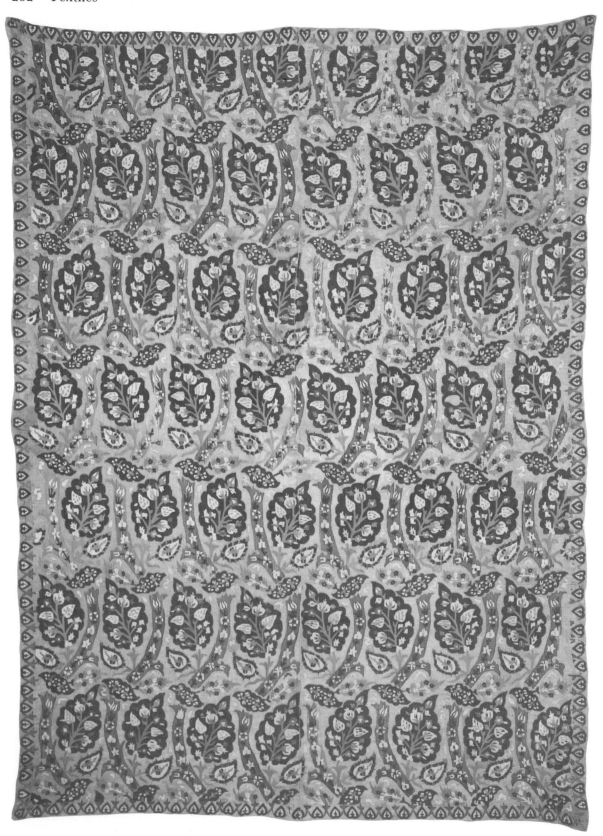

Ottoman silk embroidered
textile
18th century
8 ft. 2 in. × 6 ft.
(248 × 183 cm.)
Sold 18.4.85 in London for
£8,640 ($10,886)

Clocks and Watches

Charles II early balance spring verge
watch with seconds hand
By Thomas Tompion, London,
unnumbered
c. 1675–9
2 in. (5.1 cm.) diameter
Sold 14.12.84 in London for £27,000
($32,400)
This watch is perhaps the earliest
surviving by Tompion with a
seconds hand and heralds the
English quest for a precision
timekeeper

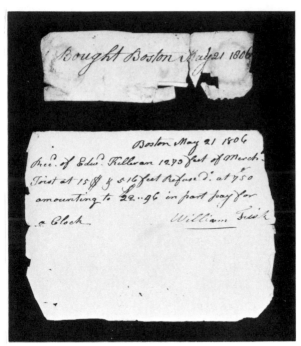

The Killeran family federal inlaid mahogany tall-case clock
Works signed and case labelled by Aaron Willard, with original bill of sale from cabinet maker William Fiske, Boston
c. 1806
7 ft. 10½ in. (239.9 cm.) high
Sold 26.1.85 in New York for $104,500 (£91,666)
Record auction price for an American tall-case clock
This clock is an important document linking the work of Aaron Willard and William Fiske

Early George II documented walnut longcase clock
By George Graham, London, No. 681
7 ft. 8½ in. (234 cm.) high
Sold 17.7.85 in London for £30,240 ($39,312)
The receipt from the maker appears to be a unique survival in
Graham's hand and is an important aid in fixing the chronology of
his *oeuvre* in relation to the serial numbers

Far left:
George II walnut equation
longcase clock
By George Graham, London,
unnumbered
7 ft. 11 in. (240 cm.) high
Sold 3.4.85 in New York for
$77,000 (£62,097)

Left:
Mid-Georgian burr walnut
longcase regulator with
compensation pendulum
By John Ellicott, London
7 ft. 8½ in. (234 cm.) high
Sold 3.4.85 in New York for
$30,800 (£24,839)

Right:
George I walnut early
longcase regulator
By George Graham, London,
No. 631
6 ft. 8 ¼ in. (204 cm.) high
Sold 14.12.84 in London for
£14,040 ($16,848)

Far right:
Mid-Georgian mahogany
longcase clock
By Matthew Dutton,
London, No. 332
7 ft. 4 in. (224 cm.) high
Sold 14.12.84 in London for
£10,800 ($12,960)

South German gilt-metal tabernacle clock
Late 16th century
12½ in. (31.5 cm.) high
Sold 19.10.84 in Amsterdam for D.fl.34,200
(£8,085)

Mahogany longcase regulator with Franklin-type dial
Signed *Vulliamy Pall Mall London*
5 ft. 11 in. (180 cm.) high
Sold 7.3.85 in London for £8,100 ($8,748)

Right:
Walnut eight-day longcase clock with planispherium dial
By Paulus Bramer en Soon, Amsterdam
Mid-18th century
10 ft. (304 cm.) high
Sold 19.10.84 in Amsterdam for
D.fl.62,700 (£14,823)

Far right:
Walnut musical longcase clock with automaton
By J.M. Juntes, Amsterdam
Late 18th century
9 ft. 2½ in. (280 cm.) high
Sold 19.10.84 in Amsterdam for
D.fl.45,600 (£10,780)

Above:
Swiss gold floral enamel quarter-repeating
cylinder watch with centre seconds
Early 19th century
2½ in. (6 cm.) diameter
Sold 3.4.85 in New York for $46,200
(£37,258)
From the collection of Stephen Richard
Currier and Audrey Bruce Currier

Above right:
Swiss gold and enamel quarter-repeating
duplex watch for the Chinese market
c. 1810
2½ in. (6 cm.) diameter
Sold 13.11.84 in Geneva for Sw.fr.55,000
(£17,741)

Right:
Swiss quarter-repeating cylinder watch with
two-tune musical automaton
c. 1810
2½ in. (6 cm.) diameter
Sold 3.4.85 in New York for $39,600
(£31,935)

Far Right:
English gold, enamel, pearl
and diamond-set verge watch
and chatelaine
Signed *Jefferys & Jones,
London, 2874*
Late 18th century
7 in. (17 cm.) long
Sold for Sw.fr.22,000
(£7,096)

Right:
French gold and enamel
quarter-repeating verge
watch and chatelaine
Signed *Baillon A Paris*
*c.*1770
7 ½ in. (19 cm.) long
Sold for Sw.fr.46,200
(£14,903)

Both sold 13.11.84 in Geneva

Stained vellum, boxwood and brass compound microscope
Stamped *GIUSEPPE*
Probably Italian
Late 17th century
8 in. (20.3 cm.) long
Sold 23.10.84 in New York for $8,800 (£7,213)

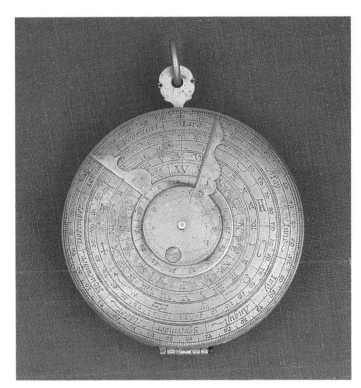

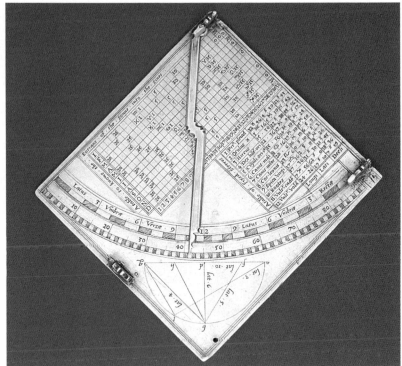

English gilt-metal equinoctial compendium compass dial
Signed *Elias Allen Fecit*
17th century
3⅛ in. (7.9 cm.) diameter
Sold 14.3.85 in London at Christie's South Kensington for
£12,000 ($13,320)

Elizabethan silver quadrant dial
Signed *Humfray Colle*
*c.*1570
2⅞ × 3¹⁄₁₆ in. (7.3 × 7.8 cm.)
Sold 13.12.84 in London at Christie's South Kensington for £62,000
($75,640)

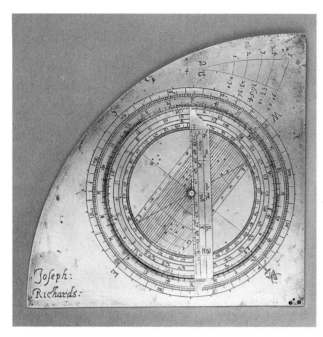

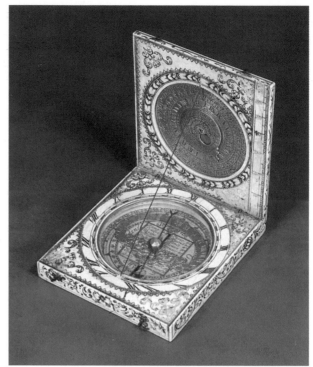

Above:
English brass quadrant
Signed *Joseph: Richards:*
17th century
6¼ in. (15.9 cm.) radius
Sold 13.12.84 in London at Christie's South
Kensington for £4,600 ($5,610)

Above right:
French ivory azimuth diptych dial
Signed *Fait Par Charles Bloud Dieppe*
*c.*1700
3⅜ × 3¾ in. (8.4 × 9.5 cm.)
Sold 13.12.84 in London at Christie's South
Kensington for £3,800 ($4,640)

Right:
French brass Butterfield-type dial
Signed *Lordelle A Paris*
1738
6¾ in. (17.2 cm.) wide
Sold 13.12.84 in London at Christie's South
Kensington for £4,600 ($5,610)

Jewellery

Diamond tiara composed of 13 graduated palm fronds with pendant diamonds
Sold 12.12.84 in London for £28,080 ($33,696)

Diamond tiara of stylized trefoil and festoon design
Sold 14.11.84 in Geneva for Sw.fr.132,000 (£42,580)
Victoria Eugènie Ena, Princess of Great Britain and Ireland (1887–1969), was a grandchild of Queen Victoria, a niece of King Edward VII and daughter of Princess Beatrice. On 31 May 1906 she married King Alfonso XIII of Spain (1886–1941) in a ceremony which not only presented a scene of pageantry such as has never been seen since in Spain but was also marred by the attack of the anarchist Morral in which 24 people died.
The new Queen was presented with a tiara and a six-row pearl necklace by the Dowager Queen of Spain, and with the present tiara, which was originally set with diamonds and turquoise, by King Alfonso. The setting of turquoise in tiaras was then made fashionable by Lady Londonderry, Baronne Leopold de Rothschild and others. In later years the Queen of Spain replaced the turquoise with more valuable diamonds and wore the piece on State occasions. Commenting on the wedding festivities in 1906, *Femina* no. 132 reported: 'In the evening there was a gala performance of *Lucie* at the Theatre Royal . . . after a wearisome day in the oppressive heat. The Royal Box was full, and the Queen was wearing her tiara set with turquoise and diamonds for the first time, a present from the King. With her were the Prince of Wales, the Queen Mother, the Princess of Wales, and the Crown Prince of Portugal. At the exit crowds blocked the way of the carriages in order to cheer the Royal Family.'

Right:
Art deco pearl and diamond
pendant suspending a
briolette-cut diamond drop
weighing 14.06 carats
Signed by Cartier, New
York, made in 1927
Sold 16.5.85 in Geneva for
Sw.fr.187,000 (£58,437)

Far right:
THE JUNE BRIOLETTE
Briolette-cut diamond
pendant set with a drop-
shaped briolette-cut diamond
stated to weigh 48.42 carats
Sold 14.11.84 in Geneva for
Sw.fr.550,000 (£177,419)

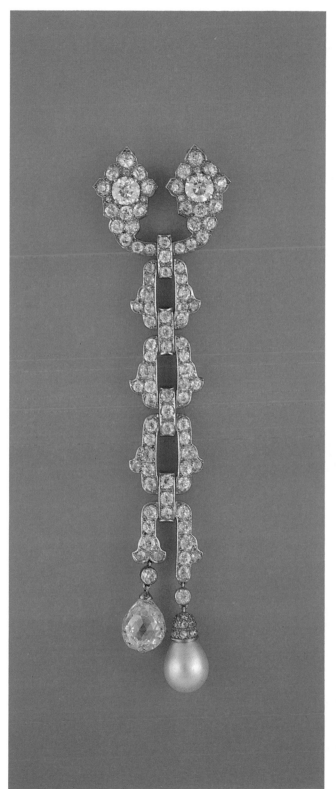

Above:
Natural pearl and diamond ornament
Gross weight 295 grains
With gemological certificate number 1924215
stating that the pearl is natural
Sold 16.10.84 in New York for $77,000
(£63,115)

Above:
Pair of natural pearl and diamond ornaments
Gross weight 412 grains
With gemological certificate number 1924207 stating that the
pearls are natural
Sold 16.10.84 in New York for $88,000 (£72,131)

Top:
Multi-gem and diamond 'Egyptian Revival' bracelet
Signed by Lacloche Paris
Sold 16.5.85 in Geneva for Sw.fr.154,000 (£48,125)

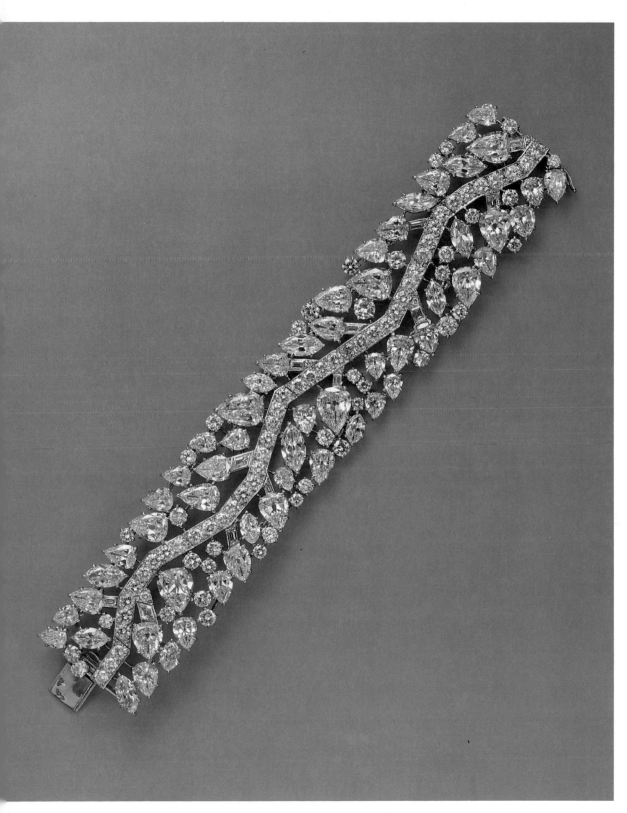

Above:
Lady's art deco rose-cut
diamond and onyx
wristwatch
By Cartier
Sold 30.1.85 in London for
£8,640 ($9,763)

Left:
Diamond bracelet
Signed by Cartier
Sold 14.11.84 in Geneva
for Sw.fr.495,000
(£159,677)

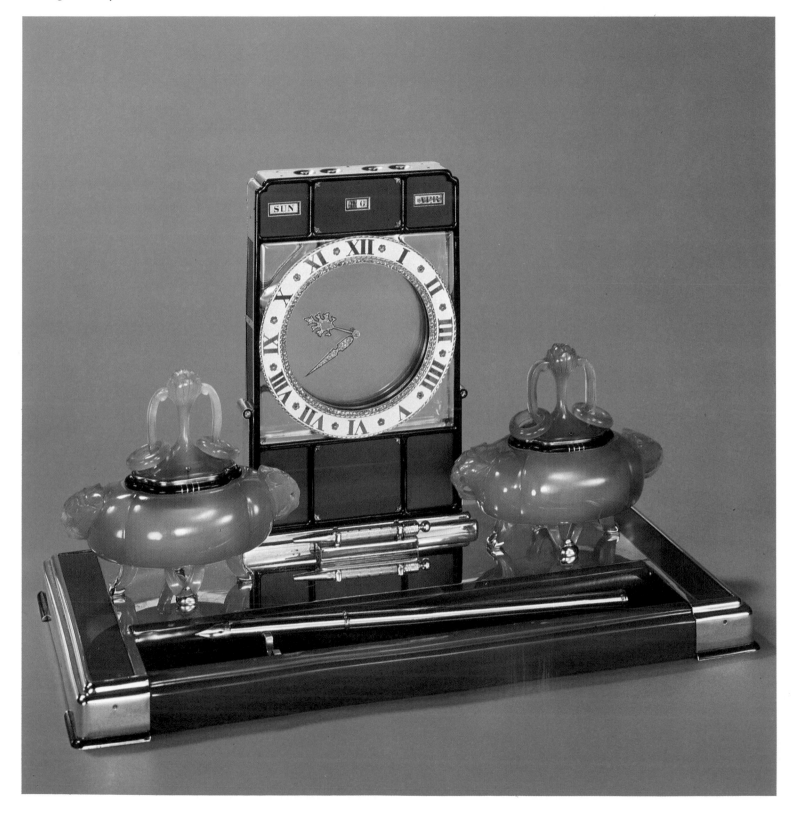

Right:
Art deco rock crystal, diamond and mother-of-pearl mystery clock
By Cartier
Sold 24.4.85 in New York for $264,000 (£209,520)

Opposite:
Jewelled agate, rock crystal, enamel and gold desk-set with mystery clock
By Cartier, made in 1925
Sold 16.5.85 in Geneva for Sw.fr.616,000 (£187,234)
The only mystery clock which Cartier incorporated into an elaborate jewelled desk-set. The model in question is the so-called 'Ecran' which first appeared in 1922.

Diamond necklace
Signed by Cartier
Sold 14.11.84 in
Geneva for Sw.fr.
990,000 (£319,354)

Right:
Art deco amber, diamond, sapphire and lapis lazuli card case
Signed by Lacloche Frères, Paris
Sold 5.12.84 in New York for $4,950 (£4,125)

Above:
Black opal of shield outline mounted as a brooch
Weight of black opal 10.12 carats
Sold 12.12.84 in London for £18,360 ($22,032)

Below:
Diamond and emerald dragonfly brooch
Signed by Van Cleef & Arpels
Sold 16.10.84 in New York for $41,800 (£34,262)
In 1939 Louis Arpels and his designer, Maurice Duvalet, originated in New York the sculptural style of jewellery seen in this dragonfly and the celebrated series of Van Cleef & Arpels ballerinas. Defined by the rose-cut diamonds which give them their shimmer, these jewels were an alternative to the gold, predominantly geometric, work of the Second World War era. They carried on a tradition of fine European jewellery composed of precious gems set in platinum or, during and shortly after the war years, in palladium. The continued to be made into the early 1950s.

Above:
Pair of pear-shaped emeralds weighing 12.63 and 12.93 carats mounted as a pair of earrings
Sold 19.6.85 in London for £124,200 ($158,980)

Diamond rectangular panel
ring
Weight of diamond 4.10
carats
Sold for £19,440 ($21,967)

Graduated imperial jade bead
two-row necklace
Sold for £140,400 ($158,652)
The colour of this jade is
known by the Chinese as
fei-tsui

Both sold 30.1.85 in London

Opposite:
Antique emerald and
diamond pendant necklace
Sold 16.5.85 in Geneva for
Sw.fr.385,000 (£120,312)

Antique emerald and
diamond brooch mounted
with a square-cut emerald
weighing 24.62 carats
First half 19th century,
probably Russian
Sold 16.5.85 in Geneva for
Sw.fr.1,320,000 (£401,215)

Antique sapphire
and diamond
necklace
Weight of three
largest sapphires
18.59, 13.84 and
9.39 carats

Pair of ear-
pendants *en suite*
Weight of two
sapphires 18.55
and 18.25 carats

Both sold
14.11.84 in
Geneva for a total
of Sw.fr.88,000
(£28,387)

Right:
Fancy blue diamond pendant
set with a pear-shaped fancy
blue diamond weighing
approximately 16.47 carats
Sold 24.4.85 in New York for
$1,375,000 (£1,000,000)

Far right:
Pear-shaped diamond
weighing 55.91 carats
With a certificate by the
Gemological Institute of
America (1972) stating that
the diamond is D colour (with
the comment 'rare light
blue') and internally flawless,
and a further certificate by
the Gemological Institute of
America (1985) for very light
blue natural colour and
internally flawless
Sold 16.5.85 in Geneva for
Sw.fr.5,500,000 (£1,671,732)

Right:
Diamond ring set with an
emerald-cut diamond
weighing 30.13 carats
With a certificate from the
Gemological Institute of
America stating that the
diamond is D colour and
clarity VSI. According to an
additional diagram the
diamond is potentially
flawless
Sold 14.11.84 in Geneva for
Sw.fr.1,870,000 (£603,226)

Far right:
Fancy blue pear-shaped
diamond of 42.92 carats
With a certificate by Gübelin
laboratories, Lucerne, stating
that the diamond is of natural
fancy-blue colour
Sold 14.11.84 in Geneva for
Sw.fr.11,000,000
(£3,548,387)

Cultured pearl necklace of 55 graduated Burmese cultured pearls measuring approximately 11.70 to 15.40 mm.
Sold 24.4.85 in New York for $220,000 (£174,600)

Diamond choker set with 45 graduated circular-cut diamonds, the centre diamond weighing approximately 8.06 carats
Total weight of diamonds approximately 100.00 carats
Although not signed, this choker was made by Harry Winston
Sold 24.4.85 in New York for $462,000 (£366,670)
From the collection of Miss Zsa Zsa Gabor

Pair of diamond pendant ear-clips with pear-shaped diamonds weighing 11.17 and 10.41 carats
Signed by Van Cleef & Arpels
Sold 16.5.85 in Geneva for Sw.fr. 935,000 (£284,194)

Fancy light yellow rectangular-cut diamond weighing 72.84 carats
With a certificate from the Gemological Institute of America stating that the diamond is of fancy light yellow natural colour, clarity VS and potentially flawless
Sold 16.5.85 in Geneva for Sw.fr.990,000 (£300,911)

Pair of briolette-cut, cushion and pear-shaped diamond pendant earrings of chandelier design
Weight of briolette-cut diamonds 6.82 and 6.57 carats
Sold 13.3.85 in London for £86,400 ($94,176)

Antique diamond and gem-set miniature bangle set with an oval bust-length miniature of Maria Alexeievna, the consort of Tsar Alexander I
Signed by Carl Kronnowetter, 1823
Sold 14.11.84 in Geneva for Sw.fr.33,000 (£10,645)
Carl Kronnowetter, son of the porcelain painter Franz Kronnowetter, was born in Vienna in 1795 and died in St. Petersburg in 1837. After 1821 he worked predominantly in Russia and painted the portraits of most of the Imperial family as well as members of the Russian court.

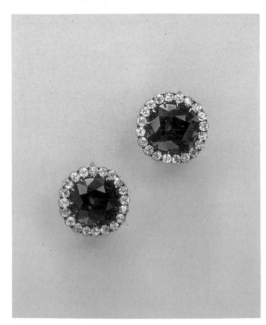

Pair of antique sapphire and diamond cluster ear-clips, each set with a cushion-shaped sapphire weighing 9.86 and 9.05 carats respectively
With an expertise from Gübelin stating that the sapphires are from Kashmir
Sold 16.5.85 in Geneva for Sw.fr.880,000 (£267,477)

Gold and Silver

Set of four George II candlesticks
By Edward Wakelin
1757
One maker's mark indistinct
12½ in. (31.7 cm.) high
Sold 11.7.85 in London for £56,160 ($77,500)

The Portland Font

CHARLES TRUMAN

Fonts in precious metals were not uncommon in England until the Commonwealth (1649–60), but the only surviving example in gold is that commissioned by the 3rd Duke of Portland to celebrate the christening of his grandson, the infant Viscount Woodstock. The font was made in the Air Street premises of the famous London goldsmith Paul Storr in 1797–8. Storr's reputation is at present undergoing consideration and it is clear that, while being a gifted craftsman, his greatest skill was in the managing of a busy and talented workshop, often producing silver and gold to the designs of sculptors and artists such as William Theed and John Flaxman. The latter had until recently been considered the modeller of the remarkable figures of Faith, Hope, and Charity which support the Portland Font. However, modern scholarship has dismissed this attribution since, although Flaxman had supplied designs for goldsmith's work as early as 1783, the style of the figures is markedly different to recorded work by the artist. It is clear that the modeller was a sculptor of great sensitivity, for the figures are without doubt the finest examples of sculpture in precious metal to have been made in England, but his identity must for the time being remain a mystery.

Shortly before the sale of the font a fascinating discovery revealed the identity of the designer of this remarkable piece. Humphrey Repton, the renowned architect and landscape gardener, wrote in his *Observations on the Theory and Practice of Landscape Gardening* (1803):

> Lest it should be objected that I am going beyond the precise boundaries of my profession, either as a landscape gardener, or as an architect, I shall observe, that the professor of taste in those arts must necessarily have a competent knowledge of every art in which taste may be exercised. I have frequently given designs for furniture to the upholsterer, for monuments to the statuary, and to the goldsmith I gave a design for one of the most sumptuous presents of gold plate which was ever executed in this country: it consisted of a basin, in the form of a broad flat vase, and pedestal, round which were the figures of Faith, Hope and Charity; the former spreading her hand over the water, as in the act of benediction; and the two latter supporting the vase, which resembled a baptismal font: the whole was executed in gold and was the present of a noble Duke to his son, on the birth of his first child.

This would appear to be the unique example of Repton designing a work in gold and it is a measure of the Duke of Portland's confidence in his young protégé that the design was entrusted to him.

THE PORTLAND FONT
George III gold christening font
By Paul Storr
1797–8
The pedestal 13¾ in. (34.9 cm.) square
Figure of Faith 7¼ in. (18.4 cm.) high
Figure of Hope 4½ in. (11.4 cm.) high
Figure of Charity 4¼ in. (10.8 cm.) high
The bowl 4½ in. (11.4 cm.) high; 8¼ (21.6 cm.) diameter
Sold 11.7.85 in London for £950,400 ($1,311,552)
From the collection of Lady Anne Bentinck

George III two-handled gold
cup and cover
By Digby Scott and Benjamin
Smith
1806
With the Latin inscription of
Rundell, Bridge and Rundell
10 in. (25.5 cm.) high
Sold 27.3.85 in London for
£108,000 ($113,400)

George II silver-gilt
toilet service
By David Willaume,
Jun.
1734
The whisks
unmarked
Sold 28.11.84 in
London for £151,200
($182,952)
Formerly in the
collection of the
Marquess of Exeter
The arms are those
of Cecil with
Chambers in
pretence for
Brownlow, 8th
Earl of Exeter, who
married in 1724
Hannah Sophia,
daughter and co-heir
of Thomas
Chambers of London
and Derby

Queen Anne silver-gilt
toilet service
By Anthony Nelme
1711
Sold 15.5.85 in
Geneva for
Sw.fr.748,000
(£228,049)

Opposite:
Pair of George II
butter dishes
By Paul De Lamerie
1734
5 in. (12.6 cm.) wide
Both sold 22.10.84 in
New York for $66,000
(£55,000)

George I seal salver
By Paul De Lamerie
1721
12¾ in. (32.4 cm.) long
Sold 28.11.84 in London for £70,200 ($84,942)

George II salver
By Paul De Lamerie
1734
24³⁄₈ in. (61.8 cm.) long
Sold 22.10.84 in New York for $253,000 (£210,833)
From the collection of Mrs Donald S. Stralem

George II chinoiserie epergne
By William Cripps
1757
22½ in. (57.1 cm.) high
Sold 22.10.84 in New York
for $33,000 (£26,830)

George II plateau
By Henry Dutton
1755
26¾ in. (68 cm.) long
Sold 22.10.84 in New York
for $46,200 (£37,870)

Opposite:
Pair of George III silver-gilt
four-light candelabra
By John Scofield
1793
26⅜ in. (67 cm.) high
Sold 22.10.84 in New York
for $82,500 (£68,750)

George IV wine cooler
Attributed to John Flaxman
By Philip Rundell
1820
Inscribed on the base 'This Wine Cooler is held in greatest estimation by Mrs Harriot Coutts, it was purchased and given to Her by dear Mr Coutts on 24 April 1821,' and on the lid 'Thomas and Harriot Coutts 24 April 1821.'
Stamped with the Latin signature of Rundell, Bridge and Rundell 20½ in. (52 cm.) high
Sold 27.3.85 in London for £133,920 ($140,616)
From the collection of The Hon. Hugo Money-Coutts

Papal presentation
dish cast and chased
with the Rape of
Europa
By Giovanni
Francesco Travani
Rome, 1670
With the mark of
Giovanni Giordani,
bollatore degli argenti
Sold 15.11.84 in
Geneva for
Sw.fr.100,000
(£354,840)

Cylindrical tankard
By Heinrich Meyer
Bergen, *c.*1640
9½ in. (24 cm.) high
Sold 18.6.85 in Amsterdam
for D.fl.91,200 (£20,727)

Latvian cylindrical parcel-gilt
tankard
By Heinrich Meyer
Riga, *c.*1680
9½ in. (24 cm.) high
Sold 15.11.84 in Geneva for
Sw.fr.39,600 (£12,774)

Circular chamber-pot
The Hague, 1687
4 in. (10.6 cm.) high
Sold 17.4.85 in Amsterdam for D.fl.68,400 (£15,545)
This chamber-pot, most probably the oldest known on the Continent and only the second known
Dutch example (the other, made in Amsterdam and dated 1750, is in the Rijksmuseum), doubled its
highest estimate to D.fl.68,400 (£15,545). From the marks it was clear that this household utensil was
made in The Hague in 1687, although the maker's mark of a lamb was not immediately identifiable.
The owner had been employed in the silver trade for some time when the chamber-pot was offered for
melting. He was taken by the object at once and was permitted to buy it for the current scrap price.
Further research on the engraved coat-of-arms revealed that the pot had belonged to Isaac van Thye
(1639–95) and Elisabeth Lestevenan, who married in 1666. The chamber-pot was a conventional part
of dining-room decoration as is bourne out by 17th- and 19th-century pictures by Jan Steen and Louis
Léopold Boilly. Indeed, between about 1770 and 1810 English sideboards had a special pot cupboard
for the use of the gentlemen after dinner when the ladies had left the room. An example in silver would
have been considered especially prestigious and it is said that on at least one occasion Louis XIV
received Polish envoys in public audience whilst making use of his own silver pot.

Collecting Early American Silver

DEAN FAILEY

Early American silver has long fascinated collectors of American decorative arts, and in fact was among the first areas of American art to attract scholarly study.

The appeal of silver to early antiquarians lies in its combination of aesthetic merit and historical interest. Silver objects fashioned throughout the colonial period were not only useful items but served as clear indicators of an individual's wealth and social status. It is not surprising, therefore, that American colonial silver kept pace with changing London fashion to a degree not usually found in the arts of cabinet making, architecture or painting.

From a historical perspective, American silver intrigued collectors because of the extensive documentation usually available on each object. Nearly all silver was marked by its maker and often additionally engraved with its owner's names, initials or presentation inscriptions. These markings allowed easy identification of craftsmen and ready association of specific objects with individuals or events of historical significance.

Recognition of American silversmiths' achievements was certainly a motivating factor in the formation of several early collections. The largest and most influential collection, particularly in its impact on the antique silver market, was formed by Judge Alfonso T. Clearwater (1848–1943) of Kingston, New York, whose 558 pieces are now the heart of the Metropolitan Museum of Art's decorative arts holdings.

Among Clearwater's contemporaries and sometime competitors were a group of Boston collectors that included Francis Hill Bigelow (1859–1933), Hollis French (1868–1940), and Dwight Blaney (1865–1944). Bigelow organized the first major exhibition to concentrate on American silver, in 1906, at the Museum of Fine Arts, Boston. He initiated a second important exhibition and catalogue at the museum in 1911 on American church silver. Together with the 1909 Hudson-Fulton Exhibition at the Metropolitan Museum of Art, these exhibits probably did more to stimulate interest and collecting activity in American silver than any event before or since.

R.T. Haines Halsey (1865–1942) must also be mentioned, not only for his specific contributions as an author of the 1906 catalogue and a lender to the Hudson-Fulton show but as the museum trustee responsible for overseeing the building of the Metropolitan Museum of Art's American Wing, which opened in 1924. Clearly this formal recognition of the importance of American art did much to encourage future generations of American collectors.

Notable successors to the pioneering group of silver collectors included Henry Francis du Pont (1880–1969), Francis P. Garvan (1875–1937), Mr and Mrs Henry N. Flynt (Mrs Flynt 1893–1971), and Philip H. Hammerslough (b.1894). Each assembled and refined collections which they presented to museums: Winterthur, the Yale University Art Gallery, Historic Deerfield, and the Wadsworth Atheneum, respectively.

Also influential in stimulating new collectors and collections were the writings and scholarship of several individuals. Following the clarion call to action by Yale professor Dr Theodore S. Woolsey in a *Harper's* article in 1896 entitled 'Old Silver', numerous catalogue essays and

several books appeared. Francis Bigelow wrote *Historic Silver of the Colonies and its Makers* in 1917, the same year that Hollis French wrote *A List of Early American Silversmiths and their Marks*. A few years earlier, in 1913, E. Alfred Jones, an English silver specialist employed by the Colonial Dames, produced a monumental work that is still a standard reference, *The Old Silver of American Churches*. The publication in 1949 of Yale silver curator John Marshall Phillips' *American Silver* established a new benchmark for writing in the field. The present generation of collectors have additionally been nurtured by the scholarship of Martha Gaudy Fales and Katheryn C. Buhler.

It is a fact, albeit a sad one, that as the years pass and our knowledge of early American silver increases, the number of fine examples appearing in the market place diminishes. Recent auction results attest to the intense competition generated by desirable forms and makers.

The sale in June 1982 of an extremely rare American silver plateau made by John W. Forbes in about 1825 for New York Governor DeWitt Clinton made headlines with the record price for American silver of $264,000 (see fig. 1). Even Judge Clearwater would have been astonished! Other rare forms of exceptional merit that we have been priviledged to sell in New York include rococo candlesticks by the New York silversmith Samuel Tingley, which fetched $71,500

1. The DeWitt Clinton Plateau
By John Forbes, New York
c. 1825
8¾ in. (21.3 cm.) high;
23 in. (58.4 cm.) wide;
63½ in. (161.3 cm.) long

2. Pair of rococo candlesticks
By Samuel Tingley, New
York
c. 1765
9 ¾ in. (24.7 cm.) high

(see fig. 2), and a handsome hexagonal baluster-form caster by the early Boston maker John
Coney, which soared to $55,000 (see fig. 4). The caster had the added glamour of being the
long-lost mate to one in the collections of the Museum of Fine Arts, Boston.

Among 18th-century American silversmiths, the work of two men is eagerly sought. Myer
Myers was an exceptional craftsman as the products of his shop confirm. A brazier by Myers
had the distinction of being one of three pieces of silver that had descended in the English branch
of the well-known New Yorker Philip Livingston. The return trip across the Atlantic proved
to be a profitable one, as the brazier fetched $18,700. The second silversmith's fame, resting
largely on his patriotic exploits during the Revolution, is such that even ordinary examples
of his work bring many times the price of a comparable piece by any other American maker.
This past season, a porringer by Paul Revere II sold for $19,800, while two years ago a neo-
classical teapot consigned by Revere's great-great-grandson achieved $39,600 (see fig. 3).

What does the future hold for the American silver market? There has not been a single major
collection of American silver to appear on the market in over 20 years and therefore patience
rather than compulsion has become the hallmark of today's collector. However, as any collector knows, this could all change with the next fall of the auctioneer's gavel.

3. Fluted body neo-classical
teapot
By Paul Revere II, Boston
*c.*1795
5⅞ in. (14.9 cm.) high

4. Hexagonal baluster-form
caster
By John Coney, Boston
1710–20
5⅞ in. (14.9 cm.) high

Objects of Art and Vertu

Gold and jewelled
hardstone vase
Probably Dresden
*c.*1715
5½ in.
(13.6 cm.) high
Sold 14.5.85 in
Geneva for
Sw.fr.264,000
(£80,488)

Far left:

CHRISTIAN FREDERICK ZINCKE
Frederick Louis, Prince of Wales
Oval, 2 in. (5 cm.) high
Sold 11.7.85 in London for £5,184 ($6,739)

Left:

JOHN SMART
A Gentleman
Signed with initials and dated 1785
Oval, 2 in. (5 cm.) high
Sold for £4,320 ($5,227)

Far left:

JOHN SMART
A Lady
Signed with initials and dated 1774
Oval, 2 in. (5 cm.) high
Sold for £6,480 ($7,841)

Left:

JOHN DOWNMAN
Sarah Hussey Delaval, Countess of Tyrconnel
Oval, 2¾ in. (7 cm.) high
Sold for £3,024 ($3,659)

All sold 27.11.84 in London

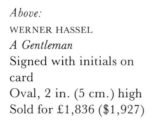

Above:
WERNER HASSEL
A Gentleman
Signed with initials on
card
Oval, 2 in. (5 cm.) high
Sold for £1,836 ($1,927)

Top:
NICHOLAS HILLIARD
A Gentleman
On vellum,
contemporary gold frame
Oval, 1⅝ in.
(4.2 cm.) high
Sold for £20,520
($21,546)

Above:
ALEXANDER COOPER
A Nobleman
Oval, 1¼ in.
(3.2 cm.) high
Sold for £3,240 ($3,402)

Above:
THOMAS FLATMAN
A Gentleman
Signed with monogram
On vellum
Oval, 2⅝ in.
(6.5 cm.) high
Sold for £8,640 ($9,072)

All sold 27.3.85 in
London

Louis XV carnet of Japanese lacquer mounted in gold set with miniatures
Paris, 1750, with the charge and décharge of Antoine Leschaudel
5¾ in. (14.5 cm.) high
Sold 14.5.85 in Geneva for Sw.fr.638,000 (£194,512)
The miniatures depict the Dauphin and the Dauphine Marie-Josèphe de Saxe and his surviving sisters, the Mesdames de France, Louis-Elisabeth (1727–59), Henriette (1727–52), Adelaïde (1732–1800), Victoire (1733–99), Sophie (1734–82) and Louise (1737–87)

Empress Elisabeth imperial presentation table snuff-box
St. Petersburg, 1761, attributed to Jérémie Pauzié
Inscribed *Objectum majoratur ponderis 115 aureorum dono ab Elisabeth Russiae Imperatrice Nicholas Esterhazy ad aulam ejus legato largitum*
3¾ in. (9.3 cm.) long
Sold 14.5.85 in Geneva for Sw.fr.770,000 (£234,756)

Louis XV gold and enamel box
By Paul Robert, Paris, 1747–8 with the charge and
décharge of Henri Clavel, the enamels perhaps by
Louis-François Aubert
3¼ in. (8.4 cm.) long
Sold 13.11.84 in Geneva for Sw.fr.297,000 (£95,806)
Paul Robert (1720–79) was apprenticed to the
goldsmith André Balmont in 1735 and attained the
maîtrise on 4 August 1747, with an address in the
Cour Neuve-du-Palais. In 1753 he moved to the Rue
Harlay, where he died on 24 August 1779.
In the mid-18th century there are frequent references
to boxes with enamelled flowers in relief, and where
these are attributed, they are given to 'Aubert'. For
example, Jean Ducrollay and the marchand-mercier
La Hoguette supplied five boxes to the Menus Plaisirs
with enamelled flowers in relief by Aubert in 1751 and
1753, and Madame de Pompadour possessed three
boxes enamelled by him at her death in 1764. The
author of these enamels would appear to be Louis-
François Aubert who worked from 1748 until 20
October 1755. Following his death, it seems probable
that his workshop continued under the control of his
widow who died in 1758.

Swiss gold, enamel and pearl singing-bird box
Signed by Jacob Frisard, Geneva, c. 1800
3¼ in. (8.4 cm.) long
Sold 14.5.85 in Geneva for Sw.fr.165,000 (£50,304)

Above left:
French empire gold snuff-box
By Adrien-Maximilien Vachette, Paris, with second standard
mark (20 ct.) for 1795–7 (or later) and warranty marks for
1809–19
3⅛ in. (8 cm.) long
Sold 28.11.84 in London for £24,840 ($30,056)

Above:
Austrian oval gold and enamel snuff-box
Signed by Philipp Ernst Schindler II, Vienna, *c.*1765
With six domestic scenes after Boucher
3 in. (7.6 cm.) long
Sold 13.11.84 in Geneva for Sw.fr.159,000 (£51,290)

Above:
Louis XVI octagonal gold snuff-box
By A.J.M. Vachette, Paris, 1787, with the poinçons of Henri
Clavel
3 in. (7.6 cm.) long
Sold 28.11.84 in London for £21,600 ($26,136)

Italian gold-mounted rock-crystal cross
Circle of Valerio Belli
c.1535
3¾ in. (9.3 cm.) long; 3 in. (7.6 cm.) wide
Sold 13.11.84 in Geneva for Sw.fr.132,000 (£42,581)
Valerio Belli of Vicenza (1468–1546) worked in Rome for Pope Leo X
(1513–22) and for Clement VII (1523–34) as a medal die-cutter,
rock-crystal carver and to a lesser extent as a goldsmith. He is
known to have signed a number of carvings on his most famous
work, the silver-gilt and rock-crystal casket of 1532 in the Museo
degli Argenti, Florence. There are close similarities between this
and the present example, particularly in the arrangement of the
figures in the scene of the Presentation in the Temple.

Pendant of enamelled gold and jewels depicting Orpheus
Probably French, *c*.1630
3½ in. (8.3 cm.) high
Sold 14.5.85 in Geneva for Sw.fr.374,000 (£114,024)

French jewelled and enamelled double-sided pendant formed as Hercules
Paris, c.1540
$2\frac{1}{2} \times 2\frac{1}{4}$ in. (6 × 5.4 cm.)
Sold 13.11.84 in Geneva for Sw.fr.1,320,000 (£425,806)
Record auction price for a piece of Renaissance jewellery

Jewel formed as a merman blowing a conch
c. 1580
3 × 2¾ in. (7.6 × 6.7 cm.)
Sold 13.11.84 in Geneva for Sw.fr.550,000 (£177,419)

Jewelled and enamelled gold pendant
formed as a warrior with a trophy of arms
Netherlandish or English, *c.*1620
2½ × 2 in. (6.3 × 5.1 cm.)
Sold 13.11.84 in Geneva for Sw.fr.68,200
(£22,000)
By order of The Audrey B. Love
Foundation from the collection of
C. Ruxton Love

Jewelled gold and cloisonné enamel cloak
clasp, one side converting to a pendant
with hinged suspension loop and seed-
pearl necklace
By Henry Wilson, *c.*1914
Each side 1⅞ in. (4.8 cm.) diameter; the
pendant 2¾ in. (7.3 cm.) long
Sold 12.12.84 in London for £10,260
($12,312)

Top centre:
Gold and enamel pendant
By Carlo Giuliano, 1865–95
Marked in two places with
applied initials
$1\frac{5}{8}$ in. (4.2 cm.) wide
Sold for £5,184 ($6,221)

Right:
Gold and enamel pendant
Signed by C. and
A. Giuliano, 1895–1912
In original fitted case with
115 Piccadilly address
$2\frac{5}{8}$ in. (6.8 cm.) long
Sold for £8,856 ($10,627)

Far right:
Gold and enamel pendant
Signed by C. and
A. Giuliano, 1895–1912
In original fitted case with
115 Piccadilly address
$2\frac{1}{4}$ in. (5.8 cm.) long
Sold for £6,480 ($7,776)

Bottom centre:
Gold, enamel and gem-set
pendant
By Carlo Giuliano, *c.*1865–95
Plaque of initials inside loop
$3\frac{1}{4}$ in. (8.3 cm.) long
Sold for £6,264 ($7,517)

All sold 12.12.84 in London

Jewelled automated silver rhinoceros
By Fabergé
2⅞ in. (7.3 cm.) long
Sold 23.10.84 in New York for $132,000
(£108,196)
Realistically modelled, the oxidized silver
finish chased to resemble the leathery
textured hide of the animal, when wound
the articulated legs, head and swishing tail
are set in motion; with a gold key and
original fitted wood case with hinged lid and
sliding side panel

Imperial two-colour gold mounted
grapeshot hand-seal
By Fabergé
Workmaster Henrik Wigström,
St. Petersburg
c.1905
2½ in. (5.4 cm.) high
Sold 23.10.84 in New York for $37,400
(£30,655)

Diamond-set nephrite
cigarette-case
*c.*1910
3 ½ in. (9 cm.) long
Sold for £10,260 ($13,240)

White guilloché enamel silver-gilt
cigarette-case
Signed with initials of Andres
Nevalainen, St. Petersburg,
1896–1908
3 ⅜ in. (8.5 cm.) long
Sold for £4,860 ($6,270)

Miniature nephrite figure of an
elephant
1 in. (2.5 cm.) long
Sold for £5,400 ($6,970)

Diamond-set nephrite
cigarette-case
Workmaster Henrik Wigström,
St. Petersburg, *c.*1900
3 ¼ in. (8 cm.) long
Sold for £5,400 ($6,970)

Guilloché enamel silver menu-
holder
Workmaster Anders Nevalainen,
St. Petersburg, 1896–1903
3 ¾ in. (9.7 cm.) long
Sold for £2,376 ($3,070)

Gem-set gold brooch
Signed with the initials of Oskar
Pihl, St. Petersburg, *c.*1890
Sold for £2,376 ($3,070)

Guilloché enamel gem-set and
nephrite vari-colour gold-
mounted parasol handle
Signed with the initials of Henrik
Wigström, St. Petersburg, *c.*1890
3 in. (7.7 cm.) long
Sold for £8,100 ($10,450)

All by Fabergé
Sold 13.6.85 in London

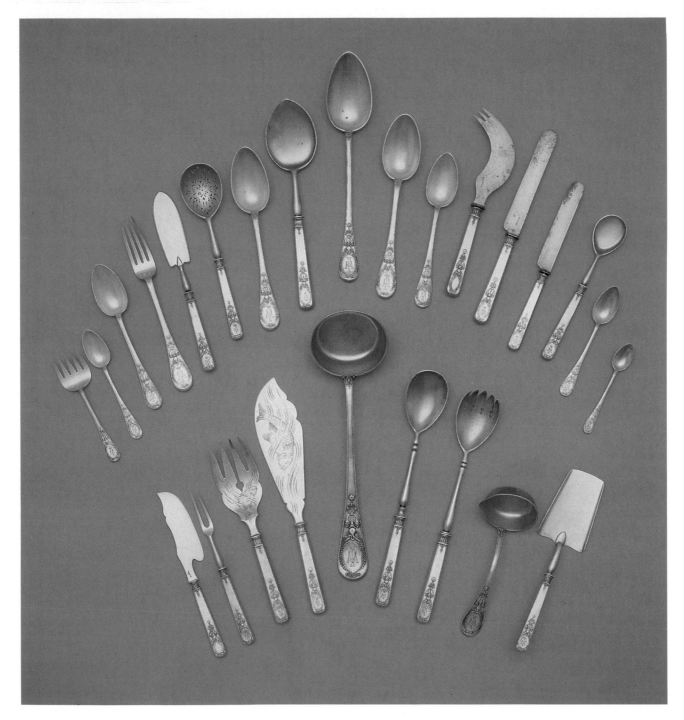

Silver flatware service, comprising 111 pieces
By Fabergé
Signed with the Imperial Warrant mark, Moscow
1899–1908
Sold 6.2.85 in London for £15,120 ($16,934)

Silver-mounted nephrite casket
By Fabergé
Workmaster Michael Perchin, St. Petersburg
Last quarter 19th century
9$\frac{1}{2}$ in. (24 cm.) high; 8$\frac{3}{4}$ in. (22.2 cm.) long
Sold 23.10.84 in New York for $30,800 (£25,245)

Silver tankard
By Fabergé
Workmaster Julius Rappoport, St. Petersburg
Signed with the Imperial Warrant mark
1899–1908
11 in. (27.5 cm.) high
Sold 12.11.84 in Geneva for Sw.fr.35,200 (£11,355)

Saint George
Asia Minor, 17th century
37½ × 27½ in. (94 × 70 cm.)
Sold 13.6.85 in London for £10,800 ($13,930)

A German silver Kiddush cup
By Hieronymus Mittnacht
Augsburg, 1761–3
With Hebrew inscription, 'Remember the Sabbath day
to keep it holy', marked on base and bowl
4¾ in. (12 cm.) high
Sold 25.6.85 in New York for $17,600 (£13,538)

Circumcision set in original walnut case, the lid inlaid with mother-of-pearl depicting a circumcision shield, knife and two cups under 'The Holy Covenant' in Hebrew, the case containing two circumcision knives with silver-mounted agate handles, a silver shield, by A.H. van Ankum, Amsterdam, c.1865, a silver probe with agate handle, a pair of silver cups, fitting into each other, the 'Kos shel Beracha' also engraved in Hebrew as a remembrance from Pincas and Mordechai Vyth to Mr Eliezer Levy Boutelje, 11 Kislev (5)625 = 10 December 1865, the 'Kos shel Meiziza' also engraved with the priestly attributes of the ewer and basin, over which the legend 'This is that belongeth to the Levites' (Numeri 8:24), some of the Hebrew characters composing the year (5)625 = 1865, probably Eastern Europe, c.1860; an oval silver sand tray, no marks, on which to depose the praeputium; a rectangular reeded silver box made at Schoonhoven in 1840 by A. Kooiman, a pair of scissors with silver handles Bois-le-Duc, c.1840, M. Wouters, and a silver powder flask, maker's mark only IN and pellet, probably Germany, c.1730, the wooden box lined with purple velvet.
3¾ in. (9.3 cm.) high; 9¼ in. (23.7 cm.) long; 5¾ in. (14.7 cm.) wide
Sold 11.12.84 in Amsterdam for D.fl.25,080 (£5,700)

Works of Art

Romano-British solid bronze figure of a
standing stag
c. 1st century AD from Southern England
6½ in. (16.4 cm.) high
Sold 16.7.85 in London for £30,240
($39,312)

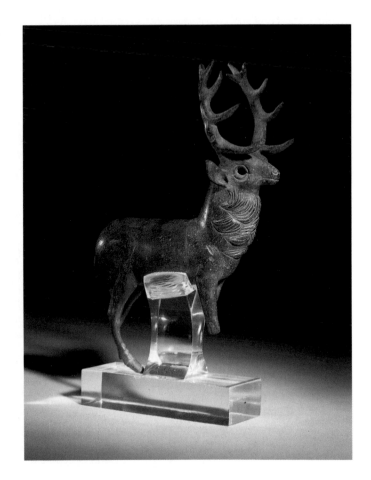

Mid-13th-century French stone head of King Herod from Chartres Cathedral
7⅜ in. (18.7 cm.) high
Sold 13.6.85 in New York for $198,000 (£152,307)

The present carving has been identified by Léon Pressouyre as the missing head of King Herod from 'The Magi before Herod', one of the relief panels which formed the choirscreen of the cathedral at Chartres. This attribution was confirmed in the early 1970s when a plaster cast of the head, made by the Metropolitan Museum of Art under the supervision of Carmen Gomez-Moreno, was successfully fitted to the body of Herod on the extant relief fragment. With the exception of a small missing chip, the decapitated body aligned perfectly with the cast. Moreover, the three-quarter angle of the head conformed with the design of the relief, in which the king, seated at the far right, turns to receive the three magi standing to his right. Structural peculiarities of the present carving as well as the fact that the right profile is comparatively unfinished reinforce this attribution.

Late 15th-century
Florentine terracotta
bust of St. Jerome
Attributed to Andrea
Verrocchio
15 in. (38 cm.) high
Sold 11.12.84 in
London for £21,600
($26,136)

Early 16th-century Paduan gilt bronze statuette of a kneeling Satyr
By Severo da Ravenna
7¾ in. (19.5 cm.) high
Sold 11.12.84 in London for £8,640 ($10,454)
This is a finely cast and chased example of the type of satyr invented by Severo da Ravenna

Late 16th-century Florentine
gilt bronze Corpus Christi
('Cristo Morto')
Solid cast from a wax model
by Giambologna
13¼ in. (33.5 cm.) high
Sold 11.12.84 in London for
£17,250 ($20,872)

Late 16th-century Florentine bronze relief of the Rape of the Sabines
Attributed to Antonio Susini, after a model by Giambologna
8½ × 10½ in. (22 × 26 cm.)
Sold 3.7.85 in London for £24,840 ($32,292)
This unpublished bronze plaque cast by the lost-wax process appears to record a small wax
model for Giambologna's much larger narrative relief which was intended to clarify the
subject of his celebrated marble group of the *Rape of a Sabine*, unveiled in January 1583.
While the composition is very similar, the details are not identical to those of the relief in
the Piazza della Signoria. This suggests that the present relief is not simply a reduction of
the finished work. Considering its small scale it is most carefully cast and worked in a way
characteristic of Antonio Susini, whereas the relief in the Piazza has a surprisingly rough,
waxy-looking surface with few traces of chasing after casting: it does not therefore convey
any greater degree of detail than the present piece. A wax model for Giambologna's relief
was recorded in the collection of his admirer and patron Benedetto Gondi, but its size was
not stated. Even if it was full size, it is probable that the sculptor would have made small
preliminary sketches in wax, one of which might have been given to Susini for finishing
and casting in bronze as a presentation piece, perhaps for the Grand Duke Francesco I de'
Medici, Giambologna's lifelong friend and patron.

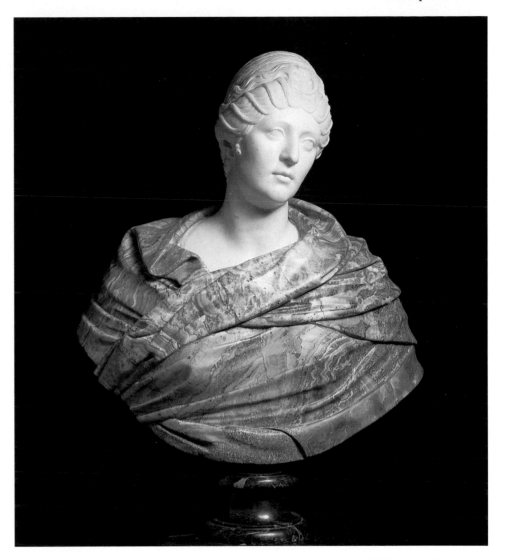

One of a pair of 17th-century Roman marble busts of Faustina (? illustrated) and
Julia Domna
After the Antique
36 in. (91 cm.) high
Sold 3.7.85 in London for £34,560 ($44,928)
These highly decorative busts are imitations of late Roman Imperial portraiture:
such busts in pairs or series were fashionable as interior decoration in Roman
palaces from the second half of the 16th century and the enhancement with
coloured marble, porphyry or alabaster shoulders is characteristic of Baroque
taste. The bust with a high bun seems to represent Faustina the Elder or Younger,
though it resembles a bust in the Bibliothèque Mazarine, Paris, which is
enigmatically labelled 'Solonina', a lady whose identity is no longer clear. The
other is clearly derived from a type generally accepted as showing the Syrian
princess Julia Domna, second wife of Septimius Severus and mother of Caracalla
and Geta, of which the best example is in the Capitoline Museum.

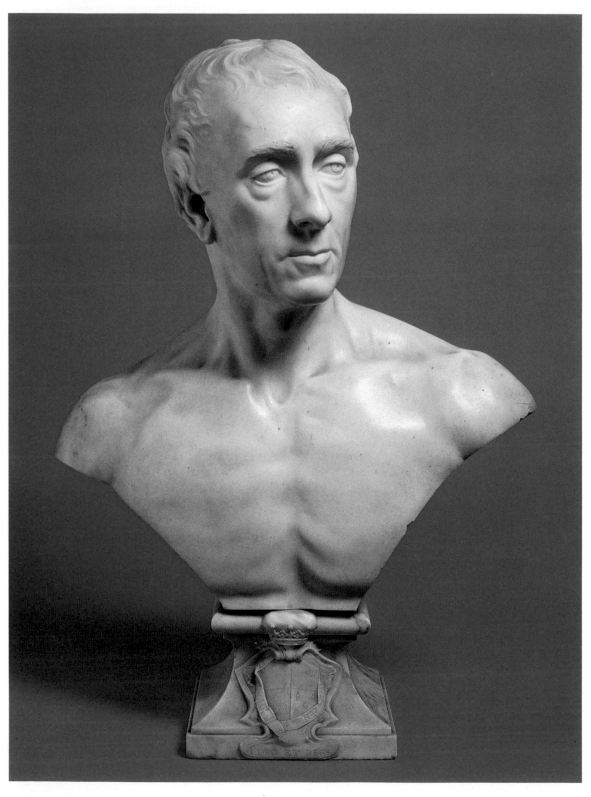

Mid-18th-century English marble bust of Philip Dormer Stanhope, 4th Earl of Chesterfield
By Louis François Roubiliac
Signed and dated on the back 'L.F. Roubiliac Sc. ad Vivum MDCCXLV' and inscribed: 'twice Embassador extraordinary to the states General Lord Steward of the Household & Lord of the Bedchamber to KING GEORGE the 2. Lord Lieutenant of Ireland & Knight of the most noble Order. of the Garter.'
On a separately carved square waisted socle with his coat-of-arms, inscribed with his motto A DEO ET REGE
29 in. (73.5 cm.) high
Sold 3.4.85 in London for £518,400 ($642,816)
Now in the National Portrait Gallery, London

One of a pair of late 18th-century southern French (Lyon) terracotta models of sejant Lions supporting coats-of-arms with the coronets of a Marquis
By Joseph Chinard
8½ × 12 in. (21 × 30 cm.)
Sold 3.7.85 in London for £8,100 ($10,530)
This unpublished pair of heraldic lions support shields bearing the arms of Nicolau de Montriblond of Languedoc and Lyonnais and of Chaponay of Lyonnais and Dauphiné: this points to the authorship of Joseph Chinard (1756–1813), the most celebrated sculptor of Lyon, who specialized in terracotta sculptures. This is corroborated by their close similarity to a lion bearing the sculptor's stamp in the Sackler Collection.

Early 19th-century Italian marble statue of Paolina Borghese Bonaparte as Venus Victrix
Attributed to Adamo Tadolini, after Canova
21½ × 35½ × 13½ in. (54.5 × 90 × 34.5 cm.)
Sold 3.7.85 in London for £11,880 ($15,444)

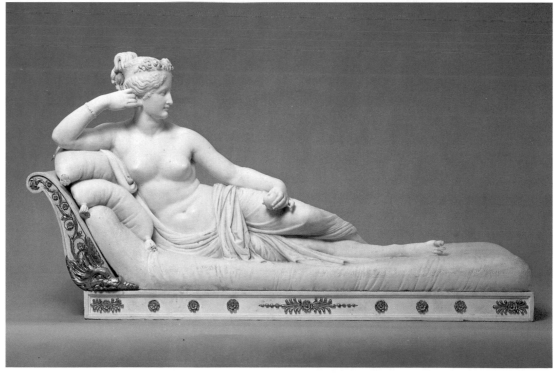

Cameo flask
25 BC–AD 25
Possibly from near Eskischehir, Turkey
3 in. (7.6 cm.) high
Sold 5.3.85 in London for £324,000 ($356,400)
Now in the J. Paul Getty Museum, Malibu, California

THE KOFLER-TRUNIGER COLLECTION

Ancient glass, formerly the Kofler-Truniger collection, was sold on 5 and 6 March 1985 for a record total of £2.4 million ($2.64 million). In a collection so rich in every major period and technique and from so wide an area, there was something to appeal to every glass collector. And major glass collectors, museum curators, dealers and students came in large numbers, realising this was an unparalleled opportunity to strengthen their own collections.

Mr and Mrs Ernest Kofler's collection was well known, having been the subject of publications and major exhibitions since 1956. They are renowned as among the foremost collectors of ancient glass this century. Their unfalteringly discerning eye for the beautiful and the interesting had led them to acquire over 40 years the finest examples of glass technique from the 14th century BC to the 7th century AD and encompassing the major glass working centres, France and Germany in the West, Italy, the Eastern Mediterranean, Egypt, and Iran in the East.

However, it was in the rare area of pre-Roman glass, in the mosaic and core-formed vessels, that the most competitive bidding arose. An amethyst and emerald green mosaic glass plate of the 1st century BC or early 1st century AD reached £43,200 ($47,520). An amethyst, white and turquoise mosaic glass footed bowl, made up of recycled ribbon and mosaic glass fragments of the late 2nd–1st century BC, fetched £41,040 ($45,144; see page 359). But it was the diminutive cameo flask, which combined rarity and exquisite quality, dating from 25 BC–AD25, which was the most keenly sought-after, being secured on behalf of the J. Paul Getty Museum for a record price of £324,000 ($356,400; see this page).

On the second day, fused mosaic glass fragments and opaque glass inlays captured the interest of Egyptian and glass collectors alike. A fused mosaic inlay of an Apis bull dating from the 1st century BC or 1st century AD reached £30,240 ($33,264). Core-formed vessels from the 6th–1st centuries BC attracted high prices, with an Achaemenid square *kohl*-flask of the 5th–4th century BC being secured by an American private collector for £54,160 ($59,576; see page 360). But it was the rare appearance on the market of Egyptian glass of such quality from the 18th Dynasty (*c.* 14th century BC) which attracted the major prices after the cameo flask. An opaque greyish-blue core-formed krateriskos with yellow and white marvered trails realised £91,800 ($100,980); a cast inlay of an 'Amarna' royal head made £86,400 ($95,040; see page 359); and a brilliant turquoise, yellow and white palm-column *kohl*-flask secured the second top price in the sale at £237,600 ($261,360; see page 359).

Above left:
Palm-column *kohl*-flask
Late Dynasty XVIII, from Amarna
Core formed
3¾ in. (9.9 cm.) high; 1½ in. (4 cm.) diameter
Sold 6.3.85 in London for £237,600 ($261,360)

Above:
Footed bowl
Late 2nd–1st century BC, Eastern Mediterranean
Mosaic glass technique
1¾ in. (4.5 cm.) high; 3½ in. (8.8 cm.) diameter
Sold 5.3.85 in London for £41,040 ($45,144)

Left:
Inlay of a royal head
Late Dynasty XVIII
Cast
1½ in. (4 cm.) high; 1 in. (2.8 cm.) wide
Sold 6.3.85 in London for £86,400 ($95,040)

Above:
Skyphos
Mid – late 1st century BC, from France
Cast and lathe cut
2¼ in. (5.5. cm.) high; 5 in. (12.3 cm.) diameter across
handles
Sold 5.3.85 in London for £45,360 ($49,896)

Right:
Kohl-flask
5th–4th century BC, Achaemenid
Core formed
3½ in. (8.8 cm.) high
Sold 6.3.85 in London for £54,160 ($59,576)

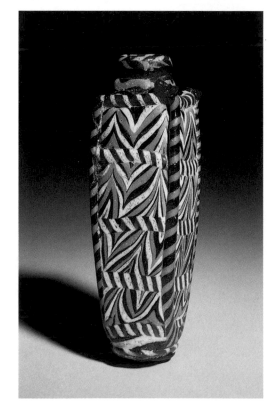

Egyptian bronze figure of
Wadjet, the lion-headed
goddess
Late Period
Inscribed round the base
'May Wadjet give life to
Prbkhr (?) son of Hor'
21¼ × 6¾ × 4½ in.
(54 × 17 × 11.5 cm.)
Sold 12.12.84 in London for
£70,000 ($85,400)

Marble head of a Maenad
Roman copy after a Greek
original of 4th century BC
10¼ in. (26 cm.) high
Sold 16.7.85 in London for
£21,600 ($28,080)

Attic red-figure
Stamnos
By the Painter of
Yale Oinochoe
*c.*460 BC
13³⁄₈ in. (34 cm.)
high; 10³⁄₄ in.
(27.5 cm.) diameter
Sold 12.12.84 in
London for £11,880
($14,375)

Yoruba wood bowl and co
By Olowe of Ise
25 in. (63.5 cm.) high
Sold 24.6.85 in London fo
£162,000 ($200,000)
By order of the
Administrators of the late
William J. Moore

Opposite right:
Fang wood female reliquary
figure
By Ntumu of North Gabon
21½ in. (55 cm.) high
Sold 28.11.84 in New York at
Christie's East for $71,500
(£58,610)

Opposite far right:
Caroline Islands wood wind
charm
Mogemog Island
17 in. (43 cm.) high
Sold 28.11.84 in New York at
Christie's East for $16,500
(£13,520)

Ottawa black-dyed tanned
skin pouch
Late 18th century
11 in. (28 cm.) wide
Sold 28.11.84 in New York at
Christie's East for $23,100
(£18,930)
From the collection of
E.B. Gray, Esq.

Ceramics and Glass

Two from a set of five Fürstenberg shaped rectangular plaques
Painted by Johann Heinrich Eisenträger
*c.*1765
5 × 6½ in. (12.5 × 16.5 cm.)
Sold 1.7.85 in London for £21,600 ($28,100)

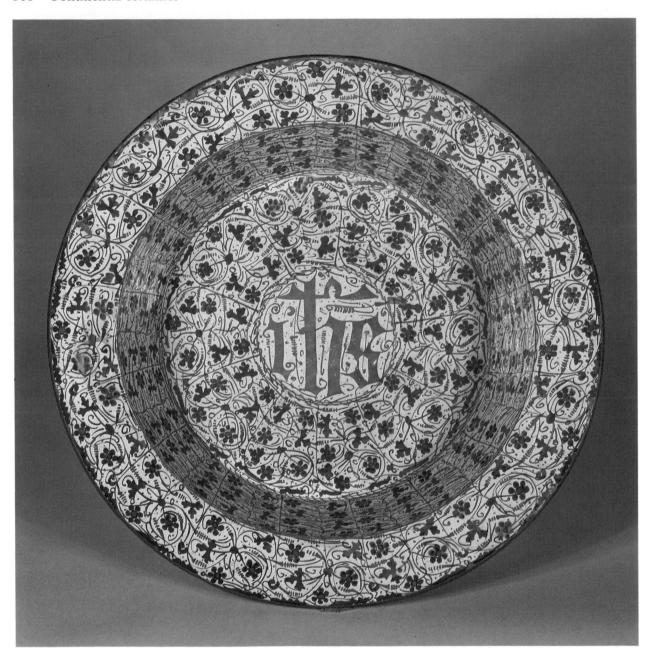

Hispano-Moresque blue and copper lustre
deep-dish
Valencia, mid-15th century
19 in. (48 cm.) diameter
Sold 1.7.85 in London for £45,360 ($58,970)

Opposite:
Tuscan two-handled armorial albarello
*c.*1470
6½ in. (16.5 cm.) high
Sold 1.7.85 in London for £32,400 ($42,120)

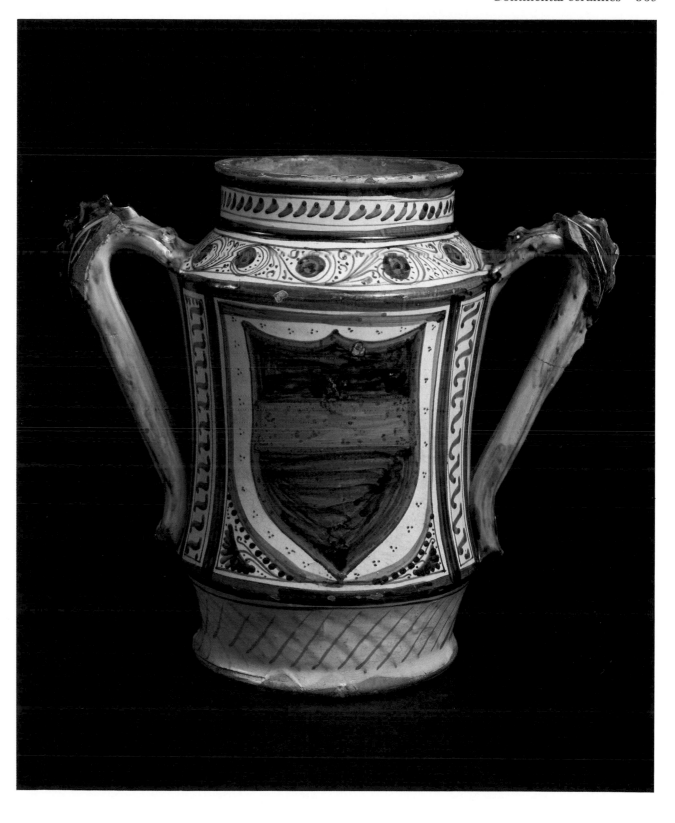

Pair of Tournai
faience figures of
pug-dogs
After the Meissen
models by
J.J. Kändler
*c.*1765
6 in. (15 cm.) high
Sold 25.3.85 in
London for £9,720
($11,372)

Pair of Strasbourg
faience partridge
tureens and covers
Paul Hannong
period
1748–54
8¼ in. (21 cm.) long
Sold 30.1.85 in New
York at Christie's
East for $18,700
(£16,400)

Centre:
Würzburg white figure of Pantalone
From the Commedia dell'Arte modelled by or after Ferdinand Tietz
1775–80
5 in. (12.5 cm.) high
Sold for Sw.fr.17,600 (£5,382)

Left and right:
Pair of Würzburg figures of gardeners
*c.*1770
6 in. (15 cm.) high
Sold for Sw.fr.41,800 (£12,782)

Both sold 13.5.85 in Geneva

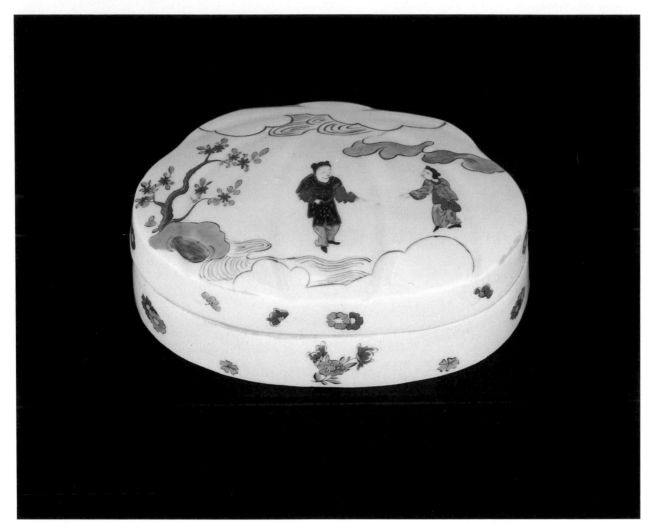

Meissen Kakiemon-shaped toilet box and cover formed as an awabi shell
1728–30
4 $\frac{1}{2}$ in. (11.5 cm.) wide
Sold 13.5.85 in Geneva for Sw.fr.66,000 (£20,183)

Meissen Bergleute
rectangular snuff-box
Painted by Bonaventura
Gottlieb Hauer
*c.*1745
3¼ in. (8 cm.) wide
Sold 3.12.84 in London for
£21,600 ($25,920)

Meissen K.P.M. oval
snuff-box
Painted after Petrus Schenck
and in the manner of
A.F. von Löwenfinck
*c.*1730
3 in. (7 cm.) wide
Sold for Sw.fr.66,000
(£20,183)

Meissen gold-mounted
K.P.M. chinoiserie oval
snuff-box
Painted by Johann Gregor
Herold
*c.*1728
3 in. (7 cm.) wide
Sold for Sw.fr.77,000
(£23,547)

Both sold 13.5.85 in Geneva

Meissen chinoiserie table-bell
c.1730
5¼ in. (13 cm.) high
Sold 12.11.84 in Geneva for
Sw.fr.88,000 (£28,387)

Meissen helmet-
shaped ewer and
basin
*c.*1740
The ewer 9 in.
(22 cm.) high
The basin 12¾ in.
(32 cm.) wide
Sold 3.12.84 in
London for £20,520
($24,624)
Now in the J. Paul
Getty Museum,
Malibu, California

Below left:
Bayreuth brown-
glazed red stoneware
circular slop-bowl
*c.*1730
6½ in. (16.5 cm.)
diameter
Sold for £1,944
($2,333)

Below centre:
Bayreuth brown-
glazed red stoneware
pear-shaped coffee-
pot and cover
Gilt in the manner of
Metzsch
*c.*1730
8 in. (20 cm.) high
Sold for £6,480
($7,776)

Below right:
Bayreuth brown-
glazed red stoneware
tea-caddy and cover
*c.*1730
4½ in. (11 cm.) high
Sold for £4,104
($4,925)

All sold 3.12.84 in
London

Opposite:
Pair of Sèvres-pattern ormolu-mounted royal-blue-ground two-handled vases and covers
Last quarter 19th century
59¼ in. (150 cm.) high
Sold 3.10.84 in London for £37,800 ($47,250)

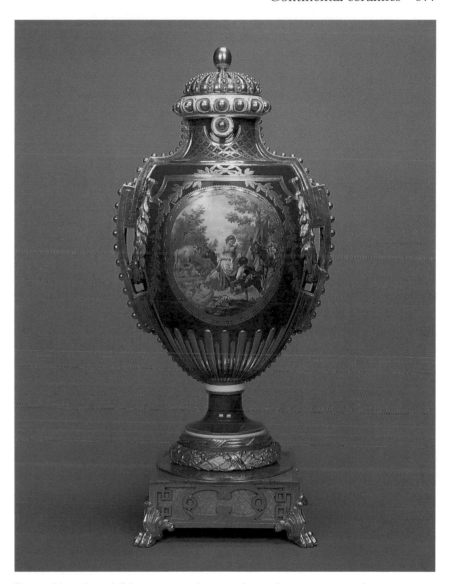

Sèvres bleu-du-roi (bleu nouveau) ground vase à panneaux and cover on ormolu base
*c.*1770
22½ in. (57 cm.) high
Sold 30.1.85 in New York at Christie's East for $46,200 (£40,530)

THE CHATEAUBRIAND SERVICE

Sèvres dessert service comprising: an oval sauce-
tureen, cover and fixed stand; four circular
pedestal bowls on spreading gilt socles; 60 plates
Sold 1.7.85 in London for £51,840 ($67,390)
The service was delivered upon the order of The
Minister of the King's Household to the Vicomte
de Chateaubriand, the Minister for Foreign
Affairs, on 21 August 1823. The order was a
supplement to the service ordered in two different
batches whilst Chateaubriand was Ambassador to
England. The previous orders were delivered on 15
April 1822 and 2 May 1822. The order of 21
August 1823 comprised:

100 assiettes plates	40/4,000	
4 corbeilles rondes	140/560	
1 jatte à pied	50	
	4,610	

It is quite clear that the present lot is from this last
delivery only. It was evidently a Royal gift. The
painters of the pieces in this service are Jacques-
Nicolas Sinnson 1795–1845, Joseph-Léopold
Weydinger 1778–1804, 1807–8, 1811, 1816–29,
and Jean François Desnoyers-Chaponnet *aîné*. The
archives at the Manufacture Nationale de Sèvres
fully record which pieces of the service were packed
in which box and the painters' register documents
which pieces were painted by which artist. Few
services can be more completely documented, as
the Archives record every stage of the decoration of
each piece.
François de Chateaubriand, 1768–1848, was a
distinguished man of letters and diplomatist. Born
in Britanny, he started his career in 1791 with a
visit to America. He travelled widely to Berlin,
Prague, Vienna and Jerusalem. He was in London
from 1792 to 1800 and again as Ambassador to the
Court of St. James in 1822. He was also
Ambassador to Berlin and Rome. The present lot
was given during his period of office as Foreign
Minister. He was an acute observer of the people
and events of his day, an extravagant and active
man, and included Madame Récamier among his
mistresses. He is perhaps most widely known
because his chef Montmiriel invented the special
filet steak cut which is known as a Chateaubriand.

Opposite:
Twenty-three figures from the Meissen *Cris de Paris* series
Sold 13.5.85 in Geneva for a total of Sw.fr.298,210 (£91,195)
Modelled in 1753 and following years this was the most extensive figure
series produced at the factory. In all, it totalled 36 characters. Many of these
have in the past not been properly identified as part of the set. However,
since they are all taken from drawings by Huet still in the possession of the
Meissen factory there can be no doubt as to the figures that actually compose
the series. More interestingly there can also be no doubt as to the correct
interpretation of each character, as these are clearly named on the original
drawings. The *Pressnummer* on each figure should correspond to a Huet
drawing, though some of the numbering is erratic. Only by looking at the
drawings is it possible to appreciate how skilfully Kändler and Reinicke
translated two-dimensional drawn ideas into the three-dimensional material
of porcelain without sacrificing any of the impact of the original conception.

Florentine famiglia gotica two-handled drug-jar
Third quarter 15th century
11½ in. (29 cm.) high
Sold 3.12.84 in London for £30,240 ($36,288)

Far right:
Worcester flared wine-funnel
c. 1755
5¼ in. (13.5 cm.) high
Sold 3.6.85 in London for
£12,960 ($16,950)

Right:
Worcester oviform vase
c. 1760
6¾ in. (17 cm.) high
Sold 1.10.84 in London for
£3,780 ($4,725)
From the collection of Brigadier
Douglas Phelps

Worcester yellow-scale
baluster milk-jug and
cover
c. 1765
5½ in. (14 cm.) high
Sold 17.12.84 in London
for £9,180 ($11,016)

Chelsea octagonal tea-
bowl and saucer
Painted in the manner of
O'Neale
*c.*1752
Sold 17.12.84 in London
for £2,808 ($3,370)

Chelsea oval sauceboat
with scroll handle
Painted in the manner of
O'Neale
*c.*1753
9 in. (22.8 cm.) wide
Sold 3.6.85 in London for
£14,040 ($17,970)

Chelsea billing dove
tureen and cover
c. 1755
18 in. (45.5 cm.)
long
Sold 23.10.84 in
New York at
Christie's East for
$18,700 (£15,330)

Pair of Chelsea
artichoke-tureens
and covers
c. 1755
6½ in. (16 cm.) high
Sold 18.3.85 in
London for £17,280
($19,353)
These are recorded
as 'Two fine
artichoaks' in the
1755 Chelsea sale
catalogue on the
fourteenth day's sale,
Tuesday 25 March,
lots 107 and 108

Pair of Worcester
hexagonal vases and
domed covers
c.1765
11½ in.
(29 cm.) high
Sold for £14,040
($17,550)

One of a pair of
Worcester powder-
blue-ground
hexagonal vases and
domed covers
c.1768
15 in. (38 cm.) high
Sold for £10,800
($13,500)

Both sold 1.10.84 in
London
From the collection
of Brigadier Douglas
Phelps

Left:
Bristol Delft blue and white documentary deep bowl
Inscribed 'IOSEPH: SPRINGALL: WHOLE: SALE: POTTER:
IN: MATTSHALL: IN: THE: COUNTY: OF: NORFOLK:'
*c.*1735
14 in. (35 cm.) diameter
Sold 3.6.85 in London for £8,640 ($11,060)

Below:
London Delft dated polychrome armorial drug-jar,
with the arms of the Worshipful Society of
Apothecaries on a shield above the motto *Opifer Que
Per Orbem Dicor*
*c.*1656
14½ in. (36 cm.) high
Sold 3.6.85 in London for £19,440 ($24,880)

Opposite left:
Worcester fluted trio
*c.*1775
Sold for £2,376 ($2,970)

Opposite centre:
Worcester faceted baluster coffee-pot and domed cover
*c.*1765
8¾ in.
(22.5 cm.) high
Sold for £2,160 ($2,700)

Opposite right:
Worcester coffee-cup and saucer from the Stormont Service
*c.*1770
Sold for £3,024 ($3,780)

All sold 1.10.84 in London
From the collection of Brigadier Douglas Phelps

Above:
Copeland blue-ground dessert-service,
comprising two lozenge-shaped cache-
pots, two tall lozenge-shaped tazzas,
four low lozenge-shaped tazzas and
18 octagonal plates
*c.*1870
Sold 18.3.85 in London for £5,184
($5,806)

Right:
Whieldon group of lovers
*c.*1750
4¾ in. (12 cm.) wide
Sold 18.3.85 in London for £8,640
($9,676)

Pair of 'Vienna' slender oviform vases, covers and waisted circular plinths
Signed Kreigsa
*c.*1880
44½ in. (113 cm.) high
Sold 18.3.85 in London for £5,616 ($6,289)

Below:
One of 12 Minton turquoise-ground dessert-plates
Attributed to Henry Mitchell, the centres painted in the manner of Landseer with wild and domestic animals in their natural habitats
Date code for 1873
10 in. (25.5 cm.) diameter
Sold 15.7.85 in London for £1,728 ($2,280)

Unrecorded signed royal armorial
goblet
By William Beilby
Inscribed *Success to the African trade of
WHITE-HAVEN*, signed below *Beilby junr.
invt. & Pinxt.*
*c.*1762
10 in. (25 cm.) high
Sold 4.6.85 in London for £56,160
($72,450)
Record auction price for any piece of
18th-century English glass

Stipple-engraved goblet
By Frans Greenwood
*c.*1744
9½ in. (24.3 cm.) high
Sold 4.6.85 in London for £32,400
($41,800)
From the collection of the Earl of
Bradford

Dated enamelled carafe
Inscribed *Tho. Worrall 1757*
9 in. (22 cm.) high
Sold 4.6.85 in London for £6,264 ($8,080)

Far right:
Plain-stemmed landscape wine-glass
By David Wolff
The Hague, 1790
6 in. (15 cm.) high
Sold 4.6.85 in London for £5,940 ($7,660)

Right:
Dated Union armorial wine-glass
By David Wolff
Inscribed DE UNIE DOOR PRUYSEN NAEST GODT
BEHOUDEN (The Union saved by God and Prussia)
The Hague, 1787
6½ in. (16 cm.) high
Sold 4.6.85 in London for £5,940 ($7,660)

Far right:
Facet-stemmed friendship wine-glass
By Jacob Sang
Inscribed DIE VRIENDSCHAP UIT DIT LEEVE SLUIT, DIE
BANDT DE ZON DE WEERELDT UIT (He who excludes
friendship from this life, Expels the sun from the
world)
Amsterdam, 1761
7 in. (17.8 cm.) high
Sold 4.6.85 in London for £8,100 ($10,450)

Right:
One of a series of 12 dated polder glasses of De
Hooge Maasdijk
1762–84
7½ in. (19.5 cm.) high
Sold 4.6.85 in London for £54,000 ($69,600)

All from the collection of the Earl of Bradford

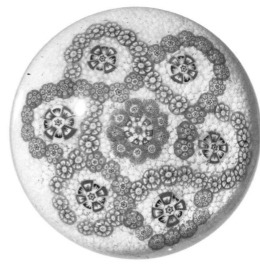

Far left:
Clichy concentric millefiori
pedestal weight
3 in. (7.5 cm.) diameter
Sold 14.3.85 in New York for
$22,000 (£19,820)

Left:
Baccarat white carpet-ground
patterned millefiori weight
3 in. (7.5 cm.) diameter
Sold 27.11.84 in London for
£3,780 ($4,574)

Left:
Baccarat large flat bouquet
weight
$3\frac{9}{16}$ in. (9 cm.) diameter
Sold 14.3.85 in New York for
$14,300 (£12,883)

Far left:
Clichy flat bouquet weight
$3\frac{1}{8}$ in. (8 cm.) diameter
Sold 14.3.85 in New York for
$20,900 (£18,829)

Far left:
St. Louis encased pink-
overlay upright bouquet
weight
3 in. (7.5 cm.) diameter
Sold 27.11.84 in London for
£6,490 ($8,360)

Left:
Baccarat flat bouquet weight
$3\frac{1}{8}$ in. (8 cm.) diameter
Sold 27.11.84 in London for
£9,720 ($12,540)

Oriental Ceramics and Works of Art

Engraved gilt-bronze censer and pierced cover
Tang Dynasty
5½ in. (14 cm.) high;
6 in. (15 cm.) overall width
Sold 6.6.85 in New York for $104,500 (£80,384)

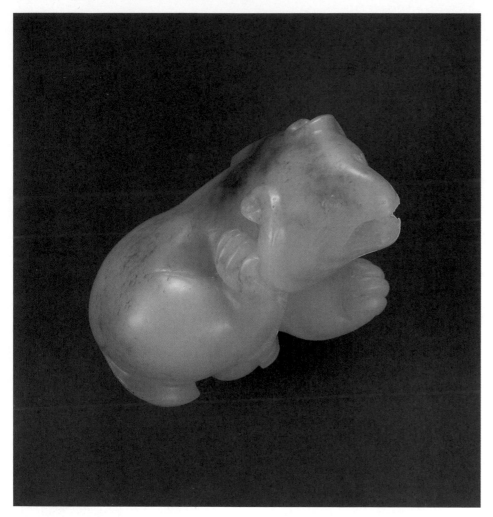

Muttonfat carving of a ruffle-necked bear
Han Dynasty
3 in. (7.5 cm.) wide
Sold 6.6.85 in New York for $88,000 (£67,692)

Gilt-bronze reliquary and
cover
Early Tang Dynasty
7 ½ in. (19.2 cm.) high
Sold 10.12.84 in London for
£73,440 ($88,838)

Blue and white and
underglaze-copper-red pear-
shaped vase
Encircled Yongzheng six-
character mark and of the
period
14 in. (35.1 cm.) high
Sold 10.12.84 in London for
£27,760 ($33,590)
From the collection of
Dr R.L. Carter

Opposite:
Blue and white dragon jar
14th century
25¼ in. (64 cm.) high; 21 in.
(53 cm.) diameter
Sold 7.12.84 in London for
£108,000 ($130,680)
Record auction price for an
Annamese work of art
This appears to be the largest
known example of Annamese
blue and white ceramics. The
style of the dragons, their fire
scrolls, the lappets and the
waves all have their parallels
in Chinese Yuan Dynasty
material.

Above:
Chinese Imari garniture
Early Qianlong
The jars 26½ in. (67 cm.)
high
The vases 19 in. (48 cm.) high
All sold 13.11.84 in London
for £20,520 ($26,471)

Left:
Pair of famille rose teapots
and covers
Qianlong
6¼ in. (16 cm.) high
Sold 29.11.84 in New York
for $41,800 (£32,656)

'European procession'
punch bowl
Qianlong
15½ in. (39.8 cm.)
diameter
Sold 9.7.85 in London
for £22,680 ($30,618)

Famille rose
European-subject
hunting bowl
Qianlong, c.1760
16 in. (41 cm.)
diameter
Sold 22.5.85 in New
York for $24,200
(£18,759)

Famille rose Dutch East India
Company cup and saucer,
with the initials V.O.C. and
the motto of the CONCORDIA
RESPARVAE CRESCUNT
*c.*1730
The saucer 4 in. (10.5 cm.)
diameter
Sold 6.6.85 in Amsterdam for
D.fl.31,920 (£7,254)
Record auction price for a
famille rose Dutch East India
Company cup and saucer

Above:
Pair of European-subject wedding
presentation plates
Qianlong
9 in. (23 cm.) diameter
Both sold 13.11.84 in London for
£9,720 ($12,539)

Right:
Encre-de-Chine Table Bay plate
*c.*1750–70
9 in. (23 cm.) diameter
Sold 6.6.85 in Amsterdam for
D.fl.44,080 (£10,018)

Far left:
Gandharan grey schist figure
of Maitreya
Pakistan, 2nd – 3rd century
48 in. (121.8 cm.) high
Sold 30.11.84 in New York
for $88,000 (£68,750)

Left:
Marble figure of Buddha
Northern Qi Dynasty,
6th century
38⅛ in. (97 cm.) high
Sold 30.11.84 in New York
for $121,000 (£94,531)

American market documentary famille rose oblong octagonal soup tureen and cover, showing the surrrender of General Burgoyne to the American General Gates, after the Battle of Saratoga

*c.*1840

13 1/4 in. (34 cm.) wide

Sold 22.5.85 in New York for $26,500 (£20,542)

This extremely rare form of decoration only exists on two other documented examples, namely, an oval platter in The Diplomatic Reception Rooms of the United States Department of State, and a punch bowl now in the White House. The surrender of Lieutenant-General John Burgoyne to the American General Horatio Gates took place on 17 October 1777. This service was probably made to commemorate the 60th anniversary of the event in 1837, and the scene is probably after a painting by John Trumbull, now in the Yale University Museum.

Wen Jia (1501–83)
Scenery of the Studio of Southern Village (Nan-cun cao-tang tu)
Ink and colour on paper
Inscribed 'In the mid-summer of Bing-zi year of Wanli era, I followed the style of Huang-ho shan ren's (Wang Meng, 1308–85) Nan-cun cao-tang tu'
Signed Wen Jia of Mou-yuan (Suzhou)
Sold 30.11.84 in New York for $71,500 (£58,606)

Opposite:
Artist unknown, but probably by Du Jin (15th century)
Fu-Sheng writing Classics in the Garden
Hanging scroll, ink and colour on silk
57 7/8 × 41 1/8 in.
(147 × 104.5 cm.)
Sold 5.6.85 in New York for $71,500 (£55,000)

Sixteenth-century lacquer Christian portable shrine or retable, known in Japan as Seigan, 'niche for a holy image'
*c.*1590–1614
19½ in. (49 cm.) high; 11½ in. (29.7 cm.) wide; 2 in. (4.9 cm.) deep; 24 in. (60 cm.) wide with doors open
Sold 22.5.85 in London for £81,000 ($105,300)

Momoyama period
Christian folding
missal stand
(Shokendai)
*c.*1600
16½ × 11 in.
(42.9 × 27.1 cm.)
Sold 27.11.84 in
London for £64,800
($78,408)

Omori School Tsuba
Dated *Meiwa kinoto rokugestsu kichinichi* (Meiwa 7, 1770), signed *Ryausai sai Omori Teruhide* (Eishu) with *kakihan*
Sold 20.3.85 in New York for $13,200 (£10,909)

Osaka School ivory netsuke of a grazing horse
Late 18th or early 19th century
Inscribed *Gechu*
Sold 2.10.84 in New York for $24,200 (£19,360)

Pair of large gold lacquer cylindrical vases, decorated in Shibayama style
Late 19th century
Each signed within a floral cartouche *Gyokukendo Kaneko san*
14½ in. (36.5 cm.) high
Sold 12.3.85 in London for £7,560 ($8,316)

Myochin School Uchidashi
Tosei-Gusoku
The *sode* dated cyclically
Kyoho Mizuno-to-u (1723) and
the *mempo* *c.*1848, the *sode*
signed *Myochin Osumi no kami
ki Munesude tsukuru*, the *mempo*
signed *Myochin Shinbachiro
Muneyuki*
Sold 20.3.85 in New York for
$25,300 (£20,909)
Record auction price for a
Japanese suit of armour

Opposite:
Myochin School russet iron
somen
17th century
The *mempo* signed *Myochin ki
Munekata*
Sold 20.3.85 in New York for
$16,500 (£13,636)

Two Ko-Imari jars and covers
c.1660–80
Both about 13 in. (33 cm.) high
Sold 2.7.85 in London for £21,600 ($28,080)

Opposite right:
Kakiemon figure of a
standing bijin
Late 17th century
14½ in. (36 cm.) high
Sold 12.3.85 in London for
£9,720 ($10,692)

Opposite far right:
Imari model of a roistering
Dutchman seated astride a
Dutch gin (jenever) cask
Late 17th century
14 in. (35.8 cm.) high
Sold 27.11.84 in London for
£18,369 ($22,216)
Originating from a Dutch
Delft design, very few of
these models are known.
A blue and white example is
in the British Museum and
there are three similar
coloured versions in Japan.
One is in a private collection,
another is in the Idemitsu
Museum in Tokyo and the
third is in the Kurita
Collection.
Volker states that the Dutch
registers refer to statuettes in
underglaze blue and it is
possible that this may include
the above.
Although most probably for
gin, other Delft models are
recorded with various
inscriptions for alcohols.

SHARAKU
Oban tate-e; okubi-e portrait of the
actor Matsumoto Koshiro IV in
the role of Sanya no Sakanaya
Gorobei, 'the fishmonger of
Sanya, Gorobei', from the play
Katakiuchi noriyai-banashi
performed at the Kiri-za
Signed *Toshusai Sharaku ga* and
published by Tsutaya Juzaburo
Sold 4.12.84 in New York for
$44,000 (£36,065)
In this role Matsumoto Koshiro
IV plays the noble fishmonger
Gorobei who aids the daughters
of the murdered Matsushita
Mikinoshin, Miyagino Shinobu,
in the play *Katakiuchi noriyai-
banashi*

SHARAKU

Oban tate-e; okubi-e portrait of the actor Ichikawa Ebizo IV in the role of Takemura Sadanoshin, father of Shigenoi from the play *Koinyobo somewake tazuna* performed at the Kawarazaki-za Signed *Toshusai Sharaku ga, kiwame* seal and published by Tsutaya Juzaburo
Sold 20.3.85 in New York for $63,800 (£52,727)

Monumental Thai stone head of Buddha
Ayuthya, 15th century
22½ in. (57 cm.) high
Sold 5.7.85 in London for £3,564 ($4,633)

Tibetan gilt-bronze group of
Mahacakravajrapani
16th century
16½ in. (42 cm.) high
Sold 22.11.84 in London for
£2,484 ($3,105)

Top:
Qajar polychrome lacquered papier-mâché
Qalamdan, the top painted with a scene of Youssef
being tempted by Zulaika
Signed *Sadiq after Lutf 'Ali Ashraf*
Dated 1201 (AD 1787)
10 in. (25 cm.) long
Sold 5.7.85 in London for £7,560 ($9,828)

Above:
Large Mamluk brass candlestick base, with areas
of silver inlay
14th century
8 in. (20.5 cm.) diameter
Sold 23.11.84 in London for £2,700 ($3,375)

Portrait of 'Imad al-Daulah, Imam Quli Khan
By Abu'l Hasan Khan Ghaffari, Sani' al-Mulk Qajar, *c.*1855–60
Oil on canvas
$25\frac{5}{8} \times 23\frac{1}{2}$ in. (72.8 × 62.3 cm.)
Sold 22.11.84 in London for £43,200 ($51,840)
A portrait of exceptional quality and a very rare example of oil painting by this artist, Abu'l Hasan Khan Ghaffari (*c.*1814–66), who was the most outstanding painter working during the reigns of Muhammad Shah and Nasr al-Din Shah.
'Imad al-Daulah, Imam Quli Khan (1814–75) was the sixth son of Muhammad 'Ali Mirza and a grandson of Fath 'Ali Shah. He was Governor of Khermanshah and Khuristan, and received the title of 'Imad in 1852–3.

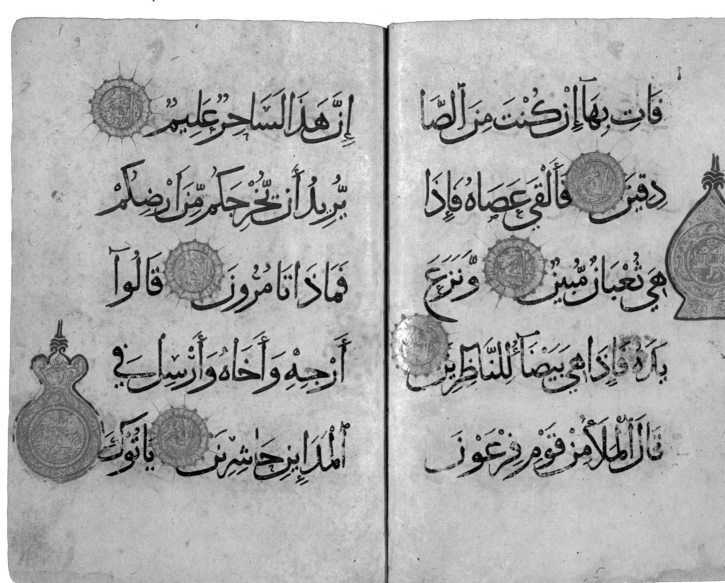

QUR'AN SECTION: JUZ IX
Seljuk, *c.* 1190
Folio 8½ × 5⅞ in. (21.5 × 15 cm.)
Sold 22.11.84 in London for £59,400 ($71,289)

The style of illumination with triple dot motif on ground of scrolling palmettes indicates a Seljuk provenance. It seems highly probable that this is one of the 30 *Juz*, mentioned extensively by Ibn ar-Rawandi in *Rahat as-Sudur* for its beautiful gilding and illumination (being a History of the Seljukids), which was written by the last of the Seljukid rulers, Tughrul III. He studied calligraphy with an uncle of Ibn ar-Rawandi, and having completed the Qur'an, spending large sums on its illumination, distributed the *Juz* to his friends.

Tughrul III was born in 1173, succeeded to the throne in 1186, and in 1188 defeated the caliphal forces at Dai-Mong near Hamadan. However, he was forced to surrender to Qizil-Arslan in 1190 and was imprisoned in a castle near Tabriz for two years. He died in 1194 when the Seljuk army was defeated outside Ray.

QUR'AN

Persia or Iraq, *c.* AD 950

Folio 3⅞ × 3¼ in. (9.7 × 8 cm.)

Sold 4.7.85 in London for £70,200 ($91,260)

An extremely rare and early example of a Qur'an written in Eastern *kufic* on vellum. By the beginning of the 10th century 'bent' or 'Eastern' *kufic* had evolved from the parent known as 'square' *kufic* as a clearly identifiable script. Usually found on paper, which was becoming widely used by this time in a vertical format, there are nonetheless a few known examples of vellum Qur'ans in public collections, notably the British Library and the Chester Beatty Library, all in a larger format.

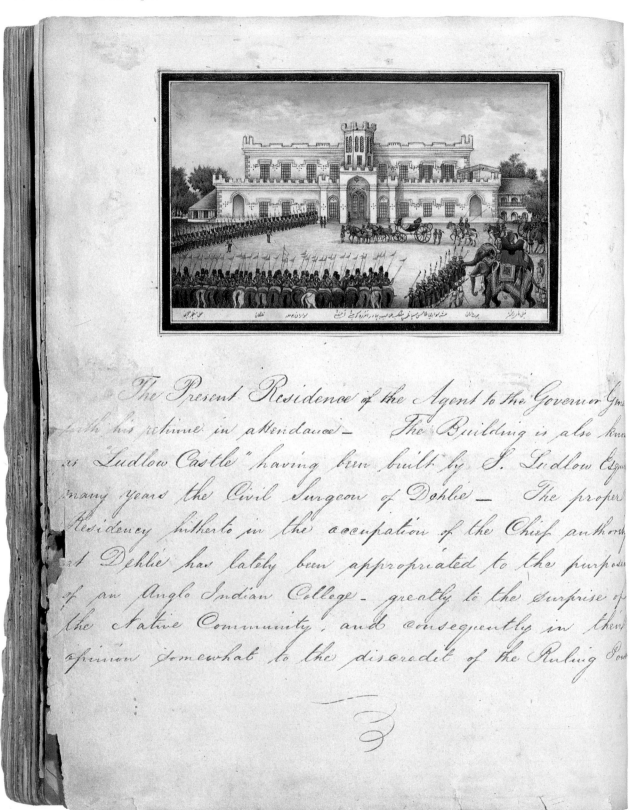

The Present Residence of the Agent to the Governor General with his retinue in attendance — The Building is also known as "Ludlow Castle" having been built by S. Ludlow Esquire many years the Civil Surgeon of Dehlie — The proper Residency hitherto in the occupation of the Chief authority at Dehlie has lately been appropriated to the purposes of an Anglo Indian College — greatly to the Surprise of the Native Community, and consequently in their opinion somewhat to the discredit of the Ruling Power

SIR THOMAS METCALFE
Reminiscences of Imperial Dehlie
Delhi, 1844
An album illustrating the principal architectural monuments, the rulers, life and ceremonial of Imperial Mughal Delhi
Contemporary black morocco binding
10 × 7¾ in.
(25.4 × 19.8 cm.)
Sold 4.7.85 in London for £23,760 ($30,888)
Sir Thomas Metcalfe followed his father, Sir Thomas Metcalfe, into the Indian service in 1813 and sailed for Delhi. He spent most of his life in or near the Mughal capital, and purchased land on the banks of the Jumna – an estate of a thousand acres, where he built Metcalfe House, surrounding it with trees, artificial lakes and beautiful gardens. In 1846 he succeeded his brother Charles to the position of British Resident and Agent to the Governor-General at the Mughal Court in Delhi and died mysteriously in 1853 from some subtle poison.

Modern Decorative Arts

'Inspiration' coffee-
service
Hand-painted Bizarre
by Clarice Cliff
Wilkinson Ltd.,
England
c.1930
The coffee-pot
8 in. (20.3 cm.) high
Sold 30.4.85 in
London for £5,184
($6,584)

Copper urn
Designed by Frank Lloyd
Wright
Probably executed by James
A. Miller for the Edward C.
Waller House,
Riverforest, Illinois
*c.*1899
18 in. (46 cm.) high
Sold 14.12.84 in New York
for $93,500 (£77,917)
Record auction price for a
Frank Lloyd Wright object

Opposite far left:
Oriental poppy leaded-glass
and bronze floor lamp
By Tiffany Studios
26 in. (66 cm.) diameter;
79½ in. (203 cm.) high
Sold 30.3.85 in New York for
$143,000 (£113,492)
From the collection of
Burt Sugerman

Opposite left:
Magnolia leaded-glass and
bronze floor lamp
By Tiffany Studios
28 in. (71.1 cm.) diameter;
79½ in. (203 cm.) high
Sold 30.3.85 in New York for
$528,000 (£436,364)
Record auction price for a
Tiffany lamp
From the collection of
David Geffen

Inlaid silver Indian-style bowl
By Tiffany & Company for the Columbian Exposition
*c.*1893
6½ in. (16.5 cm.) high; 12½ in. (31.7 cm.) diameter
Sold 23.5.85 in New York for $63,800 (£49,840)

Octagonal Honduras mahogany living-room table
Designed by Greene & Greene
Executed in the workshop of Peter Hall for the living-room of the Charles
M. Pratt House, Ojai, California
*c.*1909
54 in. (137.2 cm.) wide; 36 in. (91.5 cm.) deep; 29⅛ in. (74 cm.) high
Sold 14.6.85 in New York for $242,000 (£186,153)

Ebénè de Macassar and gilt-bronze desk
By Emile-Jacques Ruhlmann
c. 1929
82 in. (208 cm.) wide; 47 in. (119.5 cm.) deep; 30¼ in. (77 cm.) high
Sold 15.12.84 in New York for $82,500 (£68,181)
From the collection of the Museum of Modern Art, New York

'Cherokee red' enamelled steel, American walnut and brass-plated metal desk and chair
Designed by Frank Lloyd Wright for the S.C. Johnson and Son Administration
Building, Racine, Wisconsin
Executed by Steelcase
c.1936–9
28¾ in. (73 cm.) high; 84 in. (213 cm.) long; 34⅞ in. (88.5 cm.) deep
Sold 14.12.84 in New York for $77,000 (£64,167)
Record auction price for Frank Lloyd Wright furniture

Bauhaus oak lath armchair
Designed by Marcel Breuer for the Bauhaus, Weimar
1924
37 $\frac{1}{4}$ in. (94.8 cm.) high; 22 in. (56 cm.) wide; 22 $\frac{1}{2}$ in. (57.1 cm.)
deep
Sold 30.4.85 in London for £22,680 ($28,804)

Oak music cabinet on stand
Designed by C.F.A. Voysey
for W. Ward Higgs
1898
57 in. (144.9 cm.) high; 41 in.
(104 cm.) wide; 18¾ in.
(47.2 cm.) deep
Sold 30.4.85 in London for
£32,400 ($41,148)
Voysey produced most of his
best furniture designs between
1895 and 1910. It was between
these years that this particular
cabinet was designed and a
year before his famous
Kelmscott cabinet of 1899.
Both cabinets are similar but
Voysey does not in this case
employ the elaborate brass
strap hinges and mounts as
found on the Kelmscott
cabinet. The music cabinet
and the Kelmscott cabinet
were commissioned by the
same patron, W. Ward Higgs.
It is presumed that the cabinet
was used at 23 Queensborough
Terrace, Bayswater (where
Voysey designed the complete
interior), to compliment the
Kelmscott cabinet. Voysey
began to work for Ward Higgs
in 1898 and family information
suggests that work on the
house went on until about
1903.

Wakeley & Wheeler silver cup and cover
Designed by R.Y. Gleadowe
Carved and engraved by G.T. Friend and retailed by the Goldsmiths &
Silversmiths Company
Birmingham silver marks for 1938
14³/₄ in. (37 cm.) high
Sold 30.4.85 in London for £8,100 ($10,287)

Le Chavalier Normand
Enamelled cast-iron mural consisting of 109 interlocking panels from the ocean liner *Normandie*
Designed by François-Louis Schmeid
Executed at Baudin Foundry
*c.*1932
144 × 300 in. (366 × 762 cm.)
Sold 30.3.85 in New York for $110,000 (£87,301)

Boxing Gloves
A pair of chaise longues
By De Sede
*c.*1978
70½ in. (178 cm.) long; 44¼ in. (112 cm.) wide; 33½ in. (85 cm.) high
Sold 8.11.84 in London for £7,020 ($9,126)

Wall plaque
Hand-painted Bizarre
by Clarice Cliff, A.J. Wilkinson, Burslem, England
Pre-1930
17½ in. (44.3 cm.) diameter
Sold 8.11.84 in London for £8,640 ($11,232)
From the collection of S. Daniels, Esq.
It is known that Clarice Cliff was a great admirer of the Diaghilev ballet, and was inspired by the bright colours
often used in the company's décor and costumes to reproduce, in a stylized form, scenes from some of the
productions. These plaques representing dancers are extremely rare, and were most certainly painted by Cliff
herself and sometimes possibly with the help of her lifelong friend, Hilda Lovatt. It was unusual for Cliff to keep
her own work and these plaques were usually given as gifts to her several assistants, known affectionately by Cliff
as her 'girls'.

Stoneware vase
By Hans Coper
Impressed HC seal
c. 1952
13 in. (33.2 cm.) diameter
Sold 22.7.85 in London for £12,960
($16,848)

Earthenware two-handled bread crock
By Michael Cardew
Impressed MC and Winchcombe Pottery
seals
c. 1935
14 in. (35 cm.) high
Sold 19.2.85 in London for £1,620
($1,798)

A group of porcelain
and stoneware
ceramics
By Lucie Rie
Impressed LR seal
*c.*1979–81
6¾ in. (17.4 cm.)
maximum diameter;
5 in. (12.9 cm.)
maximum height
Sold individually
19.2.85 in London for
a total of £5,333
($5,919)

Minton jardinière and stand
Designed by Albert Carrier
de Belleuse
Impressed Minton 990 and
date code for 1882
66½ in. (168 cm.) high
Sold 18.7.85 in London for
£25,920 ($33,696)

Arms and Armour and Modern Sporting Guns

Brunswick brass-covered wheel-lock belt pistol
*c.*1580
31¼ in. (79.4 cm.)
Sold 18.4.85 in London for £18,360 ($23,684)
This belongs to a rare group of firearms with similar stocks bearing the monogram of Herzog Julius of Brunswick-Wolfenbuettel (1558–89, succeeded 1568). A payment to the Brunswick gunmaker Ditrich Oberst for 100 pairs of pistols and a gun with brass stocks for the wedding of Herzog Julius's son, Prince Heinrich Julius (1564–1613), in 1585, may refer to some of them.

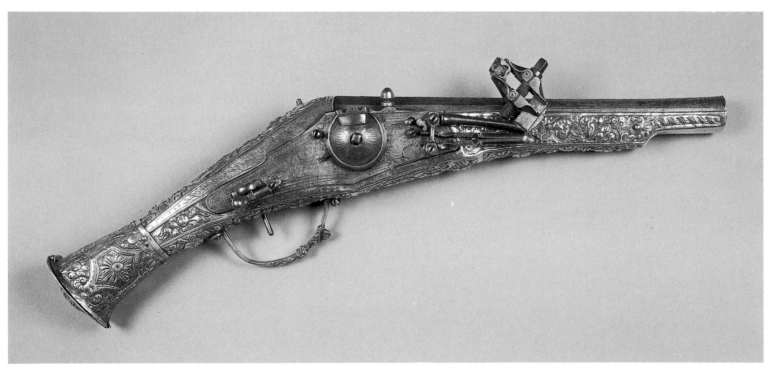

Embossed Italian
morion
Almost certainly by
Caremolo Modrone of
Mantua
c.1535–40
10 in. (25.4 cm.) high
Sold 18.4.85 in
London for £10,800
($13,932)

Saxon electoral guard comb morion
c. 1580
11 ¾ in. (29.8 cm.) high
Sold 31.10.84 in London for £10,260 ($12,517)
From the collection of Howard M. Curtis
The Curtis Collection of arms, armour and books, the most comprehensive one-owner dispersal in its specialized field for many years, totalled £275,211 ($334,656). The late Howard Curtis of Los Angeles (1927–79) was a leading Hollywood stunt man whose acrobatics include wing-walking in *The Great Waldo Pepper* and the cliff jump in *Butch Cassidy and the Sundance Kid.* Ironically, his untimely death resulted from a parachuting accident during a recreational fall.

French cased pair of exhibition rifled percussion pistols
Signed by the gunmaker 'Houllier Blanchard Breveté A Paris' and by the decorator 'J. Falloise. Gra. In. l844'
16¼ in. (41.3 cm.)
Sold 18.4.85 in London for £118,800 ($153,252)
Record auction price for a pair of pistols
Sold with two bronze medals awarded to Houllier Blanchard at the Great Exhibition of 1851 and the International Exhibition of 1862, both held in London, and a silver medal awarded at the Paris Exposition Universelle of 1867. The Reports of the Juries for the Great Exhibition record that the award was for 'showing a degree of perfection in workmanship rarely reached'. The pistols had never been sold previously, having remained in the possession of the descendants of Charles Hypolite Houllier (1811–71), founder of the firm Houllier Blanchard.

Cased Colt .44
sidehammer five-shot
percussion revolving
sporting rifle
No. 2416
Barrel 27 in. (68.6 cm.)
Sold 21.11.84 in London
for £16,200 ($20,250)

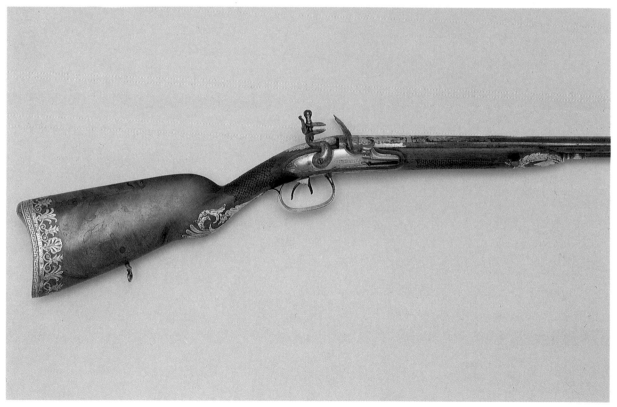

French d.b. silver-mounted flintlock sporting gun
By Fatou à Paris
Early 19th century
Barrels 32 in. (81.3 cm.)
Sold 8.5.85 in London for £23,760 ($30,888)
From the Calvin Bullock Collection (see p. 474)

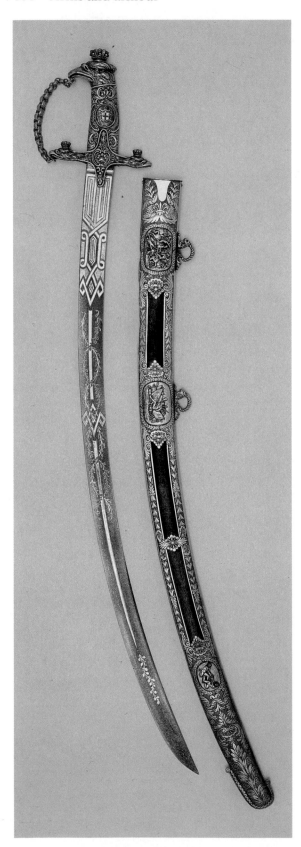

Silver-gilt mounted City of London sword
Signed Rundell Bridge and Rundell
Blade 29 in. (73.7 cm.)
Sold 8.5.85 in London for £19,440 ($25,272)
From the Calvin Bullock Collection (see p.474)
Presented to Field Marshal Count Barclay De Tolly, Commander in
Chief of the Russian Army in 1814.
This is one of four 200-guinea swords that it was resolved should be
presented to Allied Commanders, the others being Field Marshal
Blucher, Prince Schwarzenberg and Hetman Count Platoff.

'Modèle de luxe Self-Opener'
sidelock ejector 12-bore
(2¾ in.) d.b. gun
By Holland & Holland,
London
Built *c.* 1966
Sold 7.6.85 in New York at
Christie's East for $19,800
(£15,391)

Modern Sporting Guns

CHRISTOPHER BRUNKER

London's long association with the manufacture of fine sporting guns has made it the natural centre for international gun sales, but the arbitrary imposition of duty and VAT on British guns returned to the UK for sale from outside the EEC has proved a serious disadvantage for American owners, for whom no local equivalent outlet existed.

An important development, therefore, is the opening by Christie's of a modern gun department in New York, where the first major sale of sporting guns was held at Christie's East in June this year. The sale included 51 lots of modern sporting guns and about 100 lots of American collectable firearms (an established sale-category at Christie's in New York). The 'modern sporting' section, principally European arms, attracted keen international interest, which suggests that Christie's innovation of expertise and sales in New York will prove popular with American sellers and that New York's accessibility to buyers is comparable with London's.

In London, our traditional selective sales at King Street have continued to draw sellers and buyers from home and abroad, and the market has remained healthy, with about 38 per cent of the lots sold exceeding their top estimate. Our local service in this field has already been extended by the inclusion of modern firearms at Christie's South Kensington. In this category, the South Kensington sales are chiefly intended for items of moderate value, but they also offer sellers a speedier alternative to our major sales at King Street without moving out of the market centre that London affords.

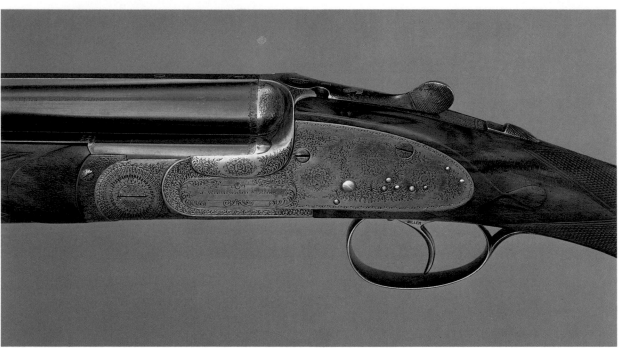

Pair of 'Under & Over' sidelock ejector 16-bore (2½ in.) d.b. guns, with extra barrels
By J. Woodward, London
Built in 1934; converted to single-trigger and restocked
Sold 19.6.85 in London for £30,240 ($40,219)
Record auction price for a pair of modern sporting guns

Pair of self-opening sidelock ejector 16-bore (2½ in.) d.b. guns, with extra barrels
By J. Purdey, London
Built in 1930
Sold 21.11.84 in London for £15,120 ($18,900)

Pair of self-opening sidelock ejector 12-bore (2½ in.) d.b. guns
By J. Purdey, London
Built in 1937
Sold 20.3.85 in London for £17,280 ($20,217)

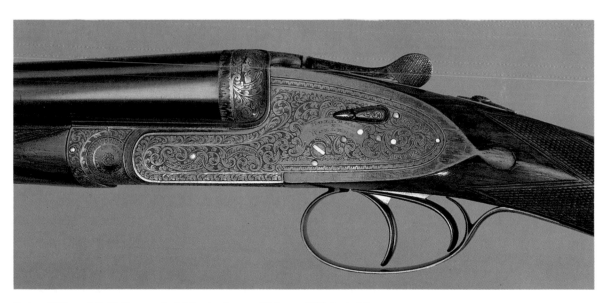

Pair of 'Royal Self-Opener' sidelock ejector 12-bore (2½ in.) d.b. guns
By Holland & Holland, London
Built in 1960
Sold 19.6.85 in London for £19,440 ($25,855)

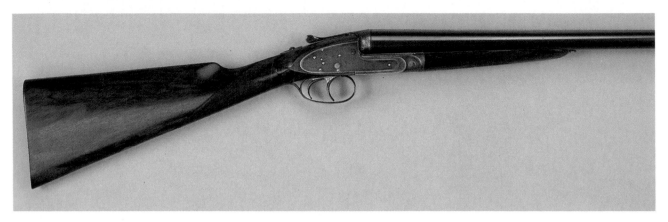

Self-opening sidelock ejector 12-bore ($2\frac{3}{4}$ in.) d.b. gun, with extra barrels
By J. Purdey, London
Built in 1936; extra barrels supplied in 1949
Sold 7.6.85 in New York at Christie's East for $11,550 (£8,978)

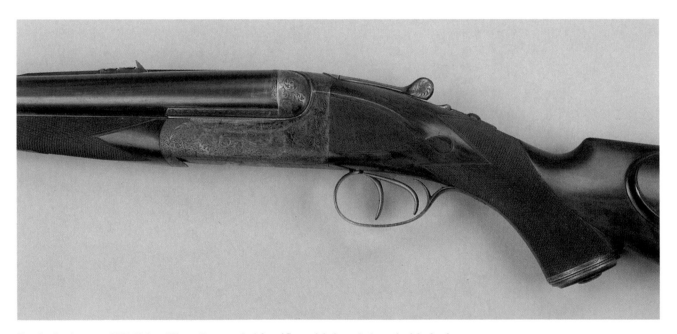

Boxlock ejector .577 (3 in. Nitro Express) d.b. rifle, with hand-detachable locks
By Westley Richards, London and Birmingham
Built in 1934
Sold 7.6.85 in New York at Christie's East for $15,400 (£11,971)

Gold-encrusted boxlock ejector 12-bore
(2 $\frac{3}{4}$ in.) d.b. gun
By J.P. Sauer, Suhl
c. 1900; Black Powder proof only
Sold 7.6.85 in New York at Christie's
East for $6,050 (£4,703)

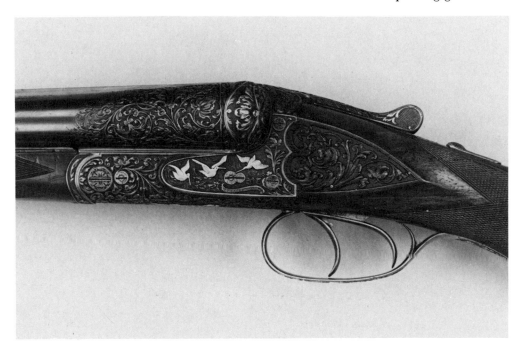

'Sporting & Military' cartridge-board
By Eley Bros., London
c. 1910
Sold 20.3.85 in London for £4,536
($5,307)

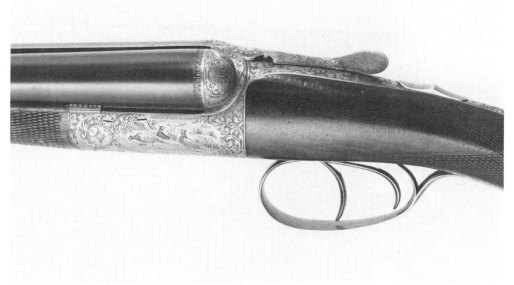

Game-engraved round-action ejector 20-bore (2 $\frac{1}{2}$ in.) d.b. gun
By J. Dickson, Edinburgh
Built in 1917; rebarrelled by G.E. Lewis
Sold 20.3.85 in London for £5,940 ($6,950)

'Daw' hammerless underlever-cocking non-ejector 12-bore (2½ in.) d.b. gun, with damascus barrels
Probably French or German c.1865 (?); rebarrelled c.1920 by H. Clarke, Leicester
Sold 19.6.85 in London for £1,404 ($1,867)
Two 19th-century authorities, W.W. Greener, *The Gun and Its Development*, and J.H. Walsh, *The Modern Sportman's Gun and Rifle*, attributed the introduction of this early hammerless system to G.H. Daw of London c.1862. However, Daw makes no mention of it in his own book, *Gun Patents* (1864), and the design is, as yet, unidentified.

Boss Patent ejector sidelever hammer 12-bore (2½ in.) d.b. gun
By Boss, London
Built c.1891 as no. 2 of a set of three for Lord Herbert Vane-Tempest; rebarrelled c.1912
Sold 21.11.84 in London for £3,888 ($4,860)
As the development of ejector systems post-dated that of hammerless actions, hammer ejector guns are relatively rare and appeal to both collectors and users. Boss hammer guns with original ejector-work are particularly scarce, as suggested by the price for this example, which was not in good condition.

Stamps

The half that is greater than the whole
Brunswick 1852 bisected 2 sgr. on letter
Sold 16.4.85 in Zurich for Sw.fr.42,750 (£12,955)

Postage Stamps and Postal History

ROBSON LOWE

LONDON

The past season has seen continued and increasing interest in classic stamps in superb condition, particularly when used on the original envelope, or with a clear cancellation indicating abnormal use. Character and quality have dominated the market, rarity having some attraction, and the ordinary still easing off in price. Proofs and essays made by the printer in the course of production of the postage stamps have been eagerly competed for.

One of the most important London sales this season was held on 4 September 1984 when over 1,000 16th-century letters addressed to the Florentine brothers Filippo and Bartholomew Corsini were sold. These merchants ran their international business from their home in Gratious (now Gracechurch) Street in the City of London, and their correspondence is the only commercial archive known to have survived the Great Fire of London in 1666. New information about the Merchant Stranger's Post and the Merchant Adventurer's Post and other courier services aroused immense interest among collectors.

Another exciting find was the letters from Lieutenant (later General) Gore-Anley to his parents, written during his service on the Nile Expedition and later during the Dongola Campaign of 1896. These letters had graphic details of the difficulties of the Expedition. The correspondence realised £7,926 ($10,086) on 13 November 1984.

Great Britain 1840 One
Penny Black
The largest known used block
Sold 27.6.85 in Zurich for
Sw.fr.54,000 (£16,354)
From the John Griffiths
Collection

Great Britain 1840 Mulready
two-pence letter sheet with a
pair of 2d.
Sold 14.11.84 in London for
£2,592 ($3,268)
From the collection of
Admiral George C. Dyer

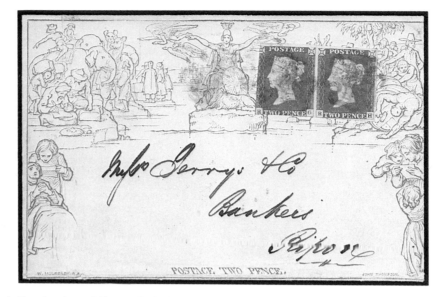

The specialized sales of Great Britain included notable properties offered on behalf of Rear Admiral Falconer Hall, Admiral George C. Dyer, and the late Commander Malcolm Burnett. Among the smaller but distinguished collections were the private delivery stamps of the Oxford and Cambridge Universities, the private telegraph companies formed by Raymond Lister, and the travelling post offices of the United Kingdom formed by Charles Mackenzie Smith. The total turnover for Great Britain was £547,641 ($711,933).

Great Britain 1890 Court
Bureau stamp used to take a
letter to the station on a
Sunday
Sold 18.4.85 in Zurich for
Sw.fr.3,940 (£1,194)
From the Denwood Kelly
Collection

Newfoundland 1860 1s. orange vermilion
Sold 26.3.85 in London for £2,052 ($2,409)

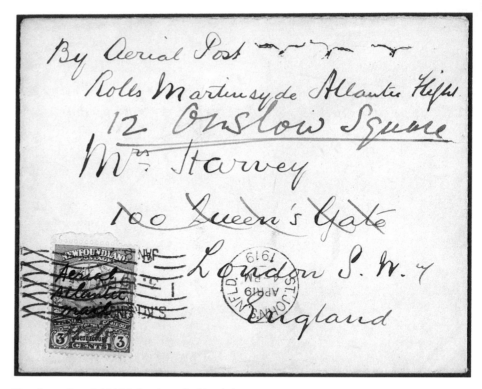

Newfoundland 1919 Martinsyde 'Aerial
Atlantic Post' 3c.
Sold 26.3.85 in London for £10,800 ($12,679)

University of Aston Development Fund: The University of Aston is one of Britain's leading technological universities and it works closely with many commercial firms who need the skills of highly trained students. During this year, a philatelist gave his collection to be sold for the benefit of the University's Development Fund. The collection was offered over five auctions and the highlight was a small sale of 85 lots comprising Newfoundland and the Maritime Provinces of Canada. This sale realised £35,355 ($45,960), but the total for the collection was well over six figures. Illustrated here are two items from the collection, including a letter carried on one of the trans-Atlantic flights made for the £10,000 prize offered by Lord Northcliffe, the owner of the *Daily Mail*. The pilot Captain F.P. Raynam, the navigator Major Charles W.F. Morgan and their aeroplane, a Rolls Martinsyde, failed at the first attempt on 19 April 1919. The second attempt on 17 July crashed after a few hundred yards and the mail was brought over by sea. The stamps (about 30) were overprinted in manuscript 'Aerial Atlantic Mail' and initialled 'J.A.R.' by Dr J. Alexander Robinson, postmaster-general of Newfoundland.

North Borneo 1884 cover
with N.B. and Straits used
together
Sold 23.10.84 in London for
£4,590 ($5,544)
From the collection of the late
Commander Malcolm
Burnett

The Asiatic market was very strong. Commander Malcolm Burnett's Brunei, Labuan and North Borneo made record prices in London. The collection of Hong Kong and Malaysia formed by Admiral George C. Dyer, US Navy retired, fetched Sw.fr.1,186,526 (£384,613) in two Zurich sales, again with several record prices.

Hong Kong 1866 cover with
4c., 6c. and 96c. olive-bistre
Sold 2.11.84 in Zurich for
Sw.fr.49,000 (£16,336)
From the Dyer Collection

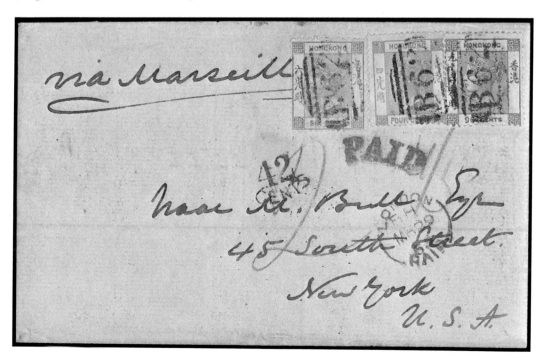

Messina to Malta 1873 with Italian 10c. and 30c. cancelled on arrival at Malta
Sold 6.6.85 in London for £972 ($1,241)

There were many fine collections included in the London sales, one of the most popular being the New Zealand formed by the late Henry L. Bartrop, sold on 24 October 1984. An incompleted die proof of the 1855 1d. brought £4,590 ($5,540) and an 1858 pin perf. 1d. dull orange used sold for £4,104 ($4,956). A mint block of 60 of the 1864 1d. carmine vermilion made £5,130 ($6,194). On 18 December 1984 a mint pair of the Niger Coast 1893 HALF PENNY on 2½d. in carmine and green went for £8,370 ($10,128). The first portion of Gerald Davis's collection of India used in Burma was eagerly competed for and a block of nine 1854 1 annas made £1,620 ($2,041). In the same sale an unused example of the Straits Settlements 30c. overprinted B for use in Bangkok fetched £3,024 ($3,810). Other features were two collections of Falkland Islands from the estate of Eric Creed of Melbourne and the Reverend Cyril Tucker, the former Bishop of Falkland Islands.

Finland 1866 Helsingfors to Stockholm
Sold 1.11.84 in Zurich for Sw.fr.16,300 (£5,361)

Sweden 1858 Stockholm to
Abo with a pair of 6 skilling
and 8 skilling
Sold 1.11.84 in Zurich for
Sw.fr.13,500 (£4,440)

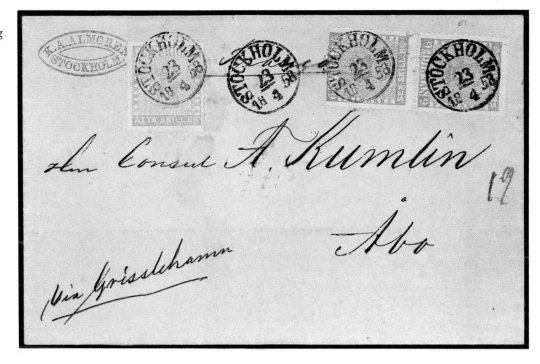

ZURICH

The 17 auctions held in Zurich included fine European covers, two of which are illustrated
here. The total turnover was Sw.fr.7,025,376 (£2,217,696).

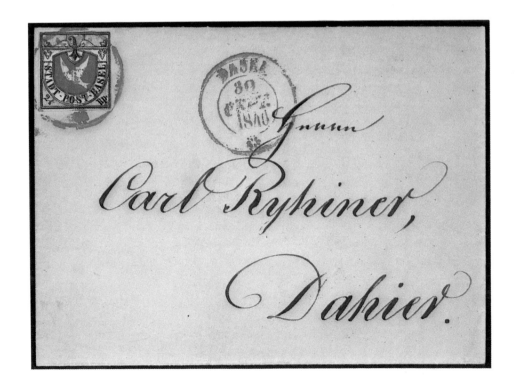

Switzerland 1846 Basle Dove
Sold 16.4.85 in Zurich for
Sw.fr.42,750 (£12,955)

Nova Scotia 1853 envelope to Madras with one 6d. and two 1s.
Sold 4.10.84 in New York for $110,000 (£88,000)

NEW YORK

Five sales were held, which yielded a turnover of $1,907,687 (£1,457,776), an increase of 128 per cent on the previous season. The sale on 3 October 1984 included a splendid array of US classics. The top prices included $12,100 (£9,680) for a mint block of twenty-two 1857 24c., $10,450 (£8,360) for the 1869 24c. with the centre inverted (repaired tear), and $25,300 (£20,240) for the 30c. with inverted flags in spite of a small thin. Next day came the incomparable collection of Nova Scotia formed by a European connoisseur which realised $273,069 (£218,455). A lovely 1856 letter bearing two 1d. and a 6d. yellow green brought $10,450 (£8,360), an 1854 cover with the 3d. blue and the 1s. cold violet fetched $35,200 (£28,160) and the Madras cover illustrated here made $110,000 (£88,000).

The March sale saw $19,250 (£16,362) paid for the US 1847 10c. mint, and in June the magnificent cover bearing a pair of the Confederate States 5c. issued in Livingstone fetched $176,000 (£130,370). A mint copy of the US 1918 24c. with inverted aeroplane made $88,000 (£67,692).

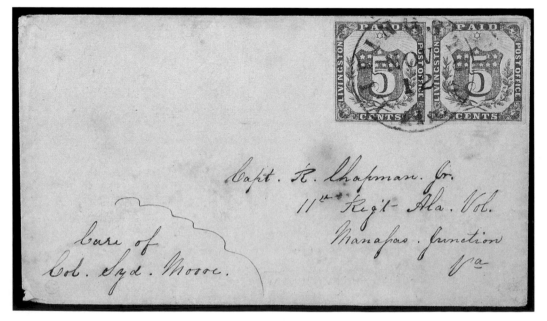

Confederate States unique pair of the Livingstone postmaster's 5c.
Sold 18.6.85 in New York for $176,000 (£135,380)

Coins and Medals

THE PULHAM HOARD

On 22 May 1983 Mr Simon Drake of Grange Farm, Pulham, Dorset, had just finished ploughing, when kicking the newly turned earth before sowing his spring barley, appropriately named Golden Promise, he noticed a gold-coloured disk. With the help of his wife Sally and a metal detector he discovered exactly 100 medieval gold coins. They were subsequently declared treasure trove and sent to the British Museum for study and recording. Since neither they nor the local Museum were in a position to purchase the coins they were returned *ex gratia* in lieu of a reward to the finder. Five were placed on display at Dorset County Museum, Dorchester, and the rest were sold on 28 May in London for a total of £67,856 ($84,820). The vast majority of coins in the hoard were Nobles (value 6/8) and from the reign of Henry VI (1422–61); Marion Archibald of the British Museum, who did an extensive study of the hoard, has calculated that it was buried *c.* 1433, and would have belonged to a very wealthy person as its face value was £32. 5s., a considerable sum in the 15th century.

Although most of the coins were fairly common, the two outstanding pieces were a Henry IV, Heavy Coinage (1399–1412), Noble of London, which fetched £5,400 ($6,750), and rarer still a Half-Noble of Henry IV from the Light Coinage (1412–13), one of only eight known examples. It sold for £6,480 ($8,100), making it the highest priced coin in the auction.

Highly Important Ancient Gold Coins

R. SANCROFT BAKER

When I joined Christie's 16 years ago the idea that a coin sale could fetch £1,000,000 was mere fantasy, especially in view of the fact that the annual total for the coin and medal department was in the region of £50,000. However, with the passing of time and inflation, such a sale took place on 9 October 1984 and it became the first time that a coin auction in England had ever fetched more than £1 million, in fact the sold total of £1.24 million was more than twice the previous record.

The coins offered were of superb quality, having been collected with care and discrimination since the early 1920s. The majority of the 313 lots were Roman gold Aurei and many of them had impressive pedigrees. Twenty-four lots had come from the famous Bement sale in 1924, while others were purchased from the collection of the great opera singer Enrico Caruso, who sold his collection of classical coins in 1923.

With so many rare coins that I could mention, I sadly have space for just a few. While the early Roman emperors were well represented, the great strength of the collection lay in later emperors such as Didius Julianus (March–June AD 193), Clodius Albinus (AD 193–7), Diadumenian, as Caesar (AD 217–18), and Laelian (AD 268), the last coin together with an example from the reign of Victorinus (AD 268–70) were part of the Planche Hoard, which was discovered in 1889.

Of the medallions in the sale, the largest was from the reign of Gallienus (AD 253–68), being the equivalent of 12 Heavy Aurei and previously unknown in gold. Another important multiple was a 2-Solidi of Constantine I (AD 307–37) from the mint of Trier, being one of three known specimens and previously in the Consul Weber Collection sold in Munich (1909). There was a similar multiple of 2-Solidi depicting Fausta, who was the daughter of Maximian I and second wife of Constantine I; this exceptional coin came from the Trau collection, dispersed in 1935, and was the only one of five specimens not to be in a museum.

The sale also had a good selection of Solidi from the Eastern Roman Empire as well as 29 gold Staters of the Kings of the Bosphorus. Of the four Greek coins in the auction, by far the most interesting was a particularly fine gold 100-Litra from Syracuse (c. 380 BC).

The last 46 lots were from the Ptolemaic series. There were some wonderful examples of Octadrachms and Pentadrachms from the reign of Ptolemy II (285–246 BC), but the best two gold coins were from the reign of Ptolemy III (246–221 BC), namely a Dekadrachm minted at Alexandria and a superb Octadrachm which was struck at Ephesus, the Greek influence being easily recognizable. The reign of Ptolemy V (204–181 BC) was represented by an unpublished gold Octadrachm.

The coin which was on the front of the catalogue caused a great deal of discussion and speculation, and ironically was one of the very few silver coins in the sale. This was the extremely rare Tetradrachm from the reign of Cleopatra VII (51–30 BC) which was minted at Askalon, now part of present-day Israel. This particular specimen had previously been part of the S.H. Chapman Collection sold in Geneva (1933). It is generally accepted to depict the finest known portrait of this Queen.

Didius Julianus
(March–June AD 193),
Aureus, £8,800 ($10,560)

Clodius Albinus
(AD 193–7), Aureus
£48,600 ($58,300)

Diadumenian, as Caesar
(AD 217–18), Aureus
£18,360 ($22,030)

Laelian
(AD 268), Aureus
£34,560 ($41,470)

Victorinus
(AD 268–70), Aureus
£9,720 ($11,660)

Constantine I
(AD 307–37), 2-Solidi
£25,920 ($31,100)

Gallienus
(AD 253–68), gold medallion
£64,800 ($77,760)

Fausta, 2-Solidi
£37,800 ($45,360)

Ptolemy III
(246–221 BC), gold
Octadrachm, £16,200 ($19,440)

Ptolemy III,
gold Dekadrachm
£34,560 ($41,470)

Ptolemy V
(204–181 BC), gold
Octadrachm, £33,480
($40,170)

Ptolemy V,
gold Octadrachm
£33,480 ($40,170)

Cleopatra VII
(51–30 BC),
silver Tetradrachm
£70,200 ($84,240)

All sold 9.10.84 in London

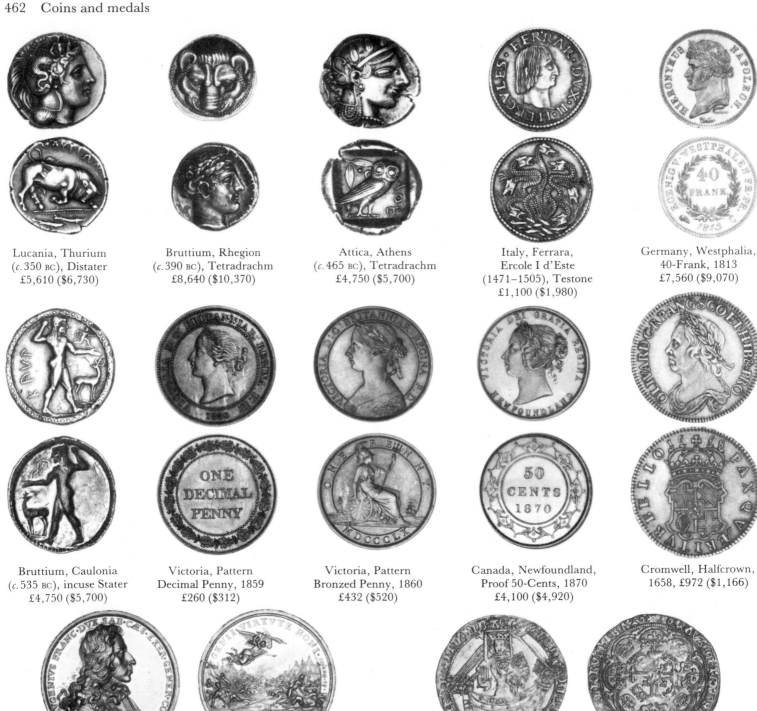

Lucania, Thurium
(*c.*350 BC), Distater
£5,610 ($6,730)

Bruttium, Rhegion
(*c.*390 BC), Tetradrachm
£8,640 ($10,370)

Attica, Athens
(*c.*465 BC), Tetradrachm
£4,750 ($5,700)

Italy, Ferrara,
Ercole I d'Este
(1471–1505), Testone
£1,100 ($1,980)

Germany, Westphalia,
40-Frank, 1813
£7,560 ($9,070)

Bruttium, Caulonia
(*c.*535 BC), incuse Stater
£4,750 ($5,700)

Victoria, Pattern
Decimal Penny, 1859
£260 ($312)

Victoria, Pattern
Bronzed Penny, 1860
£432 ($520)

Canada, Newfoundland,
Proof 50-Cents, 1870
£4,100 ($4,920)

Cromwell, Halfcrown,
1658, £972 ($1,166)

Germany, Eugen of Savoy, gold medal, 1704
£1,728 ($2,073)

Henry IV (1399–1413), Heavy Coinage, London,
Noble, £9,720 ($11,664)

Mexico, Philip V,
8-Escudos, 1702
$33,000 (£27,500)

Guatemala, Philip V,
8-Escudos, 1733
$16,500 (£13,750)

Mexico, Ferdinand VI
4-Escudos, 1747
$17,600 (£14,666)

Mexico, Guadalajara,
Ferdinand VII, 8-Escudos,
1821, $25,300 (£21,083)

Mexico, Philip V,
8-Reales, 1732
$17,800 (£14,833)

Mexico, Philip V,
4-Reales, 1732
$30,800 (£25,666)

Central American Republic,
8-Reales, 1831
$10,120 (£8,433)

Greenland, Christian VII,
1-Piastre, 1771
$23,100 (£19,250)

From Part 1 of the Norweb Collection of Mexican and Central and South American coins, sold 17/18.5.85 in
Dallas, Texas, for a total of $924,000 (£770,000)

Quarter-Dollar, 1892 O
$3,080 (£2,566)

Flying Eagle Cent,
1856
$2,310 (£1,925)

Proof 20-Cents, 1876
$3,190 (£2,658)

Gold 1-Dollar,
1855
$8,250 (£6,875)

Gold 2½-Dollars,
1841
$22,000 (£18,333)

Gold 10-Dollars, 1907
$5,575 (£4,645)

Roman Head Proof
Cent, 1792
$7,700 (£6,416)

Fugio Cent, 1787
$3,300 (£2,750)

Chain Cent, 1793
$3,740 (£3,116)

Wreath Cent, 1793
$3,300 (£2,750)

Half-Dollar, 1867
$8,800 (£7,333)

Proof Morgan Dollar, 1887
$7,700 (£6,416)

Proof Morgan Dollar, 1895
$14,850 (£12,375)

All sold in New York

Right:
The George Cross and General Service Medal, 1962, two clasps, awarded to Sergeant M. Willetts, the Parachute Regiment, £20,520 ($24,620)
Acquired by the National Army Museum
The George Cross was gazetted on 22 June 1971 and was a posthumous award

Far right:
Army of India Medal, two clasps, £1,400 ($1,680)

Below:
Battle of Britain group of seven to fighter ace Wing Commander M.L. Robinson, Royal Air Force, £3,200 ($3,840)
Acquired by the Imperial War Musuem

The Most Exalted Order of the Star of India
(GCSI) bestowed upon William Malcolm Hailey,
1932, £32,400 ($38,880)
Record auction price for a British Order

Germany, Bavaria, Order of St. Hubert, Badge
and Star, late 19th century, £11,880 ($14,250)

Photographs

JULIA MARGARET CAMERON
Joseph Joachim
Albumen print
1868
Sold 28.3.85 in London
at Christie's South
Kensington for £4,000
($4,880)

IRVING PENN
*Gaudi Cathedral (La Sagrada Familia) with Funeral Cortege, Barcelona
(1948)*
Dye-transfer print
Early 1960s
Signed, dated 1949 in ink, stamped 'Photograph by Irving Penn'
Sold 6.11.84 in New York at Christie's East for $13,200 (£10,150)
The compelling imagery that juxtaposes in seemingly
disembodied form the courtly yet somber courtege against the
eerie shell of Gaudi's acclaimed cathedral is suggestive of the
essence of Penn's vision – 'moments preserved'. For just as
Gaudi's architectural fantasies are rooted in structural reality, so
too does Penn's metaphysical image convey a greater sense of
physicality and emotive thrust. According to Penn's recollections,
this is one of three known copies to exist.

ALFRED STIEGLITZ
Poplars, Lake George
Gelatin silver print
*c.*1932
Sold 6.11.84 in New York at Christie's East for $8,800 (£6,770)

EDWARD WESTON
Two Nude Youths posed by a Swimming Pool
Platinum print
*c.*1919
Signed in pencil on the mount
Sold 6.11.84 in New York at Christie's East for $15,400 (£11,850)

MAN RAY
André Breton devant son tableau de Chirico – Hôtel des Écoles – Rue Delambre, Paris 14
Gelatin silver print
1921
Signed in pencil on the recto
Signed, titled and dated in ink and the Rue Campagne-Première stamp on the verso
Sold 6.11.84 in New York at Christie's East for $6,050 (£4,650)

ANDREW JOSEPH RUSSELL
*United States Military Railroad
Photographic Album*
Album containing 117 albumen prints
1863–5
Sold 6.11.84 in New York at
Christie's East for $25,300 (£19,460)

GEORGE N. BARNARD
*Photographic Views of Sherman's
Campaign*
Album containing 61 albumen prints
1866
Sold 6.11.84 in New York at
Christie's East for $17,600 (£13,540)

TIMOTHY H. O'SULLIVAN AND
WILLIAM BELL
*United States Explorations in Nevada
and Arizona*
Album containing 25 prints
1871–4
Sold 28.3.85 in London at
Christie's South Kensington for
£12,000 ($14,640)

*Interprête de la Legation Austro
Hongroise*
From an album containing 114
Chinese and Japanese portraits
Hand-tinted albumen prints
Sold 27.6.85 in London at
Christie's South Kensington for
£5,000 ($6,500)

Above:
G. SHEPHERD
Architectural Detail
From a collection of 53 waxed paper negatives
1853–4
Sold 27.6.85 in London at Christie's South
Kensington for £10,000 ($13,200)

Above right:
PETER HENRY EMERSON AND T.F. GOODALL
Life and Landscape on the Norfolk Broads
Album containing 40 platinum prints
Sold 28.3.85 in London at Christie's South
Kensington for £13,000 ($15,860)

Right:
WILLIAM HENRY FOX TALBOT
The Open Door
Plate VI from *The Pencil of Nature*
1844
Sold 25.10.84 in London at Christie's South
Kensington singly for £8,500 ($10,540) and as
part of the complete edition for £30,000 ($37,200)

Collectors' Sales

Hand-enamelled metal toy of an early two-seat Benz racing car
By Bing, Germany
c. 1904
11¼ in. (28 cm.) long
Sold 30.5.85 in London at Christie's South Kensington for £9,200 ($11,960)

Collecting – a Subject to be Taken Seriously

ALISTAIR SAMPSON

It is of little avail to look up the word 'collecting' in the *Oxford Dictionary of Quotations*. No *obiter dicta*, no *ex cathedra profunditi* are there recorded touching the subject. It is high time that this vacuum was filled. 'The world is divided into collectors and non-collectors' (ed. *O.D. of Q.* please note). 'Collectors are born and not made' (ditto). 'All collectors are dealers *manqués* – All good dealers are collectors at heart – The real collector never sells anything – There is no such thing as a collector.'

At one end of the spectrum we have philatelists and numismatists fulfilling their introspective destinies, sharing their delights only with their fellow *aficionados*. No residence is the more commodious, no home the more gracious through its walls being adorned with woodblock errors of colour or Edward VIII threepenny bits. These are the stuff of albums and cabinets. At the other end of the spectrum are those who seek to evoke in their homes the authentic atmosphere of yesteryear: a Queen Anne walnut chest of drawers here, a cabinet of Bow and Chelsea there, Chippendale chairs in the dining-room, pine and pewter in the kitchen, and so on. This agglomeration of goodies may well be designated 'my collection of antiques' by the owner. It is not of course collecting in the true sense, any more than is the case with the pretentious antique dealer who grandly refers to his stock as 'my collection'. A series of acquisitions is not necessarily a collection.

The true collector is caught within the thrall of a certain trait of character. It is a disease and the symptoms invariably first manifest themselves at an early age. He may well be both collecting and losing his marbles by the time he is six. Some collectors wreck their lives in pursuit of an obsession, living like church mice, accumulating with the zest of squirrels preparing for a hard winter, then leaving the Treasury and their other beneficiaries to enjoy the fruit of their labours. Others like to see their collections disposed of while they yet live.

One who chose not to live to witness the dispersal of all that he held dear was Mr Calvin Bullock of New York City, who came into this world in 1867 and quit it in 1944. He founded the international investment management firm which bears his name and in so doing doubtless made a bob or two, or to be more precise a buck or three, and therefore no doubt was able to indulge in collecting without foreswearing the good life. He later developed 'The Calvin Bullock forum for the dissemination among the business community of new ideas in the fields of government, economics, science and military affairs'. It was while thus engaged that he became conscious of Horatio 'kiss me Hardy you remind me of Emma' Nelson and Napoleon 'Waterloo, this is where I get off ' Bonaparte. He decided to form a collection devoted to memorabilia related to these two outstanding figures of their age. Between the wars he became the dominant buyer of such items and his office became a cross between Trafalgar House and Les Invalides.

On 8 May 1985, forty-one years after his death, Christie's sold the amazing collection that he, Calvin Bullock, lived and died with. The 402 lots covered a wide range. The star was without question the Vernet of *La Bataille du Pont d'Arcole*, which showed the Emperor, on 17 November

No. 1 Wall Street, New
York, Calvin Bullock's office

1796, himself holding the 'tri-color' (I quote the catalogue), urging on his grenadiers to carry
the vital bridge, thus ensuring victory over the Austrians. Sadly, heads of state no longer seem
to indulge in person in this sort of activity. Anyway, Vernet doing his bit as a war artist and
showing Bony yomping fearlessly *sur le pont*, in stark contrast to the Duke of Plaza-Toro, netted
£324,000 ($398,520; see page 63).

Leafing through surely one of the most fascinating catalogues of the year one comes upon
'lot 63, the flag which was said to have covered the body of Nelson in the cockpit of
HMS *Victory* at Trafalgar, 21 October 1805.' Wisely the cataloguer did not guarantee the authenticity of this particular shroud. He did not need to. He merely recited the inscription carried
by the oak frame. Someone was mightily impressed, as lot 63 was knocked down for £8,640
($10,627).

It is also pleasurable to record that in the course of this sale a sword (see page 444) that was
in 1814 presented by the City of London to Field Marshal Barclay De Tolly, who achieved
wonders through his 'scorched earth' policy (not to be confused with, though doubtless the inspiration of, defoliation and Agent Orange), was purchased by a Mr Paul Dwyer who is married to one Nina Barclay De Tolly so that they might give it to their 10-year-old son Alexander.

It is splendid to see such an object returning to its rightful owners. It is almost as if the Elgin marbles were being sent back to Elgin. The family paid £19,440 ($25,272), the original cost to the City of London having been 200 gns.

The Musée Nationale de France was also in there bidding, reclaiming *inter alia* Josephine's Book Box, which was stamped 'Bibliotheque de la Malmaison'.

There was a Romney of Lady Hamilton as Cassandra – at lot 223 Nelson writes to her, being somewhat knocked about after the Battle of the Nile:

My dear Madam,
I may now be able to show your ladyship the remains of Horatio Nelson and I trust my mutilations will not cause me to be less welcome, they are the marks of honor [*sic;* when did we start to put that silly 'u' in? Was it just because we wanted to make Americans feel different?].

Incidentally, when Emma did set eyes on him a month later his latest disfigurement caused her to fall into his arms in a dead faint. Considering that the poor fellow had already lost his right eye (1794) and his right arm (1797) and that this was only a trifling wound over the left eye, one cannot think what she was on about.

When one comes upon lot 268 confusion is totally confounded. The title of the lot reads, 'Napoleon I. Important and unusual series of five unpublished autograph letters to Emma.' What next? The complete correspondence between Rommel and Monty's wife? The relevation that in 1916 the Czar and the Kaiser went on a wife-swopping weekend together? Alas, although the true identity of Napoleon's Emma has never been discovered, it was not, it may be stated without fear of contradiction, Lady Hamilton.

Such was the Calvin Bullock Collection, a masterpiece of acquisition, both diverse and discriminating: minatures, objects of vertu, silver, pictures, books, letters, furniture, sculpture, *et al.* That which was lovingly put together by a great collector has now been torn asunder at auction. The catalogue will however remain a permanent memorial; others will follow in his footsteps and through his industry and scholarship much new material, including hitherto unpublished letters, has come to light.

This was just one collection of memorabilia. Within this wide field falls also everything from early Mickey Mouse souvenirs to model motorcars – when a toy Mercedes fetches £9,200 ($11,960), about the price of a second-hand grown-up version, clearly this is a subject to be taken seriously. Half of the world then will continue to invest in the established classics, the pictures and porcelain, the furniture, silver and so on which comprise a large part of Christie's turnover, whereas the other half are forever breaking new ground. What then will be the sought-after memorabilia of tomorrow? Early video-cassette recorders? Who can tell? He who can will have himself a great deal of amusement, and probably make a tidy sum into the bargin, seeking out what will be, but is not yet, save by he himself, sought-after.

The travelling writing-box of Jérome-Napoléon Bonaparte, King of Westphalia
By Martin-Guillaume Biennais
21¼ in. (54 cm.) wide; 12¾ in. (32.5 cm.) deep
Sold 8.5.85 in London for £91,800 ($110,160)
From the Calvin Bullock Collection
The box contains the following: a silver-gilt paper knife with gold-mounted mother-of-pearl handle, 1798–1809, a silver-gilt inkwell and a pounce pot both with imperial eagles in the corners and engraved with the crowned initials J and N, two silver-gilt containers similarly engraved, a straight edge and a ruler of ebony mounted in gold, a mother-of-pearl and gold measure, two pairs of gold and steel dividers, and a pencil holder, all by Martin-Guillaume Biennais, 1809–19, a spike, a pen holder, two pen knives, and a seal with alternative matrix, all of mother-of-pearl mounted in gold, an additional gold and steel pen and pencil holder, a double-ended gold pencil holder by Gabriel-Raoul Morel, a pair of vari-coloured gold and steel scissors by Pierre-François Queillé, a silver-gilt bell, a cut-glass scent bottle with enamelled gold cover, two ormolu articulated candle-branches, and two steel rectangular presse-papiers surmounted by silver-gilt lions

Above left:
Brave Little Tailor, 1938
Mickey swatting seven flies in
one blow
Gouache on celluloid applied
to a Walt Disney Productions
watercolour background
Production 2252
8⅛ × 10⅝ in. (20.3 × 27 cm.)
Sold 8.12.84 in New York at
Christie's East for $20,900
(£17,130)

Left:
Pinocchio, 1940
Gepetto discovers Pinocchio's
donkey ears
Gouache on partial celluloid
applied to a Walt Disney
Productions watercolour
background
Production 2003
Background artist Claude
Coats
7⅜ × 10¼ in. (19 × 25.8 cm.)
Sold 8.12.84 in New York at
Christie's East for $19,800
(£16,230)

Above:
Thru the Mirror, 1936
Mickey standing on a rug by
a table looking at a telephone
receiver
Gouache on full celluloid
applied to a Walt Disney
Productions watercolour
background
Production UM 41
8 × 11 in. (20.3 × 27.9 cm.)
Sold 8.12.84 in New York at
Christie's East for $12,100
(£9,920)

KATE GREENAWAY
Young Girls with a Garland of Flowers
Book illustration
Sold 24.4.85 in London at
Christie's South Kensington
for £3,400 ($4,280)

Above:
HENRY ALKEN
Hand-coloured aquatint roller, print 66 ft. in length, depicting the funeral
procession of the Duke of Wellington
Published 1853
Contained in its original glass-topped viewing box
Sold 15.5.85 in London at Christie's South Kensington for £2,400
(£3,100)

Left:
Signed postcard of Marlene Dietrich
Sold 7.9.84 in London at Christie's South Kensington for £80 ($103)

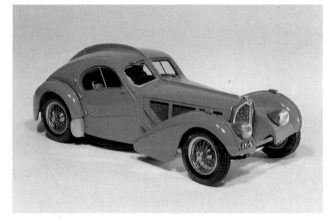

Top:
7¼ in. guage model of the GWR 4-2-2 loco and
tender No. 3067 *Duchess of Teck*
20½ × 84 in. (52 × 213 cm.)
Sold 29.4.85 at the British Engineerium, Brighton,
for £5,500 ($6,930)

Above:
Approximately ⅟₁₆ in. scale metal model of the
Bugatti 57SC Atlantic coupé, registration no. EXK 6
By Rio
4¼ × 12½ in. (10.5 cm. × 31.5 cm.)
Sold 29.4.85 at the British Engineerium, Brighton,
for £650 ($825)

Left:
French prisoner-of-war bone and horn model of a
Royal Naval 48-gun frigate
20 × 21 in. (50.8 × 53.3 cm.)
Sold 29.4.85 at the British Engineerium, Brighton,
for £12,000 ($15,000)

Above:
Painted tinplate model of a
clockwork P2 Alfa Romeo
two-seater racing car
By C.I.J. France
*c.*1926
21½ in. (54.6 cm.) long
Sold 30.5.85 in London at
Christie's South Kensington
for £800 ($1,040)

Right:
Foot figure of Gui Sieur de
Rochfort falling badly
wounded
By Courtenay, Z17
Sold 6.12.84 in London at
Christie's South Kensington
for £1,900 ($2,380)

Above:
Royal Air Force Monoplane, first version with
square wing tips
By Britains
Set no. 434
*c.*1934
Sold 29.9.84 in New York at Christie's East for
$1,870 (£1,558)

Above:
Bru bisque-headed Bébé doll
Incised 'Bru Jne 7'
20½ in. (52 cm.) high
Sold 6.3.85 in New York at Christie's East for
$6,600 (£5,076)

Right:
Bru bisque-headed Bébé doll
Incised 'Bru Jne 7'
With eight extra items of clothing, including dress
and undergarments
20 in. (50.8 cm.) high
Sold 4.12.84 in New York at Christie's East for
$8,360 (£6,850)

Far right:
Bru bisque-headed Bébé doll
Incised 'Bru Jne S'
21 in. (53.5 cm.) high
Sold 3.10.84 in New York at Christie's East for
$7,150 (£5,720)

Right:
Interchangeable cylinder
music box on stand
By Mermod Frères,
Switzerland
Retailed by Jacot Music Box
Co., New York
1900
Length of cylinder 24¾ in.
(63 cm.)
Sold 4.12.84 in New York at
Christie's East for $6,380
(£5,230)

Far right:
Musical automation of a
narghile smoker
By Lambert
23 in. (58.5 cm.) high
Sold 6.3.85 in New York at
Christie's East for $4,400
(£3,384)

Right:
Cylinder music box
By Nicole Frères, Switzerland
Serial no. 51980
1889
Length of cylinder 13¼ in.
(33.5 cm.)
Sold 4.12.84 in New York at
Christie's East for $2,200
(£1,800)

Far right:
'Eureka' phonograph
By Lioret
Sold 20.12.84 in London at
Christie's South Kensington
for £4,500 ($5,400)

Right:

Motorists or Other Interpretations of the Motor Car
A bound volume of 12 colour lithographs
after Chas Crombie
Published by Simpkin Marshall Hamilton
Kent and Co., for Perrier
Sold 12.3.85 in London at Christie's South
Kensington for £320 ($355)

Above:
Brass and copper diver's bell helmet, labelled
Siebe, Gorman & Co. Ltd., Submarine
Engineers, London; a diver's suit with lead-
weighted boots; air pump, complete with
gauge, brass fittings and handles, made by
the same company
39 in. (99.6 cm.) high
Sold 2.8.84 in London at Christie's South
Kensington for £950 ($1,225)

Right:
Desk companion comprising a clock and
calendar, the stand in the form of a bicycle
11 in. (27.9 cm.) long
Sold 25.9.84 in London at Christie's South
Kensington for £280 ($355)

Above:
Four motor car mascots, entitled
Victoire (Spirit of the Wind),
Grande Libellule, Perche and
St. Christophe
By Lalique
Sold individually 25.10.84 at
Christie's South Kensington for a
total of £2,850 ($3,614)

Left:
Selection of photographic items from
the collection of the late
W.H.G. Stevens, Esq.
The entire collection sold 21.2.85 in
London at Christie's South Kensington
for £35,000 ($38,850)

Above:
Mahogany, iron and brass triple
lantern
Sold 21.2.85 in London at Christie's
South Kensington for £2,400 ($2,660)

Left:
Prototype V.P. mono-rail camera
Sold 11.4.85 in London at Christie's
South Kensington for £300 ($390)

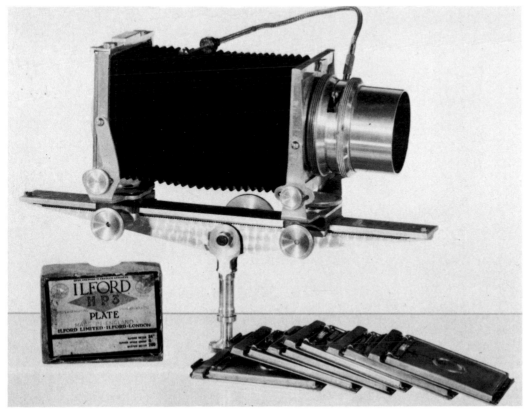

Above left:
Summer evening-dress of white silk
organza printed with red and blue
poppies
By Chanel
Model no. 36502
c. 1932
Sold 14.5.85 in London at Christie's
South Kensington for £2,200 ($2,840)

Above centre:
Chinese silk cover for the European
market
Early 19th century
100 × 90 in. (254 × 228.5 cm.)
Sold 30.4.85 in London at Christie's
South Kensington for £3,400 ($4,320)

Above right:
Gentleman's suit of deep-blue satin
French, Lyons
c. 1770
Sold 14.5.85 in London at Christie's
South Kensington for £3,000 ($3,870)

Left:
Open robe and petticoat of pink and white striped
silk brocade with garlands of flowers, with
original stomacher
The silk French
c. 1774–5
Sold 26.2.85 in London at Christie's South
Kensington for £5,500 ($5,830)
Worn by the Spanish ancestress of the vendor in
Peru in the 18th century

Fifteen-leaf fan comprising scenes by Robert Schleich, Franz Roubaud, Karl Raupp, Ladislaus van Czachorski, Franz von Stuck, Franz von Defregger, Fritz von Uhde, Eduard von Grützner, Alfred von Wierusz Kowalski, Gabriel von Max, Hermann Kaulbach, August Holmberg, Wilhelm von Diez, Enrique Serra and Wilhelm von Velten
Munich School
All signed, some dated 1903 and some 1904
35 × 53¾ in. (88 × 136 cm.)
Sold 23.4.85 in Amsterdam for D.fl.136,800 (£31,090)

Twentieth Century Entertainment

Green rubber squeaky leeks, a drooping bloom, a cloth rat, and a head chopper are not the sort of items one normally expects to find being sold at auction, yet on 30 November 1984 at Christie's South Kensington these somewhat bizarre items came under the hammer amidst avid public interest. These were just a few examples from a collection of 80 stage props belonging to the late Tommy Cooper and the saleroom was packed with fans and fellow professional magicians alike, anxious to buy a memento of their late lamented hero. In a way it was a fitting tribute to a man central to British stage and television comedy over the past 40 years.

Many of the lots were specially adapted by the great maestro himself and this of course only served to increase their popularity. A novelty saw-through-the-head, which he used with the gag 'I've got a saw head', sold with several other body penetration illusions for £150 ($183); a giant dovepan with a 5 ft. multi-coloured spring duck sold for £120 ($146); and a pair of handcuffs presented to Tommy from 'his friends at Scotland Yard' was finally knocked down for £300 ($366). However, definitely the star lot was a red fez – with a difference. It had a motorized weather vane on the top, and was used during the 1967 Royal Variety Performance with the opening gag, 'I've just been struck by lightning!'. This particular fez fetched £550 ($671), the highest price in the Tommy Cooper section of the sale, which totalled £7,500 ($9,150).

The next 80 lots were devoted to film and theatre costume, and costume design. A private collector from abroad kept the bidding energetic, purchasing, amongst other things, a dress worn by Elizabeth Taylor in the the 1963 film *Cleopatra* for £280 ($341), and a suit worn by Joan Collins in her pre-Dynasty days. At £130 ($158), this was an essential item for any serious collector of costume! However, it was Judy Garland's blouse for *The Wizard of Oz* which reached the highest price of £800 ($976), and again this went to a private collector, a schoolgirl who adored everything about Judy Garland. The Victoria and Albert Theatre Museum succeeded in buying the helmet worn by Sir Herbert Tree as Othello in 1912 for £120 ($146), the earliest item in the sale apart from a helmet from *Showboat* dated 1893.

This is the fourth sale that Christie's South Kensington have held in the film and theatre costume field, and apart from giving museums and private collectors the chance to buy the costumes, it also increases public awareness of the importance of costume in the history of cinema and stage.

The Friday morning section of the sale, including photographs, film and pop and rock memorabilia was equally well received, although the diversity of items on offer possibly contributed to the fluctuation of prices. In the pop and rock section, the Beatles, as the most influential band of the last 30 years, obviously dominated the sale both in numbers of lots and the prices realised. It is interesting to note here that in this relatively new collecting field private vendors and buyers predominate, with the highest price in the entire sale, £3,000 ($3,600), paid by a collector for a Fender Stratocaster guitar which was given to the vendor by George Harrison after an impromptu 'jamming' session at Harrison's house. Presentation 'gold' and 'platinum' discs also fetched extraordinarily high prices: one presented to John Lennon for 'Let It Be' sold for £2,600 ($3,172), and another awarded for 'Rock and Roll Music' fetched £2,000 ($2,440).

However, Beatle memorabilia was not the only category to excite competitive bidding. A pair of framed Levi jeans signed by David Bowie and sold for charity fetched an astonishing £500 ($610), and a bronze bust of Keith Richards from the Rolling Stones (with, appropriately, a real cigarette drooping from his mouth) was knocked down for £900 ($1,098).

The total for the entire two-day sale was almost £50,000 ($61,000).

Signed photograph of the
Beatles
*c.*1966
8¼ × 6 in. (21 × 15 cm.)
Sold 30.11.84 in London at
Christie's South Kensington
for £240 ($292)

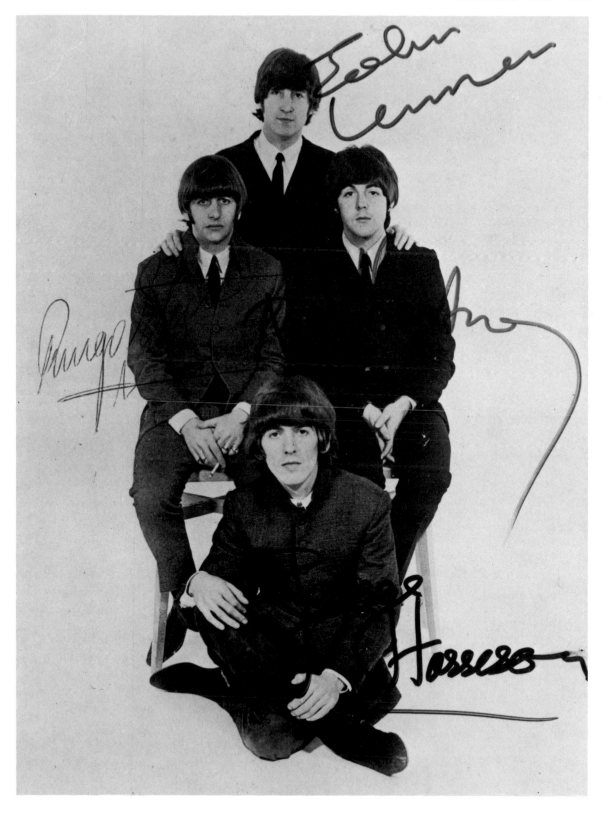

1929 Mercedes-Benz
SS 38/250
Four-seat tourer
Coachwork by Jenkins and
Pain
Sold 15.7.85 at Beaulieu for
£108,000 ($140,000)

1929 Bentley 4½ litre
drophead coupé with dickey
Coachwork by Vanden Plas
Sold 15.7.85 at Beaulieu for
£54,000 ($70,200)

1939 Rolls-Royce Wraith
Sedanca de Ville
Coachwork by Gurney
Nutting
Sold 15.7.85 at Beaulieu for
£45,360 ($58,968)

1934 Packard Twelve Series
1107 convertible Victoria
Coachwork by Dietrich
Sold 15.7.85 at Beaulieu for
£129,600 ($168,480)

KOLOMAN MOSER
Ver Sacrum, V. Jahr, XIII
Austellung Der Vereinigung
Bildener Kunst Der Österreichs
Secession
Secession Exhibition poster,
1902
Sold 1.4.85 in London at
Christie's South Kensington
for £62,000 ($76,260)
Record auction price for a
poster

Wine

M. Jacques Rouët in his Paris cellar, the contents of which were sold 19.3.85 in London

Another Record Season for Wine

MICHAEL BROADBENT, M.W.

The season just ended has seen one of the biggest percentage increases in the value of wine sold since wine auctions resumed at Christie's in the autumn of 1966: an overall 25 per cent to £7.5 million ($9.75 million), worldwide. Not only has the number of sales increased (from 44 to 50), but the size of each sale has frequently exceeded that of recent seasons, with a large number of two- and several three-session sales.

Overseas interest has been high, with American buyers taking full advantage of the strength of the Dollar, which early in the New Year nearly reached parity with the Pound, but there has also been a very noticeable increase in the number of really top-class cellars emanating from across the Channel, from Paris and Bordeaux in particular.

KING STREET

For the past three seasons we have been concentrating on two major types of sale: 'Fine Claret and White Bordeaux' and 'Fine Wines and Vintage Port'. The latter are mixed sales and include the highest quality, and oldest, claret, leading burgundy domaines, top German estates, old sherry, venerable madeira and vintage brandy. One of each type of sale is held every month in the Great Rooms. In addition we hold, from time to time, what we term 'specials', generally promotional or one-owner sales.

The number of King Street wine sales increased by three to 26 and the sold total to £5.5 million ($7.15 million) – £4 million ($5.3 million) in 1983/4 – 97 per cent of the knockdown value.

The three 'specials' this season included a first-ever sale devoted to New World wines: Australia New Zealand and California. The other two, for M. Rouët and Château Haut-Brion, are dealt with below, under The French Connection.

RETURN TO THE CITY

W. & T. Restell, the century-old family firm of wine auctioneers taken over by Christie's in 1966, used to hold regular monthly sales in the City. We returned to Beaver Hall with Christie-Restell City sales in the 1970/1 season but these were discontinued when Beaver Hall became unavailable.

There was a welcome – indeed, judging by the attendance, a greatly welcome – return to the City on 12 March 1985 when Christie's South Kensington organized a wine sale at the Chartered Accountants' Hall, conveniently situated opposite Christie's City office in Copthall Avenue. Although the sale total was, by King Street standards, modest – just over £30,000 ($39,000) – it was encouraging, and will certainly be followed up.

FINE WINE IN SCOTLAND

Our first sale in Edinburgh took place last November. Organized in association with Irvine Robertson Wines, and with the promotional support of *The Scotsman*, the sale, held at the historic

Château Haut-Brion
An anniversary sale was held
16.5.85 in London

Prestonfield House, was the culmination of a three-day event which included lectures, tastings and dinners. This was followed by a summer sale in Glasgow on Christie's own premises. The total for the two sales was £137,160 ($178,308).

CHRISTIE'S SOUTH KENSINGTON
The popular and well-attended monthly sales of bin ends and inexpensive trade stocks in the Old Brompton Road have netted £550,000 ($715,000), a healthy improvement upon recent seasons.

SALES OVERSEAS
Geneva: We have been conducting fine and rare wine sales at the Richemond Hotel since 1974. Held every spring and autumn, the 1984/5 season net total was Sw.fr.610,530 (£196,945); Sw.fr.599,943 (£175,782) the previous season.

Amsterdam: Twice yearly sales have also been held in Holland since 1976. The total sold this season was D.fl.1.4 million (£142,691), 40 per cent up on 1983/4.

Chicago: These sales which started in 1981 are now thoroughly well established. The three sales this season have netted just short of $1 million (£770,000). The four sales scheduled for 1985 will see a 30 per cent increase.

VINEXPO Bordeaux: Our very successful Bordeaux debut in June witnessed some exceptionally high prices and a total of Fr.1.3 million (£113,000), considerably in excess of expectations (see below).

THE FRENCH CONNECTION

A feature of the season has been the strengthening of our French connections. Directly, and through our agents in Paris and Bordeaux, a large volume of top-class wine from private and trade sources has been coming to London for sale. A perfect example of the former was the cellar of M. Jacques Rouët, a former managing director of Dior and a noted connoisseur, which was packed by us and shipped to London for sale in March. Every lot sold and the total was well ahead of our estimates.

On 13 June 1985, 50 years to the day that Clarence Dillon, the American banker, purchased Château Haut-Brion, his granddaughter and her husband, the Duc de Mouchy, hosted a dinner arranged by Christie's at Brooks's in St. James's. Later in the week we held a special anniversary wine sale for the Domaine Clarence Dillon. The special illustrated catalogue listed 45 vintages of Haut-Brion from 1902 to 1982 and 10 vintages of the scarce, small production Haut-Brion blanc. Once again, many individual prices, and the sale total, well exceeded estimates.

Our sale at VINEXPO was a completely new departure. Last autumn we were approached by the *Délégué Général* of the *Fédération Internationale des Vins* and the *Directeur-Général* of VINEXPO to see whether we were prepared to mount a typical Christie's fine and rare wine sale at the now highly successful Wine Fair which is held every other year in Bordeaux. With the assistance of our agent, M. Jean-Pierre Lucquiaud, and the co-operation of the leading Bordeaux auctioneer, Maître C. Jean dit Cazaux, a very well-attended sale was conducted on the last day of the Fair. High prices and a lot of good publicity ensued.

CHARITY WINE SALES

It is rather hard to keep track of the many charity wine auctions conducted by various members of the department. Top of the list for its spectacular setting, beautiful catalogue, and immaculate organization is the Napa Valley Wine Auction in California. The 5th annual sale was held this June, and another $300,000 (£230,000) or thereabouts was raised for three local hospitals. Also in the United States, sales were held for KPBS public broadcasting in San Diego and for a college of music in Detroit. In London, the Save the Children Fund and Birthright benefitted from an annual dinner and wine auction at the Savoy.

CHRISTIE'S WINE PUBLICATIONS

We currently list 21 books on wine, 8 of which are produced in association with other publishers. Only one new title was published last season, the very well-reviewed book on *Madeira* by Noël Cossart. Fully illustrated and published in both hardback and paperback, the book received a specific category award in *What Wine* magazine's book of the year competition.

Left to right:
1961 Ch. Lafite Imperial,
£3,000 ($3,900)
1961 Ch. Mouton-Rothschild
Jeroboam, £2,400 ($3,120)
1961 Ch. Lafite, 3 double
magnums, £2,700 ($3,510)

All sold 30.5.85 in London

Principal Prices 1984/5

Claret			
1870 Mouton-Rothschild	£620 ($806) per bottle	1955 Pétrus	£2,900 ($3,770) per dozen
1895 Haut-Brion	£300 ($390) per magnum	1961 Haut-Brion	£3,200 ($4,160) per dozen
1899 Mouton-Rothschild	£520 ($676) per bottle	1961 Palmer	£3,200 ($4,160) per 4
1929 Latour	£400 ($520) per bottle		double-magnums
1945 Lafite	£4,800 ($6,240) per dozen	1961 Pétrus	£9,600 ($12,480) per dozen
1945 Latour	£5,800 ($7,540) per dozen	1966 Lafite	£1,350 ($1,755) per dozen
1945 Mouton-Rothschild	Fr.15,000 (£1,300)	1966 Latour	£1,040 ($1,352) per 6
	per magnum		magnums
1946 Mouton-Rothschild	£1,300 ($1,690) per bottle	1966 Haut-Brion	£650 ($845) per jeroboam
1947 Cheval-Blanc	£420 ($546) per magnum	1966 Mouton-Rothschild	£980 ($1,274) per dozen
1947 Pétrus	£620 ($806) per bottle	1970 Pétrus	£2,150 ($2,795) per dozen
		1975 Pétrus	£2,300 ($2,990) per dozen

White Bordeaux

1858 Yquem	£460 ($598) per bottle
1861 Yquem	£560 ($728) per bottle
1865 Yquem	£760 ($988) per bottle
1921 Yquem	£340 ($442) per bottle
1928 Yquem	£420 ($546) per bottle
1929 Climens	£270 ($351) per bottle
1967 Yquem	£350 ($455) per magnum
1929 Haut-Brion Blanc	£300 ($390) per bottle
1970 Haut-Brion Blanc	£650 ($845) per dozen
1978 Haut-Brion Blanc	£680 ($884) per dozen

Burgundy

1945 La Tâche	£540 ($702) per bottle
1947 La Tâche	£480 ($624) per bottle
1953 Romanée-Conti	£300 ($390) per bottle
1961 Romanée-Conti	£840 ($1,092) per magnum
1966 Romanée-Conti	£3,700 ($4,810) per dozen

White Burgundy

1969 Montrachet DRC	£4,400 ($5,720) per dozen
1971 Corton-Charlemagne, Latour	£1,150 ($1,495) per dozen
1978 Montrachet, Laguiche	£1,400 ($1,820) per dozen

Rhône

1911 Châteauneuf-du-Pape	£105 ($136) per bottle
1961 Hermitage, La Chapelle	£1,700 ($2,210) per dozen
1971 Hermitage, La Chapelle	£460 ($598) per dozen
1972 Hermitage, La Chapelle	£620 ($806) per dozen
1982 Grillet	£240 ($312) per dozen

Hock

1949 Marcobrunner TBA	£165 ($214) per bottle
1953 Winkeler Hasensprung TBA	£105 ($136) per bottle
1959 Kreuznacher Brückes TBA	£75 ($97) per bottle

Australia/California

1959 Grange Hermitage, Bin 95	£185 ($240) per dozen
1965 BV Cabernet-Sauvignon	£320 ($416) per dozen

Champagne

1914 Moët & Chandon	£110 ($143) per bottle
1943 Bouzy-Rouge (Clicquot)	Fr.56,000 (£4,800) per 6 magnums
1947–73 Krug	Fr.40,000 (£3,500) per 6 magnums
1949 Roederer Cristal	£700 ($910) per dozen
1955 Dom Pérignon	£800 ($1,040) per dozen
1959 Dom Pérignon rosé	£1,400 ($1,820) per dozen
1961 Krug	£550 ($715) per dozen
1961 Bollinger RD	£160 ($208) per magnum
1961 Dom Pérignon	£720 ($936) per dozen
1969 Roederer Cristal	£750 ($975) per dozen

Port

1887 Taylor	£520 ($676) per 3 bottles
1896 Croft	£130 ($169) per bottle
1927 Graham	£135 ($175) per bottle
1927 Taylor	£520 ($676) per 3 bottles
1931 Noval Naçional	£840 ($1,092) per bottle
1935 Taylor	£1,350 ($1,755) per dozen
1945 Graham	£1,350 ($1,755) per dozen
1945 Taylor	£1,750 ($2,275) per dozen
1947 Noval Naçional	£200 ($260) per bottle
1955 Taylor	£680 ($884) per dozen
1963 Croft	£420 ($546) per dozen
1963 Fonseca	£420 ($546) per dozen
1963 Noval Naçional	£1,200 ($1,560) per dozen
1963 Taylor	£440 ($572) per dozen

Madeira

1792 Blandy's	£280 ($364) per bottle
1795 Terrantez	£220 ($286) per bottle
1862 Terrantez	£150 ($195) per bottle

Chartreuse

1878–1903	£140 ($182) per litre

Cognac

1811 Napoléon GFC	£270 ($351) per bottle
1812 Impérial GFC	£340 ($442) per magnum
1858 Monnet	Fr.12,000 (£1,050) per bottle

Collectors' Pieces

Gold Pocket Corkscrew, Paris, 18th century, record auction price for a corkscrew	£3,800 ($4,940)

Contributors

MICHAEL BROADBENT Master of Wine and head of Christie's Wine department, as well as President of the International Wine & Food Society, Chairman of the Wine Trade Art Society, and a former Chairman of the Institute of Masters of Wine. Prolific writer and much-travelled lecturer, he is the author of *The Great Vintage Wine Book*.

CHRISTOPHER BRUNKER Director in charge of Modern Sporting Guns at Christie's.

JEFF CLEMENTS Fellow of Designer Bookbinders and President of the Society in 1981–3. His fine bindings are in numerous public and private collections in both Europe and the USA. He is Chairman of the Faculty of Art and Design and Head of the Department of Graphic Design at Bristol Polytechnic.

ROBERT CUMMING Principal and founder of the Christie's Fine Arts Course. Prior to joining Christie's in 1978 he worked in the Education Department of the Tate Gallery. Author of two books, *Just Look and Just Imagine* and the *Christie's Guide to Collecting*, he is also on the council of the Friends of the Tate Gallery and the Exhibitions Sub-Committee of the Arts Council.

DEAN FAILEY Vice-president of Christie's New York with responsibility for American Furniture and Decorative Arts, and formerly curator of the Bayon Bend collection of American Decorative Arts in Houston, Texas. He is the author of *Long Island is My Nation*, an in-depth study of American decorative arts from Long Island.

DAVID FRASER Assistant City Museums officer of the Museums and Arts Gallery in Derby. He was responsible for the 1979 exhibition of Joseph Wright of Derby to celebrate the centenary of the Derby Art Gallery, and is currently contributing to *Iconography of Landscapes*.

JUDITH GOLDMAN The founding editor of *Print Collector's Newsletter* and Managing Editor of *Art News*. She has just completed a book on James Rosenquist entitled *Life and Paintings* and is the adviser on prints for the Whitney Museum in New York City.

JOHN HERBERT Former Director of Press and Public Relations at Christie's and Editor of *Christie's Review of the Season* since 1959.

PHILIP HOOK Director of the Nineteenth Century Picture department at Christie's since 1981. He frequently appears on the BBC's Antiques Roadshow as a picture expert.

REBECCA JOHN Granddaughter of Augustus John and great niece of Gwen John. She is currently working on the biography of the late Admiral of the Fleet Sir Caspar John, her father, who died last year.

RICHARD KINGZETT Director of Thomas Agnew and Sons, where he specializes in Old Master Paintings. He is the author of a volume on Samuel Scott for the Walpole Society.

RONALD LIGHTBOWN Keeper of Metalwork at the Victoria and Albert Museum. He is the author of several books, including works on Botticelli and on Donatello and Michelozzo. His *catalogue raisonné* of the work of Andrea Mantegna will be published by Phaidon Press in 1986.

ROBSON LOWE He has conducted stamp auctions since 1936 and has written several standard works, including the five-volume *Encyclopedia of Empire Postage Stamps* and *The British Postage Stamp*, the latter written for the National Postal Museum, for which he is Philatelic Adviser. The firm of Robson Lowe has become a part of the Christie's Group.

CHRISTOPHER PONTER Specialist on tax advice and planning C.G.T., C.T.T., and exemption legislation. A director of Christie's with responsibility for sales to the nation in lieu of tax, and a former senior examiner of the chattels side of the Estate Duty Office.

FRANCIS RUSSELL Director of Christie's who specializes in Old Master Paintings and Drawings. A frequent contributor to the *Burlington Magazine* and advisor to the Treasure Houses of Britain exhibition in Washington.

ALISTAIR SAMPSON After switching from the Bar to antiques on his fortieth birthday, he is now a partner in the firm bearing his name selling porcelain and furniture and is on the council of BADA. He also writes a regular column in *Punch*.

RAYMOND SANCROFT BAKER Director of Christie's in charge of the Coins and Medals department.

CHARLES TRUMAN Recently joined Christie's as a director of the Silver and Objects of Vertu department, having previously worked at the Victoria and Albert Museum in the Metalwork department.

MARINA VAIZEY Art Critic on the *Sunday Times* and formerly on the *Financial Times*. Author of numerous books, including *The Artist as Photographer*, her monograph on Peter Blake is shortly to be published. She is also a member of the Arts Council.

PAUL WHITFIELD Group PR & Marketing Director of Christie's and formerly for 10 years in the Furniture department, after which he worked in senior management positions at Christie's South Kensington and King Street.

Christie, Manson & Woods Ltd.

EUROPEAN SALEROOMS

Head Office
Christie, Manson & Woods Ltd.
8 King Street
St. James's
London SW1Y 6QT
Tel: (01) 839 9060
Telex: 916429
Chairman: J.A. Floyd

South Kensington
Christie's South Kensington Ltd.
85 Old Brompton Road
London SW7 3JS
Tel: (01) 581 7611
Telex: 922061
Chairman: W.F. Brooks, F.S.V.A.

Scotland
Christie's & Edmiston's Ltd.
164–166 Bath Street
Glasgow
Tel: (041) 332 8134/7
Telex: 779901
Chairman: Sir Ilay Campbell, Bt.

Robson Lowe at Christie's
47 Duke Street
St. James's
London SW1Y 6QX
Tel: (01) 839 4034

39 Poole Hill
Bournemouth
Dorset
Tel: (0202) 292740

Italy
Christie's (International) S.A.
Palazzo Massimo Lancellotti
Piazza Navona 114
Rome 00186
Tel: (396) 654 1217
Telex: 611 524
Tom Milnes Gaskell
Maurizio Lodi-Fé

The Netherlands
Christie's Amsterdam B.V.
Cornelis Schuytstraat 57
1071 JG Amsterdam
Tel: (3120) 64 20 11
Telex: 15758
Cables: Christiart, Amsterdam
Harts Nystad

Switzerland
Christie's (International) S.A.
8 place de la Taconnerie
1204 Geneva
Tel: (4122) 28 25 44
Cables: Chrisauction, Geneva
Telex: 423 634
Hans Nadelhoffer
Richard Stern
Georges de Bartha

UNITED STATES OF AMERICA SALEROOMS AND REPRESENTATIVES

Christie, Manson & Woods International, Inc.
502 Park Avenue
New York, N.Y. 10022
Tel: (212) 546 1000
Cables: Chriswoods, New York
Telex: 620721
President: Christopher Burge
Executive Vice Presidents: François Curiel,
Stephen S. Lash

Christie's East
219 East 67th Street
New York, N.Y. 10021
Tel: (212) 606 0400
Telex: 672-0346
President: J. Brian Cole

BEVERLY HILLS
Terry Stanfill
Russell Fogarty
Hillary Holland
342 North Rodeo Drive
Beverly Hills, Ca. 90210
Tel: (213) 275 5534
Telex: 6711872

BOSTON
Elizabeth M. Chapin
Edgar Bingham, Jr.
32 Fayette Street
Boston, Mass. 02116
Tel: (617) 338-6679

CHICAGO
Frances Blair
Laura Gates
200 West Superior
Chicago, Illinois 60610
Tel: (312) 787 2765

DALLAS
Carolyn Foxworth
7047 Elmridge Drive
Dallas, Texas 75240
Tel: (214) 239 0098

PALM BEACH
Helen Cluett
225 Fern Street
West Palm Beach, Fla. 33401
Tel: (305) 833 6952

PHILADELPHIA
Paul Ingersoll
Francis Gowen
P.O. Box 1112
Bryn Mawr, Pa. 19010
Tel: (215) 525 5493

SAN FRANCISCO
Ellanor Notides
3516 Sacramento St.
San Francisco, Ca. 94118
Tel: (415) 346 6633

WASHINGTON
David Ober
Nuala Pell
Joan Gardner
1234 31st Street N.W.
Washington, D.C. 20007
Tel: (202) 333 7459

REPRESENTATIVES

Great Britain and Ireland

Christie's in the City
Simon Birch
10/12 Copthall Avenue
London EC2R 7DJ
Tel: (01) 588 4424

Highland
John Douglas-Menzies
Mounteagle, Fearn, Ross-shire
Tel: (086283) 2866

Grampian
Lord Inverurie
The Stables, Keith Hall
Inverurie, Aberdeenshire
Tel: (0467) 24366

Perthshire
Sebastian Thewes
Strathgarry House
Killiecrankie by Pitlochry
Perthshire
Tel: (079681) 216

Argyll
Sir Ilay Campbell, Bt.
Cumlodden Estate Office
Crarae, Inveraray, Argyll
Tel: (0546) 86633

Edinburgh
Michael Clayton
5 Wemyss Place, Edinburgh
Tel: (031) 225 4756/7

Ayrshire
James Hunter Blair
Blairquhan, Maybole, Ayrshire
Tel: (06557) 239

Northumbria
Aidan Cuthbert
Eastfield House, Main Street
Corbridge, Northumberland
Tel: (043471) 3181

North-West
Victor Gubbins
Eden Lacy, Lazonby, Penrith, Cumbria
Tel: (076883) 8800

Yorkshire
Sir Nicholas Brooksbank, Bt.
Mrs Veronica Brook
46 Bootham, York
Tel: (0904) 30911

West Midlands
Michael Thompson
Stanley Hall, Bridgnorth, Shropshire
Tel: (07462) 61891

Midlands Office
The Hon. Lady Hastings
Mrs William Proby
The Stables, Milton Hall, Peterborough
Tel: (073121) 781

East Anglia
Iain Henderson Russell
Stuart Betts, M.C., F.G.A. *Consultant*
Old Bank of England Court
Queen Street, Norwich
Tel: (0603) 614546

Mid-Wales
Sir Andrew Duff Gordon, Bt.
Downton House, New Radnor
Presteigne, Powys
Tel: (0242) 518999

Cotswolds
Viscount Ebrington
111 The Promenade, Cheltenham, Glos.
Tel: (0242) 518999
Rupert de Zoete *Consultant*

West Country
Richard de Pelet
Monmouth Lodge, Yenston
Templecombe, Somerset
Tel: (0963) 70518

South Dorset & Solent
Nigel Thimbleby
Wolfeton House, Dorchester, Dorset
Tel: (0305) 68748

and at:

Bournemouth
39 Poole Hill, Bournemouth, Dorset
Tel: (0202) 292740

Cornwall
Christopher Petherick
Tredeague, Porthpean
St. Austell, Cornwall
Tel: (0726) 64672

Devon
The Hon. George Lopes
Gnaton Estate Office
Yealmpton, Plymouth, Devon
Tel: (0752) 880636

South East
Robin Loder
Leonardslee Gardens
Lower Beeding, Nr. Horsham
West Sussex
Tel: (040376) 305

Kent
Christopher Proudfoot
The Old Rectory
Fawkham, Dartford, Kent
Tel: (04747) 2854

Ireland
Desmond Fitz-Gerald, Knight of Glin
Glin Castle, Glin, Co. Limerick
Private Residence:
52 Waterloo Road, Dublin 4
Tel: (0001) 68 05 85

Northern Ireland
John Lewis-Crosby
Marybrook House, Raleagh Road
Crossgar, Downpatrick, Co. Down
Tel: (0396) 830574

Channel Islands
Richard de la Hey
58 David Place, St. Helier, Jersey
Tel: (0534) 77582

Overseas

Argentina
Cesar Feldman *Consultant*
Libertad 1269, 1012 Buenos Aires
Tel: (541) 41 1616 or 42 2046
Cables: Tweba, Buenos Aires

Australia
Sue Hewitt
298 New South Head Road
Double Bay, Sydney, 2028
Tel: (612) 326 1422
Cables: Christiart Sydney
Telex: 26343

Austria
Vincent Windisch-Graetz
Ziehrerplatz 4/22, 1030 Vienna
Tel: (43222) 73 26 44

Belgium
Richard Stern, Janine Duesberg
Christie, Manson & Woods (Belgium) Ltd.
33 Boulevard de Waterloo
1000 Brussels
Tel: (322) 512 8765 or 8830
Telex: 20380

Brazil
Maria-Thereza de Azevedo Sodre *Consultant*
Av. Rui Barbosa, 582
22250 Rio de Janeiro
Tel: (5521) 551 1467
Telex: 212 3323

Canada
Murray Mackay
Christie, Manson & Woods
International, Inc.
94 Cumberland Street, Suite 803
Toronto, Ontario M5R 1A3
Tel: (416) 960 2063
Telex: 06-23907

Denmark
Birgitta Hillingso
Dronningens Tvaergade 10
1302 Copenhagen K
Tel: (451) 32 70 75
Telex: 21075

France
Princesse Jeanne-Marie de Broglie
Laurent Prevost-Marcilhacy
Christie's France SARL
17 rue de Lille, 75007 Paris
Tel: (331) 261 1247
Telex: 213468

Hong Kong
Alice Yuan Piccus
3607 Edinburgh Tower
The Landmark
15 Queen's Road Central, Hong Kong
Tel: (8525) 215396/7
Telex: 72014

Israel
Christie's in Israel
2 Habima Square, Tel Aviv 64253
Tel: (9723) 202 930/204 727
Telex: 35770

Italy
Milan
Giorgina Venosta
Christie's (Italy) S.r.l.
9 via Borgogna, 20122 Milan
Tel: (392) 794 712
Telex: 316464

Turin
Sandro Perrone di San Martino
Corso Matteotti, 33, 10121 Turin
Tel: (3911) 548 819

Lucca
Bruno Vangelisti
Via S. Donnino 8
55100 Lucca
Tel: (39583) 43715

Japan
Sachiko Hibiya
Ichibankan Bldg., B1
3–12, Ginza 5-chome
Tokyo 104
Tel: (813) 571 0668
Telex: 29879

Mexico
P.O. Box 105–158
Mexico 11570
Tel: (525) 531 1686/1806

Monaco
Christine de Massy
Christie's Monaco S.A.M.
Park Palace
5 bis, Avenue St. Michel
98000 Monte Carlo
Tel: (3393) 25 19 33
Telex: 469870

Norway
Ulla Solitair Hjort
Riddervoldsgt. 10b, Oslo 2
Tel: (472) 44 12 42

Portugal
Antonio M.G. Santos Mendonça
R. Conde de Almoster, 44, 1° Esq.
1500 Lisbon
Tel: (351) 78 63 83
Telex: 12839

Spain
Casilda Fz-Villaverde y Silva
Valenzuela 7, Madrid 28014
Tel: (341) 232 66 27
Cables: Christiart, Madrid
Telex: 46681

Sweden
Lillemor Malmström
Artillerigatan 29
11445 Stockholm
Tel: (468) 620 131
Telex: 12916

Baroness Irma Silfverschiold
Klagerups Gard, 230 40 Bara
Tel: (4640) 44 03 60

Switzerland
Maria Reinshagen
Christie's (International) A.G.
Steinwiesplatz, 8032 Zürich
Tel: (411) 69 05 05
Telex: 56093

Venezuela
Alain Jathiere
Apartado 88061
1080 Caracas
Tel: (582) 962 1755
Telex: 24950

West Germany
Jörg-Michael Bertz
Inselstrasse 15
D-4000 Düsseldorf 30
Tel: (49211) 4982986

Isabella von Bethmann Hollweg
Wentzelstrasse 21, D-2000 Hamburg 60
Tel: (4940) 279 0866

Charlotte Fürstin zu Hohenlohe-
Langenburg
Residenzstrasse 27, D-8000 Munich 2
Tel: (4989) 22 95 39

Monsieur Gérald Van der Kemp, President d'Honneur of Christie's Europe, is based in our Paris Office.

Index